The Subject of Psychosis: A Lacanian Perspective

The Subject of Psychosis: A Lacanian Perspective

Stijn Vanheule
Ghent University, Belgium

First published 2011 by
PALGRAVE MACMILLAN

Palgrave Macmillan in the UK is an imprint of Macmillan Publishers Limited, registered in England, company number 785998, of Houndmills, Basingstoke, Hampshire RG21 6XS.

Palgrave Macmillan in the US is a division of St Martin's Press LLC, 175 Fifth Avenue, New York, NY 10010.

Palgrave Macmillan is the global academic imprint of the above companies and has companies and representatives throughout the world.

Palgrave® and Macmillan® are registered trademarks in the United States, the United Kingdom, Europe and other countries.

ISBN 978-0-230-27664-2

This book is printed on paper suitable for recycling and made from fully managed and sustained forest sources. Logging, pulping and manufacturing processes are expected to conform to the environmental regulations of the country of origin.

A catalogue record for this book is available from the British Library.

A catalog record for this book is available from the Library of Congress.

10 9 8 7 6 5 4 3 2 1
20 19 18 17 16 15 14 13 12 11

Transferred to Digital Printing in 2012

Contents

List of Figures   vi

Acknowledgements   vii

Introduction   1

Part I   First Era: The Age of Imaginary Identification

1   Psychosis as a Disorder at the Level of the Imaginary   9

Part II   Second Era: The Age of the Signifier

2   Towards a Structural Study of Psychosis   33

3   Foreclosure and Its Vicissitudes   50

4   A Novel Approach to Hallucinations   81

5   Delusions Scrutinized   96

Part III   Third Era: The Age of the Object *a*

6   The Object *a* and Jouissance in Psychosis   125

Part IV   Fourth Era: The Age of the Knot

7   Psychosis within the Logic of Knotting and Linking   151

Notes   172

References   179

Index   188

List of Figures

2.1	Signifier and signified	37
2.2	The logic of signification	43
3.1	Metonymy	53
3.2	Signifier and signified	53
3.3	Metaphor (I)	55
3.4	Metaphor (II)	55
3.5	Impact of the signifier on the signified	56
3.6	Metaphor of the Name-of-the-Father	58
3.7	Maternal desire	59
3.8	The Name-of-the-Father substitutes maternal desire	60
3.9	Recognition between master and slave	62
3.10	The creation of phallic signification	63
4.1	Scholastic model of perception	83
4.2	Effect of the *perceptum* on the *percipiens*	85
5.1	Autonym	109
5.2	Schreber's delusional metaphor	119
6.1	The matheme of the division of the Other	129
6.2	Partial objects and corresponding objects *a*	133
7.1	Trefoil knot	156
7.2	Borromean rings	156
7.3	Trefoil knot deduced from the Borromean rings	160

Acknowledgements

The idea for this book grew out of my teaching at Ghent University, where in one lecture series I cover principles of Lacanian psychoanalytic therapy with psychosis. Using Lacan's (1959) article 'On a Question Prior to any Possible Treatment of Psychosis', the enthusiasm of my students combined with their unremitting struggle to read this text forces me each year to explain Lacan's ideas on psychosis as clearly as possible, while still staying close to the original sources.

Many colleagues and friends supported me in writing this book – 'bad for your career!'. Paul Verhaeghe introduced me to Lacanian psychoanalysis and has always supported me in finding my way with the material. Other colleagues and collaborators at the Department of Psychoanalysis and Clinical Consulting at Ghent University have provided me with useful feedback on various drafts of this book: Filip Geerardyn, Mattias Desmet, Reitske Meganck, Virginie Debaere, Julie De Ganck, Wim Galle, Abe Geldhof, Ruth Inslegers, Nathalie Laceur, Wim Matthys, Els Ooms, Kaatje Van Roy, Glenn Strubbe, Eline Trenson and Jochem Willemsen. Lewis A. Kirshner, a visiting researcher at my Department, has been a most inspiring interlocutor. Even when they are not aware of it, the following people have also played an important role for me when writing this book: Lieve Billiet, Giancarlo Dimaggio, Derek Hook, Lieven Jonckheere, Anne Lysy, Kareen Malone, Jacques-Alain Miller, Erwin Mortier, Els Vandenbussche and, last but not least, Sandra Van der Mespel. Finally, I am very grateful to Clare Murphy for her excellent work on copy-editing this book. Thanks to all of you.

Introduction

Jacques Lacan's oeuvre covers a period of more than 50 years, during which time he developed a theory that innovated psychoanalytic practice and introduced a new method of reflecting on human subjectivity. His work continues to be read today and is well known for being powerful, intriguing, baroque and complicated, all at the same time. The theory he formulated represents a work in progress of a restless, inquiring mind and needs to be studied with appreciation for how his concepts and ideas evolved over time. The purpose of this book is to clarify his particular approach to the clinic of psychosis. The principal themes running through his work concern the ways in which psychotic experiences are structured and how psychoanalysis can provide a useful framework for the treatment of psychosis.

During the nineteenth and early twentieth centuries psychosis was largely understood in terms of organic mechanisms: its symptomatology was seen as a surface phenomenon of presumed underlying disturbances in the brain. While Lacan was interested in the strict neurobiological work of his forbearers, particularly because of its detailed observation of the functioning of psychotic patients, he felt nonetheless that these theories neglected the complexity of psychotic experience. The main factor left out of consideration was the question as to how psychosis affects subjectivity. One of the central aspects of Lacan's work is his exploration of how the experience of self and other is organized in psychosis and how stability can be achieved despite the disruption that characterizes it. At first Lacan addressed these questions by focusing on identification, suggesting that identification with a specific type of image marks the turning point in psychosis. Later he put this view aside, contending that what matters in psychoanalysis is the materiality of speech. He argued that language makes up the experience of subjectivity and that

1

psychosis is marked by the absence of a crucial signifier. This absence implies a specific type of subject–Other experience, one in which mechanisms of identification play only a secondary role. As his seminar progressed, however, Lacan twice revised these ideas: First, he stressed that in psychosis the subject–Other relation entails a different experience of corporeality and a different relation to the drive; second, he began to focus on the systemic interplay between the registers that he places at the basis of human functioning: the Real, the Symbolic and the Imaginary.

I propose that Lacan's work on psychosis can best be framed in terms of four eras or broad periods. In each period a different set of key concepts can be discerned, together with a number of crucial texts containing references to psychosis. In this book I present a close reading of these texts. The central ideas are explained and contextualized in terms of Lacan's broader oeuvre. Related texts, such as those of Freud, de Clérambault and Merleau-Ponty, are discussed. I argue that the empirical field of psychoanalysis should include detailed case studies, and to this end I discuss one case study from each period of Lacan's work. These case studies were central to Lacan's explanation of his ideas. I have not included case studies from my own clinical practice nor from that of other psychoanalysts, nor do I address other theories of other authors working with Lacanian psychoanalysis. In this respect I have limited myself to examining the logic articulated within Lacan's oeuvre. My guiding principles were that Lacan's ideas on psychosis should be presented as clearly as possible and that shifts in his conception of psychosis should be framed in the context of his broader work. Through this approach, I hope to contribute to the academic and clinical study of Lacanian theory.

The *first era* I discern in Lacan's work covers the 1930s and 1940s and focuses on identificatory mechanisms, which I discuss in Chapter 1. Lacan brings psychoanalytic concepts into dialogue with psychiatric theory, and gradually emancipates the psychoanalytic thesis from the psychiatric. He stresses that psychosis involves an imaginary mode of relating to the world. At the basis of this relation he proposes that an identificatory structure can be found in which the ego is captured by an ideal image. What is typical of psychosis is the inability to recognize that one is captured by the images one actually imposes upon the world, rendering it deeply threatening. Key texts in this period include Lacan's doctoral thesis (1932), which has not yet been translated into English, and his article Presentation on Psychical Causality (Lacan, 1947). The case of Aimée, a paranoid patient Lacan worked with during an internship and discussed in his doctoral thesis, is pivotal for this era.

The *second era* I distinguish covers the 1950s, when Lacan refers to psychosis in terms of language-based structures. Central to this period is his year-long seminar on psychosis (Seminar III; Lacan, 1955–56), which gave rise to the text On a Question Prior to Any Possible Treatment of Psychosis (Lacan, 1959). During this time Lacan provided his most extensive discussion of the topic of psychosis, proving himself a truly innovative thinker. His reinterpretation, or 'structural analysis' (Lacan, 1959, p. 449), of Daniel Paul Schreber's (1903) autobiography is crucial in this phase of his work. I devote four chapters of my book to this era.

Chapter 2 comprises an overview of the basic tenets of Lacan's structural approach to psychosis during the 1950s. Two important sources of inspiration are reviewed: the work of linguists Ferdinand de Saussure and Roman Jakobson. I examine Lacan's theory of the predominance of the signifier in the unconscious, and discuss his concepts of 'structure' and 'subject', which arguably receive a strongly materialist interpretation in his work. Compared with the other chapters of this book, here I concentrate my analysis less on psychosis but instead examine key concepts of Lacan's work from that decade. The concepts of structure and subject are the cornerstones of what I call his second paradigm, in which psychosis is studied structurally in terms of how the Symbolic is organized. The next three chapters build on this analysis and attempt to shed light on how Lacan conceptualizes psychosis during this period.

Chapter 3 examines the idea of foreclosure. Starting from the anthropological studies of Claude Lévi-Strauss, I explore Lacan's idea that a foreclosure of the so-called signifier of the Name-of-the-Father lies at the basis of psychosis. I also investigate his suggestion that in psychosis a process of metaphorization does not take place. Four logical consequences of foreclosure are discussed: (1) the idea that in psychosis the subject threatens to remain undefined; (2) the suggestion that the other is perceived as fundamentally capricious; (3) the thesis that the unconscious obtains a status of externality; and 4) the proposal that imaginary identification might compensate for the negative effects of foreclosure.

In Chapters 4 and 5 I show how this paradigmatic shift towards a structural model of psychosis enabled Lacan to reconceptualize commonly accepted ideas about hallucinations and delusions, respectively. In Chapter 4 I demonstrate that in Lacan's theory hallucinations are not thought of as perceptions without an object, but as perceptions that subvert the subject. Chapter 5 discusses delusions demonstrating how ruptured metonymy can be found at their basis and how failing metaphorization can be compensated for through the creation of a delusional metaphor.

The *third era* proposed in this book comprises his tenth seminar onwards (1962–63), when Lacan begins to elaborate his theory of the so-called object *a*. Problems that were previously approached in terms of the logic of the signifier are now addressed in terms of the limits of the Symbolic. Lacan embraces the new idea that some aspects of Being are Real and cannot be grasped via language. The two key concepts he used to address the domain of subjectivity that appears at the limit of the Symbolic are 'jouissance' and the 'object *a*'. The complex notion of jouissance denotes a mode of satisfaction or drive gratification beyond pleasure, and the object *a* refers to what remains of the mythical partial object after the assumption of language. In this period of Lacan's work, references to psychosis are spread across several seminars and texts (Lacan, 1965, 1966b, 1968). He argues that in psychosis the object *a* is not separated from the subject, whereas in neurosis such a separation has taken place. With the concept of jouissance he makes clear distinctions between paranoia and schizophrenia, and addresses the question of how problems with regard to jouissance might trigger acute delusional episodes. In Chapter 6 this line of thinking is explored using the fictional case of Lola Valerie Stein, from Marguerite Duras's (1964) novel *The Ravishing of Lol V. Stein*.

The *fourth era* I discern in Lacan's work on psychosis includes his 23rd seminar (Lacan, 1975–76), where knot theory is used to operationalize the interrelations between the Real, the Symbolic and the Imaginary. The central question he is then working with concerns how a link can be made in the relation between the Real, the Symbolic and the Imaginary, the three registers that make up psychical reality. Lacan proposes the symptom as the systemic element that binds these registers, such that the link comprises a systemic whole that is more than the sum of its parts. In these years the Name-of-the-Father is redefined as the symptom of neurosis. In psychosis no use can be made of such symptoms, which implies that psychical reality is organized through tailor-made solutions he calls 'sinthoms'. The main case Lacan uses to reflect on such singular inventions is that of James Joyce. In Chapter 7 I discuss these last developments in Lacan's work on psychosis.

The attentive reader will observe that some of the ideas reviewed during my discussion of these four periods are complementary, while others are somewhat contradictory. For example in the 1950s, Lacan strongly defended a categorical view of neurosis and psychosis, arguing that both are structured by clearly distinct Symbolic mechanisms called primal repression and foreclosure. In the 1970s this was no longer the case. Neurosis and psychosis were then seen as modes of knotting the Real, the Symbolic and the Imaginary that have strong resemblances, despite independent characteristics. While writing this book I attempted neither to resolve nor to conceal such contradictions. The more critical reader can decide how to proceed with them. Furthermore, it will become clear that as time progressed the level of abstraction in Lacan's work increased considerably. Up until the 1960s, Lacan's discussion of psychosis frequently referred to the work of other authors, and largely aimed to connect theoretical ideas with clinical case material. From the 1960s onwards, his ideas on psychosis were formulated in a more fragmented way, with a stronger focus on conceptual rather than clinical implications. This more abstract discussion of psychosis is evident in my last two chapters, which are more theoretical than the preceding five. Personally I strongly appreciate Lacan's late work, but I believe that it is of utmost importance that his concepts and ideas be studied in terms of the different phases in his theoretical development. Furthermore, I believe that the clinical relevance of these ideas should be further examined, integrated with case studies and brought into dialogue with other theories. I hope my book stimulates such research.

Part I

First Era: The Age of Imaginary Identification

1
Psychosis as a Disorder at the Level of the Imaginary

An encounter with psychosis and psychoanalysis

Contrary to Freud, who first trained as a neurologist, Lacan started his career as a psychiatrist and focused on psychosis. Between 1927 and 1931 he underwent training in several psychiatric clinics. At the Sainte-Anne hospital he worked under the supervision of Henri Claude, and at the Special Infirmary of the Paris police headquarters, under Gaëtan Gatian de Clérambault (Roudinesco, 1994). Henri Claude was one of the first clinicians in France to institutionalize the teaching of psychoanalysis, where he combined psychodynamic theory with biological determinism. This theoretical position was subsequently elaborated and termed Organo-Dynamism by Henri Ey, a pupil who trained under Claude together with Lacan. Gaëtan Gatian de Clérambault, on the other hand, was less influential at that time, perhaps because he was not a university professor. This is reflected in Lacan's doctoral thesis, where de Clérambault is only a minor reference (see Lacan, 1932, pp. 126–34, 355). It was nevertheless de Clérambault that Lacan (1966c, p. 65) would later refer to as his 'only master in psychiatry', largely owing to his systematic method of examining case studies, which Lacan replicated in his thesis (Lacan, 1947, p. 138). In the period between 1909 and 1933 de Clérambault wrote about the mechanisms of disruption in mental life preceding the crystallization of delusions (de Clérambault, 1942, pp. 455–655) using concepts such as 'mental automatism' and 'passivity syndrome'. These ideas were highly influential to Lacan, who regarded them as 'closer to what can be constructed on the basis of a structural analysis than any other clinical approach in French psychiatry' (Lacan, 1966c, p. 65). In Chapter 5 I join Lacan in this viewpoint and argue that in de Clérambault's work the basis for what

Lacan later qualifies as ruptures in the process of metonymy can be found.

Although Lacan had already written a number of clinical studies on psychosis in the 1920s and 1930s, it is in his doctoral thesis that we find a more systematic theoretical exposition of the pathology. It is also here that the foundations of his psychoanalytical theory can be found. Essentially this work contains two parts: a literature review focusing on delusional processes and the predetermining role of personality, followed by the case of Aimée where he elaborates these ideas. The text is limited to a discussion of paranoia, which is the form of psychosis Lacan most often referred to throughout his work. As a matter of fact, in his choice of case studies Lacan seems to have had a preference for the more organized psychotic problems than those in which disintegration and chaos are pivotal. Aimée, Schreber, Lol V. Stein, and James Joyce are all cases in which a form of psychotic logic comes to the fore, against a background of a relatively 'normal' social and intellectual functioning. With such a mixture of ordinary and extraordinary features, these case studies reveal certain key characteristics of psychosis [1] and are illustrative of the structure of psychosis.

A critique of psychological and biological models of psychosis

The literature review of Lacan's doctoral thesis examines the psychological and biological models of psychosis. In his discussion of the psychological models the works of Bleuler, Kretschmer and Jaspers are the main points of reference. Lacan had been familiarized with these German psychiatrists through his teachers and a clinical placement he underwent in the famous Burghölzli clinic in Zurich (Roudinesco, 1994). From Bleuler's work Lacan retains the idea that at the core psychotic outbreaks are constituted by 'reactions of the subject to vital situations' [2] (Lacan, 1932, p. 77). Such vital situations refer to sexual and professional problems that exceed an individual's capacity to cope, and that 'touch his affectivity in a profound way'.[3] Within this logic, delusional developments, which have a somatic, sensorial, affective and ideational component, are reactive to 'internal conflicts' (Lacan, 1932, p. 81). From the work of Kretschmer, Lacan retains the idea that a so-called sensitive character often lies at the basis of paranoia and that in the aetiology of psychosis a specific type of event or experience can be found: 'the original experience that determines psychosis, is the one which reveals to a subject "his own insufficiency, humiliating him at the ethical level"'[4] (Lacan, 1932, p. 92). Situations that provoke such experiences include ethical conflicts with respect to sexuality, professional failure and conflicts in social relations. Lacan qualifies these so-called *reactions* as psychogenic. The assumption is that the development of psychosis can be adequately understood in terms of reactions of the personality to vital situations and events: 'these reactions are characterised by their integration in a *comprehensible* psychological development, by their dependence of the *conception* that a subject has *about himself*, and by the *tension* that is inherent to his [the personality] relations with the *social* environment'[5] (Lacan, 1932, p. 105). Lacan concludes that such psychogenic reactions are an 'efficient cause'[6] in the development of psychosis, in that they are 'determining of the structure and of the permanence of the symptoms'[7] (Lacan, 1932, p. 347). From these premises Lacan indicates that clinical analyses depend on the application of 'all one's capacity of sympathy'[8] (Lacan, 1932, p. 224). Later, when he grew more critical of his dissertation, he criticized such comprehension-based approaches. Several examples of this can be found in his third seminar (Lacan, 1955–6) and in his article On a Question Prior to Any Treatment of Psychosis (Lacan, 1959). I will return to this in Chapter 5.

With respect to biological models of psychosis, Lacan expresses a critical attitude at the very outset of his doctoral thesis, which was not common within the tradition of French psychiatry at that time. Clinicians, such as Claude, de Clérambault and many others, largely accepted that the cause of psychotic disturbances could be found in the brain; psychological disturbances were the mere expression of a cerebral lesion. They advocated the development of refined clinical descriptions of psychosis, but attributed all psychotic peculiarities to neurological abnormalities. In 1932 Lacan's attitude in this debate is rather balanced. He believes that organic processes play a 'non specific' role in the development of psychosis and that they make up so-called 'occasional causes', in that they determine 'the onset [*déclenchement*] of psychosis'[9] (Lacan, 1932, p. 347). The concept *déclenchement* refers to the moment of onset or to the triggering of a mechanism, and fits with the conception of psychosis as an organic illness. It denotes the moment at which pathogenic processes, to which a person was predisposed, are set in motion leading to the initial manifestation of symptoms. Interestingly, Lacan retains this concept in his later work even when he leaves organic explanations out of consideration. Nevertheless, it is worth noting that in his early writing the concept of *déclenchement* has a strictly biological meaning. For example, in his very first article, on ocular movement, *déclenchement* was used with reference to how reflexes are triggered (Alajouanine et al., 1926). He also used this concept just prior to his dissertation in an article on the structure of paranoia to denote what we would now call stressors that turn vulnerability into a disorder (Lacan, 1931). Stressors or 'triggering causes', he notes, are 'an endogenic or exogenic toxic episode, an anxiety process, an infectious affection, an emotional trauma' [10] (Lacan, 1931, p. 18). What is not explained in Lacan's dissertation is how exactly he sees the determining role of brain mechanisms in the triggering of psychosis. Later in his work he is more explicit on this matter, indicating that a 'libidinous biological defect' [11] causes psychosis and that at the moment a psychosis is triggered a biological mechanism must be active (Lacan, 1938, p. 67). However, this line of reasoning was not elaborated further, indicating his disinterest in cerebral models of psychosis and his disbelief in the idea that psychosis can be completely understood in terms of disturbed cerebral processes.[12]

One reason for this reserve seems to reside in the fact that no matter how material they may seem to be, brain mechanisms are always theoretically presumed, and cannot be directly observed: 'the clinic doesn't show us these mechanisms' [13] (Lacan, 1931, p. 440). Lacan (1955–6, p. 65) suggests that all modern research starts from the presumption that there is something 'absolutely nondeceptive' in the objects that are studied and the methods used to study them. Indeed, data that indicate brain mechanisms must always be *derived* from observable phenomena, which in turn are *presumed* to be precise indicators of these mechanisms. Without an 'act of faith' that instils belief in the truthfulness of this approach (Lacan, 1955–6, p. 65), even the most apparently objective research collapses.

However, the main reason for Lacan's disinterest in biological models is not because he believed that they were wrong, but because they didn't provide him with clinically useful tools for the study and treatment of psychosis. In terms of this reservedness, he states: 'Admittedly, in the study of psychosis, every day seems to bring some new *organic* correlate; upon taking a close look at these: these correlations, which we don't consider discussing, only have a partial reach, and only take an interest from the doctrinal point of view they claim to be reinforcing' [14] (Lacan, 1932, pp. 15–16). This statement not only indicates that a co-occurrence between two phenomena does not justify linear causal conclusions; it also suggests that whereas biological studies are relevant in terms of building brain models of psychosis, they leave many other factors out of consideration. For example, biological models do not address psychosis qua lived experience, while clinical insight into the lived experience might be very important. The relevance of such studies is therefore thought to be largely doctrinal: they reinforce or condemn abstract ideas of psychosis, but do not offer much in terms of how to orient oneself clinically with such patients.

Lacan's problem with both psychogenic and organogenic accounts of psychosis is not so much that they bear witness of theoretical preferences, but that they are *non-specific* and do not inform us on how therapeutic work with individual patients should be organized (Lacan, 1932, p. 347). In other words, they only inform us about factors and conditions that are usually related to psychosis. They build upon information that is generally true for all cases belonging to a certain group, such as the stressors that are typically associated with the onset of psychosis or the genes that are usually involved in the intergenerational transmission of psychosis. Nowadays we would say that such knowledge builds on what can be statistically detected in a sample, and that it gives us a global understanding of psychosis: a thread of information that can be generalized across cases. However, each case of psychosis will always only partially match such generalized knowledge. Lacan (1932) argued that the treatment of specific cases of psychosis necessitates an understanding of the *specific causes and conditions* that lead to a psychotic outbreak. This implies a detailed focus on the biographical context, the specific life events, as well as the lived experience, as illustrated in his discussion of Aimée. In his later work, Lacan further elaborated this interest in both the *specific* and the *clinical case*. He points out that rather than focusing on universal truths, psychoanalysis should concentrate on the singular and the particular (e.g. Lacan, 1961–2, 1966a).

Despite his reticence towards 'non-specific' biological explanations, Lacan was very interested in the clinical descriptions that authors had been developing within this paradigm. He refers to studies in France that centred on the concept of *psychological or mental automatism*, and to the German research tradition that focused on the concept of *process* (Lacan, 1932, p. 108). Both approaches explain psychosis by referring to mechanisms that automatically take place in the personality. Once the underlying mechanism is triggered, the disorder that ensues is a self-deploying system. In this view, psychosis is an illness like many others, the course of which can be predicted in advance. In Lacan's (1932, pp. 127–33, 207–17) discussion of the course of psychosis, three periods can be discerned. First we have an acute phase, [15] during which so-called elementary phenomena or disruptions in mental life can be observed. Characteristic of this phase is that a new, heterogeneous element, which some have qualified as 'xenopathic' or 'parasitic', enters mental life and evokes perplexity in the patient (Lacan, 1932, pp. 127,

131). Next is a 'phase of affective meditation' [16] (Lacan, 1932, p. 209), in which feelings of estrangement, anxiety, inhibition, depression or depersonalization stand to the fore, and finally a 'phase of delusional organization' [17] (Lacan, 1932, p. 209). Central to this last phase is that a delusion, which mainly consists of interpretations, is elaborated. Lacan suggests that in their study of the course of psychosis organicists tend to concentrate on the first phase and dismiss the study of delusions (Lacan, 1932, p. 217).

The originality of Lacan's doctoral thesis is not so much in the idea that organic processes and vital conflicts play a role in the causation and deployment of psychosis, albeit a non-specific one, but that he discerns a third pathogenic factor: 'the specific cause' of psychosis [18] (Lacan, 1932, p. 347). Lacan's discussion of this additional third factor appears in the case of Aimée. Indeed, this discussion comprises his first attempt to describe aspects of psychosis via psychoanalytical theory, and aims to explain 'the meaning of the delusion' [19] (Lacan, 1932, p. 252). Attention is paid to the so-called typical identification process, the psychological mechanism in which a psychotic person is trapped, which is considered to be the specific cause of psychosis. In subsequent work in the 1930s and 1940s, Lacan further elaborates this psychoanalytical perspective and more clearly emancipates the psychoanalytical thesis from the psychiatric one. It is noteworthy, however, that in his doctoral dissertation the use of psychoanalysis is still a bit confused (Cox-Cameron, 2000), and very much consistent with the post-Freudian interpretations he would later harshly criticize (Lacan, 1959, pp. 453–7).

The encounter with Aimée

Lacan studied the case of Aimée, who has meanwhile been identified as Marguerite Pantaine Anzieu, [20] during his internship in the Sainte-Anne hospital (Allouch, 1994; Cox-Cameron, 2000; Roudinesco, 1994). Aimée was interned in 1931 following a violent knife attack on the actress Huguette Duflos, who is named Mme Z in the case study. With regard to this attack, Aimée stated: 'I did it, because they wanted to kill my child' [21] (Lacan, 1932, p. 157). Upon his examination of the case, Lacan concludes that she has a fairly complex delusion in which elements of erotomania, persecution, ideas of reference, jealousy and grandeur can be discerned.

Aimée was 38 years old when she carried out the knife attack. She was separated from her husband and had been living alone in Paris for six years; her son lived outside Paris with his father and Aimée's sister, who took care of him. Lacan's case study shows that paranoid symptoms were already present during her first pregnancy and the stillbirth of this baby, and returned at the birth of her son leading to a six-month hospitalization. She had a close but complex relationship with her mother: 'We were two friends' [22] (Lacan, 1932, p. 220). Aimée's mother also had a history of paranoid traits, and remarkably gave Aimée the name of her older daughter, who tragically died during her pregnancy with Aimée (Allouch, 1994; Cox-Cameron, 2000; Roudinesco, 1994).

At first Aimée's fears for her son's safety were vague, but upon her arrival in Paris her certainty of the threats towards him obtained a name: 'One day, she says, as I was working at the office, and just like always searching in myself from where these threats against my son could come from, I heard my colleagues talk about Mme Z. I then understood that she was the one that had it in for us' [23] (Lacan, 1932, p. 162). It was a befriended colleague, Mme C de la N, who first mentioned Huguette Duflos, and who chatted in Aimée's presence about the actress's habits and success (Lacan, 1932, pp. 226–7). Later on, the number of persecutors increased and soon several famous Parisians were accused of threatening her and her son. For example, she saw allusions to her private life in the works of the novelist Pierre Benoit (Allouch, 1994), which prompted her to approach him and ask for justification. She herself meanwhile fostered the idea of what she called realizing 'the reign of the good', where women and children could have a good life (Lacan, 1932, p. 166), and appealed to a number of authorities to intervene in the cruelties taking place. Edward VIII, the Prince of Wales at that time, was one of the people she appealed to. She sent him her books and fostered erotomanic ideas about him, but he never personally responded to her. When her culminating fear of being threatened became overwhelming, Aimée bought a hunting knife from a specialist manufacturer and finally attacked Huguette Duflos, who sustained only minor injuries.

Aimée remarkably wrote two novels, neither of which were ever published. However, Lacan (1932, pp. 181–99) included extracts of these novels in his dissertation, noting how they do not bear witness of stereotypical psychotic narratives, such as repetitive or returning phrases and incomprehensible allusions, which he had previously studied in the writings of a psychotic woman (Lacan et al., 1931). Instead, Aimée's work is well written and crucial delusional themes are expressed in a clear narrative structure.

In his discussion of pathogenic processes, Lacan points to two personality characteristics that are clearly present in the case of Aimée: psychasthenia, which would explain her inability to find adequate ways of dealing with hatred, and a sensitive nature, which accounts for her susceptibility to conflict (Lacan, 1932, pp. 234, 243). Lacan refers to the work of Janet and Kretschmer to explain these personality character-istics, which he understands as determining the way Aimée reacts to vital conflict. In this respect he goes against any idea that a single per-sonality type would form the basis of paranoia [24] (Lacan, 1932, p. 50). Even then he concludes that personality traits cannot univocally define a predisposition to psychosis (Lacan, 1932, p. 346); instead he points to abundant ego-dystonic elementary phenomena, which supports the idea that a process of psychosis has been triggered. However, for Lacan cerebral models are insufficient in explaining the logic of Aimée's delu-sion (Lacan, 1932, p. 217). He argues that in this case study classic organic and psychogenic models may provide a good context to start from. Yet detailed insight into the pathogenesis of the case, or more particularly, the '*meaning* of the delusion', necessitates an additional perspective that highlights *specific* causes (Lacan, 1932, pp. 347, 352). At this point Lacan turns to psychoanalytical theory in order to frame the logic that is implicit to Aimée's delusions, and her way of relating to others.

The most original idea in his thesis is the suggestion that Aimée is overwhelmed and captivated by her close relationships with certain oth-ers. For example, in terms of her relationship with her colleague, Lacan states that Mme C de la N's actions 'contrast with those of our subject "like an object to its mirror image" ' [25] (Lacan, 1932, p. 226) and that 'of the two friends, one was the shadow of the other' [26] (Lacan, 1932, p. 227). In his subsequent articles, which focus on psychosis in terms of a disorder at the level of meaning, and more broadly in his works on imag-inary identification, mirror terminology is used extensively (Vanheule and Verhaeghe, 2009). The roots of this mirror-and-meaning paradigm can be found in his doctoral dissertation (Lacan, 1932, pp. 219–44).

This notion of a *captivation by the other as a mirror image* not only implies that Aimée relates to others in terms of resemblances, but also that the self-other differentiation is weak, leading to confusion, affec-tive ambivalence and feelings of intrusion. Lacan indicates that Aimée deals with these aversive experiences by means of externalization. She displaces them onto celebrities that in some way or another incarnate an ideal image of how she would like to be, but with whom she has no personal relationship. Aimée's presumed persecutors, such as Huguette Duflos, and the people towards whom she has an erotomanic attitude, such as Edward VIII, fit this criterion. Within this logic the assault on Huguette Duflos can be interpreted as an attack on an externalized ideal image of what Aimée herself would like to be, namely a worldly woman: 'a woman who, to a certain degree, enjoys liberty and social power' [27] (Lacan, 1932, p. 253). In the same vein Lacan (1933, p. 28) argues that 'Aimée hits the brilliant being she hates, precisely because she represents the ideal she has about herself'. [28] In other words, the selection of Huguette Duflos as victim is not determined by the actress's actions towards her attacker, but by her mere resemblance to an image or prototype that Aimée both loves and hates, but above all, cannot distance herself from. Her persecutors are 'doubles, triples and successive "editions" of a *prototype*' [29] (Lacan, 1932, p. 253).

Aimée's way of relating to others, whereby a relatively unfamiliar other, one who incarnates an ideal image of a person, is perceived as having it in for her, bears witness to an *erotomanic* attitude or a passionate delusion. Her conviction is that, no matter how concealed it might be, she is the centre of the other's attention. In an erotomanic delusion the initiative is *'attributed to the object'* [30] (Lacan, 1932, p. 263). Typical for erotomania is that the perceived preoccupation by another might, in some instances, or as time progresses, be experienced as overly intrusive. In some cases this leads to asking the other for explanations for his or her interference, as Aimée did with the novelist Pierre Benoit, or to counteractions that aim at stopping the other, as with Huguette Duflos. Lacan summarizes this by stating: 'Aimée hits her exteriorized ideal in her victim, just like the *passionate* hits her unique hated and beloved object' [31] (Lacan, 1932, p. 253).

A further conclusion he makes is that she is a case of *self-punishing paranoia*. This is a diagnostic category Lacan invents in his dissertation. On the one hand it indicates that the act was self-directed. Through her assault, Aimée attacks an externalized aspect of herself. On the other hand Lacan qualifies the attack as a true punishment: by attacking an innocent other Aimée violates the law, and is actually punished for what she did. Punishment has a relieving and almost curing effect on Aimée, which according to Lacan suggests that this is what she was unconsciously aiming for (Lacan, 1932, pp. 248–54).

Lacan situates the roots of Aimée's way of relating to others in her relationship with her older sister. In response to a number of difficulties between Aimée and her husband, this sister joined the household after eight months of Aimée's marriage. From the outset, married life posed problems for Aimée. At first there were rows, but gradually she sunk into episodes of mutism and suffered from several bodily, phobic and obsessive complaints. During her pregnancies and upon the stillbirth of her first child and the birth of her son, these problems intensified, but did not give way to a systematized delusion. Aimée's sister was a young widow. She entered the household with the aim of bringing stability, but also had 'an enormous need for affective compensation' [32] (Lacan, 1932, p. 230). Lacan suggests that while Aimée recognized and valued her sister's contributions – her sister represented the image of the person she failed to be (Lacan, 1932, p. 232), she also felt dominated and humiliated by the fact that her sister occupied *her* place as a mother. Aimée suspected that she was plotting against her with her husband. Lacan concludes that Aimée's grievance with her sister, which is centred on the idea that she has stolen her child, makes up the theme around which the delusion is systematized.

In discussing the nature of Aimée's prototypical relationships, Lacan introduces a battery of psychoanalytical concepts. These concepts are not explained in detail and their added value is not always clear. Besides some vague reservations formulated in the conclusion of his dissertation, he does not present much by way of a critical discussion of his psychoanalytical arguments. Indeed, as he doesn't do much more than note similarities between certain aspects of Aimée's functioning and previously formulated aspects of psychoanalytical theory, one has the impression that he is still exploring psychoanalytical theory, without mastering its complexities.

For example, Lacan proposes that Aimée's relationship with her sister shows an affective fixation to the fraternal complex (Lacan, 1932, p. 261) and that, in her way of dealing with conflict, she makes use of the defence mechanism of negation, or *Verneinung* (Lacan, 1932, pp. 232–3), and repression (Lacan, 1932, p. 263). More generally, he points to a libidinal fixation to the sadistic–anal phase, which would explain why her super-ego is so severe, and why she unconsciously wants to punish herself (Lacan, 1932, p. 259). The fact that Aimée felt 'masculine' and 'attracted' to her friend Mme C de la N (Lacan, 1932, pp. 227–8) is explained in terms of homosexual tendencies (Lacan, 1932, p. 261). This is reminiscent of Freud's (1911, 1922) suggestion that a warded-off homosexual phantasy could lie at the basis of paranoia. [33]

In his discussion of Schreber, Freud concluded that 'the familiar principal forms of paranoia can all be represented as contradictions of the single proposition: "*I* (a man) *love him* (a man)"' (1911, p. 63). The types of delusion thus explained are persecution, erotomania, jealousy and grandiosity. In each of these cases a characteristic initiative is attributed to the other; in each case the 'I' as subject is innocent in relation to what takes place. In delusions of persecution the contradiction concerns the idea of loving, which implies that the central proposition 'I *love* him' is replaced by the idea 'I *hate* him'. In a subsequent step this idea is 'transformed by projection' (Freud, 1911, p. 63). Projection means that 'an internal perception is suppressed, and instead, its content, after undergoing a certain kind of distortion, enters consciousness in the form of an external perception' (Freud, 1911, p. 66). '*He hates* (persecutes) *me*' thus becomes the proposition of persecution. In erotomania another element is chosen for contradiction. This time a change takes place at the level of the gender of the other. The basic erotomanic proposition is: 'I do not love *him* – I love *her*', which is subsequently transformed via projection into the idea 'I observe that *she* loves me'. The erotomaniac only responds to the loving initiative of the other. In delusions of the jealous type, the initiative of loving the man is attributed to the partner, which leads to suspicion and to feelings of being betrayed. 'It is not *I* who loves the man – *she* loves him' is the proposition that is central to jealousy. Freud (1911, p. 65) states that in delusions of grandeur, the transformation is most radical, and 'concerns the proposition as a whole'. He says that the central proposition is rejected, and replaced by the idea: '*I do not love at all – I do not love anyone*', which is equivalent to the grandiose delusional idea: 'I only love myself'. Strictly speaking this conclusion is not correct. The principal transformation taking place in the transition from 'I love him' to 'I only love myself' concerns the object of the proposition: the object is the same as the subject, while the subject and the verb of the proposition remain constant. The principal difference with other types of delusion seems to be situated at the level of projection. In the grandiose delusion the formulation is not further transformed via projection onto others.

Lacan rather uncritically applies these ideas to the case of Aimée (Cox-Cameron, 2000), suggesting that they 'brilliantly explain the structure of the delusion' [34] (Lacan, 1932, p. 262) and concludes that homosexual impulses are present in Aimée's relationship to Mme C. de la N (1932, p. 264). He indicates that these impulses are 'revealed by the delusion', yet, 'strongly sublimated' (Lacan, 1932, p. 264) and 'repressed' (Lacan, 1932, pp. 279, 301). Lacan also indicates that Freud's depiction of the process of transformation sheds light on the erotomanic aspect of Aimée's delusion and explains the persecutory and jealous themes expressed in her delusional life. In an article on the Papin sisters, two young women who brutally killed their bosses, Lacan (1933, p. 27) adds that next to the homosexual impulse, a murderous, and often sadomasochistic, impulse can be found at the basis of paranoia. Remarkably, he states that paranoid psychosis is 'curable' (Lacan, 1932, p. 347) and that the therapy of psychosis should focus on resistances and defence mechanisms: 'the therapeutic problem of psychosis necessitates a *psychoanalysis of the ego* rather than a psychoanalysis of the unconscious; this means that it is in a better study of the *resistances* of the subject and in a new experience of their *manoeuvre* that he will have to find his technical solutions' [35] (Lacan, 1932, p. 280).

In his 1959 article On a Question Prior to the Treatment of Psychosis, Lacan fiercely criticized psychoanalytical explanations of psychosis that focus on defence mechanisms and disturbed instinctual impulses. In doing so he does not refer to his earlier work from the 1930s, but focuses on his contemporaries from the 1950s who are actually engaged in this line of reasoning. Indeed, his critique on the 'simplistic' and 'uncritical' ideas of his contemporaries largely applies to his own earlier work. In arguing against a focus on the ego and the defence mechanism of projection, Lacan states that 'there is no relation between affective projection and its supposed delusional effects' (Lacan, 1959, p. 453). In terms of Freud's suggestion that diverse delusions might be comprehended as ways of negating the proposition 'I love him', he underlines the 'logical problems formally involved in this deduction' (Lacan, 1959, p. 453). Furthermore, homosexual impulses, or any instinctual deviance, are no longer thought to be at the basis of psychosis: 'Homosexuality, which is supposedly the determining factor in paranoiac psychosis, is actually a symptom articulated in the psychotic process' (Lacan, 1959, p. 455). As we will demonstrate in Chapter 5, the concept of feminization better articulates what is at stake: Schreber makes no homosexual object choice, but finds no hold in the phallus.

In the world of French psychiatry and psychoanalysis, Lacan's doctoral dissertation had a mixed reception (Roudinesco, 1994). Few of his contemporaries discussed the thesis at all, or examined the theoretical and clinical consequences of the claims he made. Freud, for example, was sent a copy, but never reacted. The only person to review it in depth upon its publication was Henri Ey (1932). Ey appreciated Lacan's review of the literature, described his discussion of Aimée as brilliant but also pointed to the embryonic status of some of his more creative theoretical reflections. Paul Guiraud (1933) was more critical. He rejected Lacan's criticism of biological models, mocked his literary writing style and denounced his aggressive tone. Later discussions of the dissertation were more favourable, but clearly influenced by admiration for his later writing. From the 1950s onwards, Lacan grew silent about his doctoral thesis, and never profoundly examined his earlier ideas. Apart from some critical notes, no serious evaluation of these former viewpoints can be found in his later work (Lacan, 1975–6, 1976a). Many seem to have followed Lacan in this later reservedness and refrained from studying the dissertation, which is counterproductive for those who want to grasp the evolution of his work. Remarkably, Lacan's dissertation met with much approval among a number of Paris surrealist artists of the 1930s, with whom Lacan was acquainted. The artist Salvador Dali, for example, used Lacan's dissertation to refine his so-called paranoid–critical method. Lacan's description of paranoid functioning was inspirational for Dali's elaboration of a surrealist approach to reality (Dali, 1933, 1973; Garrabé, 1979). In his autobiography, Dali (1973, p. 171) illustrates the intellectual status this work had for him by stating: 'Lacan has thrown a scientific light on a phenomenon that was obscure for most of our contemporaries – the expression paranoia – and has conferred it its true meaning'. [36]

Imaginary identification as the 'psychical cause' of paranoia

In his work from the 1930s and 1940s, Lacan further elaborated on one of the most original ideas in his thesis, namely that Aimée is swamped and captivated by her close relationships to idealized others. This line of reasoning eventually constituted his broader paradigm for explaining psychosis and is elaborated in his essay The Family Complexes (Lacan, 1938) and in his article Remarks on Psychic Causality (Lacan, 1947). In both articles *paranoia* is understood as marked by a developmental arrest at an early stage of ego-formation, the so-called mirror stage, when a narcissistic relation to reality and a specular relation to others are still prevalent. The result of this arrest is that an imaginary mode of relating to the world is predominant. *Schizophrenia* in its turn is defined as a regression to the developmental phase preceding the mirror stage, which is the weaning phase (Lacan, 1938, p. 44).

Lacan situates the mirror stage, or phase, at the origin of subject formation (Lacan, 1947, p. 150). In the 1930s and 1940s he conceptualized the mirror stage in developmental psychological terms, as a formative period in infantile development that typically takes place when a child is between 6 and 18 months old (Lacan, 1949, pp. 75–6). From the 1950s on, with the introduction of the schema of the two mirrors (see Vanheule and Verhaeghe, 2009), he gradually starts discussing the mirror stage in terms of a mode of relating to others, which he qualifies as Imaginary. From then on it no longer refers to a chronological phase, in which development could be 'arrested' or to which one could 'regress', but to a typical way of relating to the other.

In the 1930s and 1940s, Lacan situated the mirror stage in the middle of three developmental phases. These phases are outlined in his essay The Family Complexes (1938), where Lacan examines child development. Here he states that development is not just a matter of biological maturation, but embedded in social interactions and fundamentally influenced by the child's familial context. This developmental context is also the basis for his explanation of psychopathology. In this respect he focuses on developmental arrests and fixations that cohere with specific pathological traits. The three phases discerned include the weaning complex, the intrusion complex and the Oedipus complex. For Lacan the term complex refers to a typical way of relating to objects, which is enacted over and again (Lacan, 1938, p. 28). What is typical of each complex is that a specific image is central to the child's actions (Lacan, 1938, p. 72). In the weaning complex this image is the breast, in the intrusion complex it is the mirror image and in the Oedipus complex it is the image of the father (Miller, 2005).

The weaning complex is characterized by the mutual affective bond that is installed between child and caregiver through nursing. With reference to neurological and hormonal data on newborns, Lacan speculates that humans are born prematurely, which makes the child particularly dependent on care. This 'prematurity at birth' (Lacan, 1949, p. 78) is overcome via a close attachment to the mother, a bond that evokes 'a privileged psychic satisfaction' [37] in the mother (Lacan, 1938, p. 34). The object that the child relates to during the weaning phase is not the mother as a person, but the (image of) the mother's breast. This relation implies that in the child's mind, the breast more strongly belongs to himself than to the mother. The mother is not yet discerned as a distinct entity to whom characteristics, such as possession of the breast, can be attributed. A close attachment to her is created via the object breast. Given the fact that the activity of feeding is experienced as pleasurable, the child aims to repeat this activity, progressively establishing an attachment to caregivers. After six months the importance of suckling declines and the mirror phase begins, whereby the primitive subject identifies with externally perceived mirror images. The three principal effects of this process of identification are the constitution of the ego, the resolution of the so-called 'physical phase' of relating to the world, and that the individual's relation with fellow human beings (*semblables*) undergoes a 'metamorphosis' (Lacan, 1947, pp. 153–4).

In his conceptualization of the mirror phase, Lacan (1938, 1947, 1949) makes a parallel with insights from ethology on how animal development is triggered and shaped by *Gestalts*. He uses examples, including that of the female pigeon, whose gonads only start to mature conditional upon the observation of a congener or its own image in a mirror; and the migratory locust, which becomes gregarious only upon seeing a look-alike during a certain phase of its development. If a migratory locust is not confronted with such an image, it remains solitary. Lacan argues that, in a similar way, *Gestalts* guide human development but are embedded and transmitted within a cultural context. Culture and familial history mould all possible images with which humans identify, and it is primarily within the familial context that they are expressed. Lacan therefore prefers the Latin term 'imago' or image over *Gestalt*. His use of the term imago echoes Jung's use of this concept but, even more so, the fundamentally cultural assumption of Christian theology that man is shaped after the *imago dei* – the image of God.

The basic problems the infant overcomes during the mirror stage are organic disturbance and discord, which are an effect of the child's lack of sensory and motor coordination. The infant's non-integrated experience of the body in combination with the thrust of the libidinal drives is a perfect cocktail for a generalized state of malaise (see also Lacan, 2004, pp. 75, 162). In Lacan's interpretation, the ego comes into being as a defence against this troubling state. In other words, through the infant's identification with a mirror image, an experience of totality and a feeling of identity [38] are acquired. In this type of identification the infant first distinguishes an externally perceived image (i.e. the image of the self that is seen in a mirroring surface, or an image of someone else that is treated as equivalent to oneself), and subsequently concludes that there is an 'I' to which this image refers. Within this logic, discerning a mirror image *precedes* the formation of the ego. This means that the materials constituting identity come from without. Biological maturation at most accounts for a preparedness to perceive the mirror image, not for the events that lead to its adoption or for the shape it will actually take. In this sense, the primitive ego corresponds to the body image and offers the infant an opportunity to experience itself as a unity. Along this way the mirror image functions as an 'ideal ego' for the ego. It is the successful version of itself, which the ego tries to coincide with in order to achieve an experience of self-mastery or self-realization. Commenting on this self-mastery, Lacan ironically states that the mirror image, as an ideal ego, is an 'orthopaedic' instance. It offers a feeling of unity, and enables the human being to anticipate a state of completion, which is not actually realized but virtually foreseen. The aspect that becomes masked along this way is the basis of incompletion and discord that marks a person's actual functioning (Lacan, 1949, p. 78).

The assumption of an ego and the idea that the ego corresponds to an ideal ego principally give rise to jubilance and playfulness in the child (Lacan, 1949, pp. 75–6). Jubilance coincides with the experience of self-recognition. Playfulness in its turn arises once the ego has been established, and indicates that the child is pleased by the experience of independence from his environment. As soon as the infant can crawl and walk, much of its play is based on exploring this image of itself as an autonomous being, for instance by running around tables, or by walking away from its parents when they sit down for a rest. The enjoyment of these activities is based on a new-found autonomy in relation to a static environment.

Lacan describes the cultural and familial transmission of the human mirror image. However, his earlier discussion of the course of this transmission, the role of the primary caregiver and the affective bond that is established during the weaning phase remains vague. What is lacking in this respect is a discussion of the role played by the recognition of the primary caregiver. In the mirror phase, the child cannot assume a mirror image by itself. The assumption of a mirror image is mediated by the caregiver's encouragement and validation. A self-image is only assumed when it is confirmed as a mirror image by the one who stands next to the child. Similarly the child only makes fun of running around tables or away from its mother and father because of their witnessing presence. The caregiver's position as witness is a necessary support for the acknowledgement of the child's autonomy. In the 1950s, when imaginary identification is discussed in terms of the schema of the two mirrors, Lacan is more explicit on the role of the other. From then on the mirror is explicitly used as a metaphor for what the calls the Other, which refers to the function of a recognizing third person that is underexposed in the earlier work (see Lacan, 1961, p. 565).

In 1938 Lacan's perspective on the mirror stage has a clear developmental thread. Nevertheless, his later work is more concerned with the way in which elements of psychical functioning reminiscent of the mirror stage are expressed in later life, and give rise to an '*imaginary mode*' of relating to the world (Lacan, 1947, p. 149). For example, in 1949 he states that he uses the example of the mirror stage 'given the light it sheds on the *I* function in the experience psychoanalysis provides us of it' (Lacan, 1949, p. 73). In other words, the theory of the mirror phase is used in order to clarify the functioning of the ego in adult life. With respect to psychosis he argues that 'the fundamental structure of madness' can be observed in the development of the primitive ego, which makes the logic of the mirror stage worthy of close examination (Lacan,

1947, p. 152). By making this claim Lacan suggests that the core characteristic of madness concerns an *identificatory structure*. The essence of psychosis is, in other words, not made up by a frailty or an unfortunate event, but by a mode of identification. This identification is magnified in psychosis, but can be more generally recognized in the human subject as such, which the theory of the mirror stage illustrates.

Lacan (1947, p. 153) goes even further in his argument, and claims that imaginary identification makes up the *psychical causality* of psychosis. I believe this claim is too teleological and therefore non-tenable. The claim suggests that an identification early in life produces later psychosis. Given the fact that a psychoanalyst works only with narrated reality, and that narratives on past events are not factual, but shaped by language and influenced by all kinds of later events, Lacan simply doesn't possess the correct data for making such claims. Only prospective longitudinal data would make such conclusions credible. I believe that this is probably why he didn't repeat his claim in his later work. With his shift in the 1950s to the epistemological framework of structuralism, comments pertaining to the factual causes of psychosis disappear. What then comes to the fore is a more detailed account of the logic or the structure of the psychotic experience, which he will address by examining the organization of the psychotic person's discourse.

As indicated above, in the 1930s and 1940s this step was not yet made and the focus is directed towards imaginary identification. This stress on identification is perhaps what made Lacan's early work so attractive to the surrealist movement. In their artistic activity surrealists were looking for a novel non-conventional approach to reality. This led many of them to study psychiatric textbooks, like the work of Kraepelin, for example (Garrabé, 2005). What Lacan's work added to the classic psychiatric perspective was the idea that the basic structure of paranoia is present in a person's functioning before the outbreak of psychosis, and that it concerns a mode of identification in social relationships. This identification is not necessarily indicative of a disorder and can be recognized as an aspect of human functioning, as illustrated by the theory of the mirror stage. The reason why Lacan's work was attractive for surrealists is probably because of the suggestion that through imaginary identification an element of paranoid functioning is characteristic of everybody. Salvador Dali (1933, 1973) most explicitly cultivated this latent element of paranoia and tried to systematize it in his paranoid–critical method of approaching reality.

In line with his ideas on the parallel between madness and the mirror stage, Lacan (1947, 1949) qualified any kind of self-knowledge that is obtained during the mirror phase as 'paranoid' and as 'alienated'. He points to the externally oriented basis of self-knowledge, which seems to be constructed in three steps. The first step in the construction of self-knowledge concerns the detection of an image in the outside world, or more broadly a unit of information that is alien to the subject. In the mirror stage this is the mirror image, which in a second step is perceived to refer to the subject, and experienced as revealing something about its own being. Given its revelatory character in a third step the image is adopted via identification. Identification is in this context purely imaginary, in that it is solely oriented on the image as a *Gestalt*. The reason why the mirror image is adopted during the mirror stage concerns the satisfying experience of totality it entails. The actual state of the infant is one of discord. The mirror image suggests that discord can be overcome, and is therefore idealized for the promise it implies. Through identification the identity of the subject is equated with the identity discerned in the unit of information, and as a result the element that is initially experienced as alien is experienced as the subject's own. Hence Lacan's claim that identification comes down to alienation. With regard to the alienated nature of self-knowledge, Lacan states that the way in which the primitive subject deals with the mirror image constitutes the basis for later positions towards knowledge. It reflects the 'basic ontological structure of the human world' (Lacan, 1949, p. 76). This means that all knowledge the 'I' has about its own being in the world comes from without. All self-knowledge is imported, and accidentally revealed at crucial moments in life.

As indicated above, Lacan qualifies knowledge not only as alienated, but also 'paranoid' (Mills, 2003). The reason for this lies in the parallel he discerns between the mirror stage and clinical paranoia. At the onset of a psychotic outbreak, during the so-called 'fertile moments' of the delusion (Lacan, 1947, p. 139) where elementary phenomena manifest, the same way of relating to units of information as that of the mirror phase can be observed. In both cases, an external unit of information is adopted uncritically because of its reputed value in revealing a truth about the subject's being. Lacan (1947, 1949) critically argues that both bear witness of a general structure of misrecognition. What is not recognized in each situation is that an 'act of faith' lies at the basis of adopting the external unit of information. Without hesitation [39] the subject believes that his own being is identified by what is revealed.

In terms of the mirror phase, misrecognition concerns the equation between the mirror image or ideal ego, and the subject's being: the feeling of unity introduced by the ideal ego is an illusion that blinds the ego to everything that does not fit the image. Although Lacan (1938, 1947, 1949) describes the process of mirroring as a necessary stage in human development, he also strongly emphasizes that it implies a more generalized deluded stance vis-à-vis reality, others and one's own body. It results in 'mihilism': the violent tendency to consider everything from the perspective of me (Lacan, 1961–2, lesson 15 November 1961).

In cases of psychosis, the same tendency towards misrecognition can be found. During a psychotic episode, the psychotic subject does not recognize that he actually imposes his own mental state, or 'the law of his heart', onto the world: 'It is an insane enterprise, rather, in that the subject does not recognize in this havoc the very manifestation of his actual being, or that what he experiences as the law of his heart is but the inverted and virtual image of that same being' (Lacan, 1947, p. 140). From this perspective, psychosis is marked by an inability to recognize that one is captured by the images one actually imposes upon the world. In 1949 (p. 80) Lacan formulates this idea as follows: 'the subject's capture by his situation gives us the most general definition of madness – the kind found within the asylum as well as the kind that deafens the world with its sound and fury'. Within this logic a person like Aimée is trapped within her own paranoid knowledge as she cannot take the reflective distance or symbolic meta-perspective necessary to recognize her own implication in what is happening to her (see Lacan, 1947, pp. 138–9). What she misrecognizes is precisely what she both adores and disputes in others; an ideal image of how she would like to be. Aimée does not realize that she actually imposes her own ideal ego upon others. Paraphrasing Lacan (1947, p. 141), Aimée is mad precisely insofar as she does not recognize that she herself contributes to the havoc against which she revolts. In this sense, madness is not considered as 'a contingent fact' that merely expresses latent biological frailties (Lacan, 1947, p. 144). It is the direct effect of an identificatory structure: 'the risk of madness is gauged by the very appeal of the identifications on which man stakes both his truth and his being' (Lacan, 1947, p. 143).

'*Hainamoration*' and '*jealouissance*': Two outcomes of imaginary identification

In his discussion of the mirror phase and psychosis, Lacan points to a number of typical affective outcomes and interpersonal interpretations that are associated with imaginary functioning. These are adequately grasped by his later neologisms *hainamoration* and *jealouissance* from seminar XX (Lacan, 1972–3, pp. 90–1). Both are condensations of existing words. *Hainamoration* is a contraction of the words *haine* (hate), *amour* (love) and *adoration* (adoration), and expresses how affects are intermingled in an imaginary relation: each time one of these affects is expressed, the other themes will be present as well. *Jealouissance* is a condensation of *jalousie* (jealousy) and *jouissance*. It expresses how *jouissance*, meaning an experience of enjoyment beyond lust, is found in the jealous hate of another being.

Hainamoration and *jealouissance* particularly occur during the second moment of the mirror stage. The first moment of the mirror phase is the identification with a self-image, which results in the constitution of the ego and the establishment of physical and mental boundaries. These boundaries delineate the primitive subject's being from the outside world. Once this narcissistic ego has been established, in the second moment of the mirror phase the infant begins to discern other beings or alter-egos. Others can only be discerned as distinct entities when the ego has been installed as a point of reference. Developmentally speaking, the figure of the other, in the sense of semblable or equal, comes into being when an elementary level of self-experience is established. Entities resembling the ego can be differentiated, and rapidly populate the primitive subject's world. This leads to a 'metamorphosis' of the individual's relation to the other. Whereas others were first experienced as vague elements in the environment, they now prove to be semblables and do not leave the ego unaffected (Lacan, 1947, p. 154).

By discussing the imaginary relation between the ego and his semblable, Lacan principally aims to characterize a mode of interaction that logically precedes regulation via cultural laws and convention. The idea is that social relationships are mediated by laws and conventions and this mediation takes shape during the Oedipal phase, which follows the mirror stage. The basis of the social relation, by contrast, is made up during the second period of the mirror stage. During this period a climate of struggle, suspicion and admiration is established in relation to the other, which deeply influences the way subsequent interpersonal relations are interpreted. In an explicit reference to Hegel (1807), and an implicit allusion to Kojève (1947), Lacan (1953–4, p. 277) says that a life and death struggle 'for pure prestige' characterizes this imaginary relation to the other. The semblable is a rival, in relation to whom elimination seems to be the safest option. In fact, this is the strategy of which Aimée bears witness. Her act of violence was directed towards limiting the imaginary other that came too close. In 1938 Lacan (p. 43) suggests that an alternative for setting a limit lies in the pact or the contract, which implies subordination to rules of convention and to symbolic laws. Whereas this idea is embryonic in the 1930s, in the 1950s it will make up his new paradigm on psychosis.

In the mirror stage love and adoration can be principally recognized in the attraction towards the mirror image. Its reflection of totality delights the subject, which can be observed in the jubilant and triumphant reactions following the actual assumption of the mirror image. Love and adoration can be recognized in the positive reaction towards those who support the adoption of the mirror image. Hate will be experienced in relation to anyone or anything that disrupts the privileged relation with the mirror image. Such disruptions will give rise to images of fragmentation, in which the acquired state of wholeness is experienced as disintegrating.

In his discussion of the intrusion complex, which coincides with the mirror phase, Lacan (1938, pp. 43–5) indicates that in the mirror stage hate actually has three faces. The first way in which hate can manifest is via intrusion. Intrusion is experienced in relation to those who disrupt the cherished relation between the ego and its ideal image. The ego's typical reaction is to hate the intruder. Second, hate can manifest via rivalry. Rivalry is experienced when an ego compares itself with a semblable and when both are perceived to relate to the same ideal. This provokes competition around being the best in fulfilling the ideal, and gives rise to a desire to eliminate the rival other. The third way in which hate manifests is jealousy. Jealousy is experienced when the ego concludes that the semblable with which one is competing has the advantage, and has something one lacks. Jealousy reflects the desire to have this advantageous position for oneself, and the wish to eradicate the frustrating other. The concept *jealouissance*, which stresses the experience of enjoyment-beyond-lust that comes with jealousy, indicates that the imaginary experience of hate is more than a simple psychological reaction. Jealousy and hate put the body into a state of uproar; acts of revenge provide an unequalled satisfaction and any symbolic compromise will be experienced as a frustration. Conversely, Lacan (1949, p. 79) also points to the effect of the body on imaginary experience. He argues that for the ego manifestations of the drive will always carry a threat of danger. The drive is not incorporated by the ego: the ego came into being as a reaction against the organic discord the drive makes up. As a result, any experience of the drive will give rise to an experience of imminent danger that comes from without. Imaginary interpersonal interpretations will aim to give this danger a face.

Whereas Lacan discusses the reactions of *hainamoration* and *jealouissance* more extensively in relation to the mirror stage and imaginary relations in general, he discerns the same reactions in paranoia, where they give shape to typical delusional themes (Lacan, 1938, 1947). In this respect, megalomania and erotomania bear witness of love and adoration, whereas delusions of intrusion, persecution and jealousy bear witness of hate and *jalouissance*.

Conclusion

The first period in Lacan's work on psychosis situates itself on a turning point between tradition and innovation. At first Lacan is fairly traditional in his viewpoints. His doctoral thesis elaborates a critique on the then established biological and psychological models of psychosis, but remains vague in terms of formulating alternative viewpoints. His discussion of Aimée brings him to detect a specific mode of relating to others, but at this stage a broad conceptual discussion of the nature of the imaginary relation is still lacking. He loosely refers to elements of Freudian theory and concludes that self-punishing paranoia depicts a somewhat novel type of psychosis. Lacan's work becomes more innovative when he elaborates his theory of the mirror stage. At first this stage refers to a developmental process, but later on he uses it to discuss the structure of imaginary relations to the world, as can be observed in paranoia. What is important here is that this line of reasoning focuses on identification and relationship patterns. It enables Lacan to shift away from his earlier Freudian-based explanation of psychosis in terms of homosexual impulses. With the theory of the mirror phase, delusional themes are framed as consequences of a broader strategy of misrecognition. The basis of it is an identificatory structure, whereby the ego is alienated to and captured by an ideal image. Disbelief in this image is impossible, and this impossibility defines madness.

Part II

Second Era: The Age of the Signifier

2
Towards a Structural Study of Psychosis

Lacan's switch from the Imaginary to the Symbolic

In the 1950s, almost parallel with the beginning of his public seminar in psychoanalysis, Lacan's focus on psychosis changed. Inspired by the increasingly influential structuralist movement that shaped the domain of linguistics and ethnography, and guided by his belief that psychoanalysis should be revived by reading Freud's texts to the letter, Lacan argues that the basic problem of psychosis concerns the position of the subject in relation to language, or more broadly in relation to what he calls the register of the Symbolic. The register of the Symbolic is thereby conceptualized in opposition to the register of the Imaginary. In this opposition the Imaginary is not fundamentally redefined, but subordinated to language-based structures. Lacan assumes that the Symbolic determines imaginary modes of relating to oneself and to the world: 'Imaginary effects, far from representing the core of analytic experience, give us nothing of any consistency unless they are related to the symbolic chain that binds and orients them' (Lacan, 1957a, p. 11). In other words, imaginary phenomena, such as the tension between the ego and the ideal ego, should not be studied as such, but should be considered in terms of laws that are implicitly present at the level of the Symbolic (Ragland-Sullivan, 1986). In allusion to Plato's cave, imaginary phenomena are only 'shadows and reflections' (Lacan, 1957a, p. 11) of what is really at stake, which is the way in which the subject is determined by language. In his focus on language and on the Symbolic Lacan finds inspiration in the work of Ferdinand de Saussure, the founder of structural linguistics, in addition to the work of linguist Roman Jakobson and anthropologist Claude Lévi-Strauss. In the spirit of these authors Lacan seeks to articulate the structure that characterizes psychosis, meaning the laws that determine the subject's position towards the Symbolic and towards others in psychosis.

During this time Lacan considered psychosis in terms of a non-event at the level of the Symbolic. Whereas neurosis was characterized by a process of metaphorization, due to which the subject and the other are determined in relation to the law, in psychosis this process of metaphorization fails. This creates a fundamental instability, both in terms of how the other is experienced and the way in which subjectivity takes shape. The term 'foreclosure', which I discuss in detail in Chapter 3, is used to refer to this absent metaphorization. Lacan uses this concept to elucidate full-blown psychosis, with hallucinations and delusions, as well as ordinary or discrete forms of psychosis, where mental stability is obtained via imaginary identifications.

These ideas on the structure of the Symbolic in psychosis were first formulated during one of his year-long seminars (Lacan, 1955–6) and in the subsequent article On a Question Prior to any Possible Treatment of Psychosis (Lacan, 1959). This paper is a synthesis of his seminar, but also contains a number of novel elements that were further elaborated in later seminars and papers. While Lacan stayed quite close to common psychiatric models of psychosis during the first phase of his work, from the 1950s onwards he diverges from these models as well as elements of Freudian theory he had previously embraced: the idea of projection is left behind and the concept of foreclosure is used in the place of Freud's concept of rejection. With this theoretical shift he begins to formulate novel ideas on the nature of psychosis and the status of hallucinations and delusions. Attention is no longer paid to intra-psychical processes, but instead to the way in which the subject is determined by the structure of speech. What is important about this move is that psychosis is studied with a focus on the subject–Other relationship. His principal idea is that in psychosis the subject has a different relation to the Other than in neurosis, and therefore the structure of psychosis should be clarified. This would offer clinicians a theoretical compass that can guide their practice. In other words, because psychoanalysis is a *conceptually based practice* a conceptual model of the structure of psychosis is needed before one can properly question the treatment of psychosis, as well as the effects of such treatment.

Lacan's focus on the *structure* of psychosis as manifested in *speech* means that any conclusion drawn from his teaching on the biological, psychological or social cause of psychosis is spurious. A structural approach provides logical models of how specific psychological problems are organized, but provides no basis for causal inference. On the basis of such models, clinical material, including information gathered during clinical interviews or psychoanalytical sessions, can be examined with a focus on their internal organization: What is a person's position towards his own speech? Or towards his past? How does he relate to others in social situations?... However, an analysis of the structure of speech should not lead to far-reaching claims concerning actual events that may have taken place in reality. Lacan's structural model clarifies the logic of psychotic functioning, but does not propose to explain the so-called biopsychosocial factors that may have caused psychosis.

This chapter gives an overview of the key concepts in Lacan's work from the 1950s. The notions of signifier, signification and the subject are explained, and the status of the subject in psychosis is explored. In the next three chapters the concept of foreclosure and the status of hallucinations and delusions will be discussed.

The Lacanian signifier

As indicated above, Lacan's discussion of psychosis in the 1950s focuses on the register of the Symbolic. In this context he adopts the notions 'signifier' and 'signified' from the linguist Ferdinand de Saussure (e.g. Lacan, 1953, p. 26, 1957b, p. 415). de Saussure's (1916) study of linguistics concentrates on the structure of language. The way in which speech is actually produced in daily life and the relation between language and the outside world, or between language and its referents, are largely left out of consideration. Instead, his work focuses on the internal organization of the linguistic system.

At the basis of de Saussure's work the 'linguistic sign' is deconstructed in terms of 'signifier' and 'signified' (de Saussure, 1916, p. 102). The signified concerns the concept or the idea that the linguistic sign conveys, while the signifier refers to the material side of the sign. The signifier is the 'acoustic image' or the 'sound image' that by which the sign is made up: 'The sound image is sensory, and if I happen to call it "material", it is only in that sense, and by way of opposing it to the other term of the association, the concept, which is generally more abstract' (de Saussure, 1916, p. 66). In stressing this idea of the acoustic image, de Saussure assumes that the aspect of sound is pivotal in both spoken and written language. For example, a person reading text automatically converts the written traces into sounds that are mentally experienced. The concept 'signifier' refers to this mental experience of sound. He calls it an *image* to the extent that the signifier concerns 'the psychological imprint of the sound', and not sensory perception (de Saussure, 1916, p. 66). In this respect de Saussure distinguishes signifiers from phonemes: phonemes refer to vocal activity whereas signifiers refer to mental representations. Thus considered, the words we use are combinations of sound images, which we conventionally agree have a semantic or grammatical value. Furthermore, de Saussure (1916, p. 113) argues that 'the bond between the sound and the idea is radically arbitrary'. This means that the relation between signifier and signified is random, there is no inherent reason why particular signifiers are used to refer to particular ideas. In other words, only convention explains their connection, hence the diversity of languages.

A further characteristic de Saussure attributes to the signifier is that it is an entity in language because of the fact that it is distinguished and differentiated from other signifiers: 'The linguistic entity is not accurately defined until it is delimited, i.e. separated from everything that surrounds it on the phonetic chain' (de Saussure, 1916, p. 103). This means that continuous flows of speech can only be decoded if we are able to distinguish separate signifiers, to which different signifieds can be attributed. More broadly, this idea implies that the identity of a given element in language, like a signifier, can only be defined based on this element's dissimilarity from other elements. Structuralist authors typically take this as a basic tenet: dissimilarity defines identity, while resemblance indicates absolute non-identity (Milner, 2002, p. 108). de Saussure goes on to state that, contrary to what might be said about a notation system, there is no exact correspondence between signifier and signified. Dictionaries might indicate that certain signifieds are connected to specific signifiers, but once language is used these strict lexical connections become more relative. Grammar and syntax have a fundamental effect on the creation of meaning. de Saussure (1916, p. 112) therefore concludes that in language two 'planes' or 'curves' can be distinguished: 'the indefinite plane of jumbled ideas' and 'the equally vague plane of sounds'. These planes are not related in terms of fixed connections, which Lacan (1957b, p. 419) also stresses with his idea that there is an 'incessant sliding of the signified under the signifier'. Yet the moment language is used, the curves are connected. In speech or writing signifiers are related to signifieds, which results in the creation of 'signification' or signifying units. Lacan (1955–6, 1957b) refers to this process with the concept 'punctuation'. Punctuation leads to the creation of a momentary link between signifier and signified: 'A signifying unit presupposes the completion of a certain circle that situates its different elements [signifier and signified]' (Lacan, 1955–6, p. 263). This idea of the creation of a momentary link between signifier and signified returns in Lacan's more metaphorical expression that speech hooks the signifier to the signified (Lacan, 1955–6, p. 299) or creates 'button ties' in discourse (Lacan, 1957b, p. 419). Their effect is that the sliding of the signified under the signifier comes to a halt.

With respect to the way humans deal with language, de Saussure proposes that the signified predominates over the signifier. This accent on the concept or the idea assumes that language is used to transfer and express meaning, and reflects an idealist assumption on human functioning: the mental (signified) prevails over the material (signifier) (Badiou, 1982). Lacan (1957a, 1957b) clearly argues for the opposite. He exchanges de Saussure's idealist assumption for a materialist viewpoint, and considers the signifier, qua element of the Symbolic, as primordial to the signified, qua element of the Imaginary. He argues that at the level of the unconscious, the signifier predominates and even makes up the logic of how symptoms are organized. To formally depict the primacy of the signifier Lacan frequently uses the following notation (Figure 2.1), whereby the fraction bar indicates that the signifier (S) prevails over the signified (s):

$$\frac{S}{s}$$

Figure 2.1 Signifier and signified

Lacan refers to this formula as an 'algorithm' (Lacan, 1957b, p. 428). Mathematically speaking, to define such formal notation as an algorithm might sound invalid since it is not a calculation method. As Miller (2010, p. 13) indicates, Lacan's formulae are 'imitation mathemes' that reflect an *effort* towards mathematization or logical formulation. What Lacan provides with his formula is a schematic or logical expression of the relation between the signifier and the signified, and not an arithmetic device. The Lacanian formula is the abstract expression of a theoretical idea, and aims at grasping the structure of the problems under discussion. Throughout his work Lacan developed many formulae with a similar status as the formula depicting the relation between the signifier and the signified. These make sense in terms of his structural approach to science, and express his belief that the laws of composition among the elements that make up structures can be expressed in formulaic terms. The formulae describe the internal organization of phenomena or problems; they specify the elements that make up the phenomenon or problem, characterize interrelations between these elements and indicate how effects are determined by the interrelations between elements.

An example of Lacan's materialist view of the signifier in the unconscious can be found in the Freud-Fliess correspondence of 1887–1904.[1] In one letter (dated 29 December 1897) Freud discusses a man, Mr. E, who had an 'anxiety attack at the age of ten when he tried to catch a black beetle' (Masson, 1985, p. 290). During a session Mr. E, when speaking about his anxiety attack, connected the idea of the beetle (*Käfer* in German) to the word ladybug (*Marienkäfer* in German). Before making this connection Mr. E had been talking about his mother, who was called Marie. In other words, the topic of his mother constituted the basis upon which further associations were made. In the path of associations the word 'Marie' led to the word *Marienkäfer*. Furthermore, when talking about his mother Mr. E mentioned that as a child he had heard a conversation between his grandmother and aunt. Freud states that this conversation was about the marriage of his mother, where 'it emerged that she had not been able to make up her mind for quite some time' (Masson, 1985, p. 290). As a child Mr. E grew up with a French-speaking nurse, and therefore learned to speak French before German. Regarding the following session with Mr. E, Freud states that just prior to the session 'the meaning of the beetle [*Käfer*] had occurred to him; namely: *que faire?* = being unable to make up one's mind...' (Masson, 1985, p. 290). The French expression *que faire?*,[2] which means 'what to do?', expresses his mother's hesitation about her marriage, an idea that Mr. E obviously shies away from. The example shows that in discovering the unconscious determination of this patient's anxiety attack, the signified 'bug' or 'beetle' is misleading: anxiety doesn't arise in relation to the particular species of insects involved. What matters is the acoustic image or the signifier: for this man, who subsequently spoke German, *Käfer* sounds like the expression *que faire* from the language of his childhood. This acoustic image, which we can denote as '*Käfer/que faire*' corresponds to two underlying ideas: 'bug' and 'mother's hesitation about her marriage'. The anxiety entering consciousness is connected to the word 'bug', while simultaneously the truth is repressed. What really concerns him is his mother's hesitation about her marriage, of which he, as her child, is the product.

The path towards this subjective truth can only be followed via the traces of the signifier and therefore by carefully circumventing the signified that first entered consciousness. Lacan's idea is that the unconscious follows the logic of the signifier and that the analyst's task consists of hearing the signifiers that echo in an analysant's speech.[3] In his opinion symptoms and formations of the unconscious, like dreams, are rebuses, the hidden meaning of which can be detected by hearing the signifiers that are implied (e.g. Lacan, 1953, 1957b; Miller, 1998). As such we could even make a further step in unravelling Mr. E's associations, and *hear* that the French verb *marier*, which means 'to marry', also echoes in the sound image of *Marienkäfer*. *Que faire?* is only the first part of the question that is expressed in *Marienkäfer*, while *marier* is the grammatical subject that this question actually addresses.

The signifying chain, the Other and the process of signification

Another idea Lacan adopts from Ferdinand de Saussure (1916) is that the moment language is used in speech, signifiers are linked in signifier-to-signifier connections or chains. Signifiers connect in 'signifying chains', says Lacan (1957b, p. 418), like links in a necklace. de Saussure refers to these signifier-to-signifier connections with the term 'syntagm' (de Saussure, 1916, p. 124), indicating that it is via syntax that signifiers make up meaningful series. Examples of syntagms are words, word groups and sentences. In each case, signifiers are clustered and connected in a linear relationship of adjacency. Both Roman Jakobson and Lacan follow de Saussure in this idea. Jakobson (1953, p. 565) concludes that the principle of connecting signifiers makes up a specific dimension or axis in language: 'Syntax is concerned with the axis of concatenation'. In a broader time frame these signifying chains make up the *diachrony* of language. This means that by linking signifiers in linear chains the dimension of *time* is introduced. On the one hand adding a new signifier implies that preceding signifiers obtain a status of anteriority. On the other hand the linear connection of signifiers in speech is open ended and leads to the anticipation of additional signifiers. The articulation of each signifier sets up the expectation of yet another signifier that will further complement the chain. To depict the diachronic connection between signifiers Lacan uses the formula: S1 → S2. This formula indicates that a given signifier (S1) should always be studied in terms of its reference (→) to another signifier (S2).

In clinical contexts the idea of the signifying chain is important to Lacan. The chain of signifiers is the sole context from which the value of a signifier can be grasped: 'Only signifier-to-signifier correlations provide the standard for any and every search for signification' (Lacan, 1957b, p. 418). In so saying, Lacan radicalizes a viewpoint that can also be found in the work of Jakobson and de Saussure. Jakobson (1953) argued

that both convention and context are important for the accurate interpretation of speech and writing. Convention gives the interpreter an
idea of the meanings or signifieds that are usually attributed to a word.
Such conventional meanings can be found in a dictionary, yet such definitions are not sufficient for an accurate interpretation of a given chain
of signifiers. Language is not just a code whereby words have standard
meanings. Grammar and context also determine the sense of the words.
This implies that, for the interpretation of a word or a syntagm, the
broader signifying chain must be taken into account. Lacan (1956c) radi-
calized this viewpoint and argued that in clinical contexts, conventional
understanding should be minimized, while contextual understanding
should be maximized.

In this respect Lacan (1959, p. 460) opposes his approach to interpretation to Carl Gustav Jung. Whereas Jungian psychoanalysis assumes
that symbols, as they appear in dreams for example, have standard
meanings that can be decoded, Lacan stresses the contextual determination of meaning. He argues that 'the signifying articulation' (Lacan,
1959, p. 460) itself determines the meaning of a given element in discourse. In a clinical context, signifiers should be primarily understood
in terms of the signifying chain the patient produces and clinicians
should refrain from interpreting them in terms of their own preconceived knowledge. The single relevant basis for interpreting elements
from a person's discourse is the context made up by this discourse itself.

The *Käfer* example illustrates how understanding the conventional
meaning of a word does not help the analyst grasp its unconscious determination; nor would the interpretation of 'bug' as an archetypal symbol
of resurrection. Such interpretations even deafen the analyst from hearing the signifiers that circulate in a person's discourse, and consequently
interfere with the work of accessing unconscious material. The only way
to adequately understand the relevance of a particular signifier (S1) is
by listening to the chain of signifiers in which it is embedded ($\rightarrow$ S2).
In clinical work relying on conventional signifieds is problematic, not
only because it leads to the imposition of the therapist's preconceived
ideas, but because in doing so one joins the ego in its defensive focus
on certain signifieds (Lacan, 1955–6). Contrary to what he argued in
his doctoral thesis, from 1949 onwards Lacan argued that focusing on
the ego is counterproductive in psychoanalysis and obfuscates any work
with the unconscious.

Next to the syntagmatic or diachronic dimension in language, de
Saussure and Jakobson also distinguish a so-called associative, paradigmatic or synchronic axis. Lacan refers to this as the dimension of

synchrony, which, following Jakobson, he opposed to diachrony (e.g. Lacan, 1955–6, 1957b). Synchrony means that when a signifier is diachronically chained in speech, it simultaneously echoes many other signifiers that are not actually articulated, but are connected to it associatively. For example, at the synchronic level one could make the assumption that Mr. E's idea of the *Marienkäfer* was also related to the French verb *marier*/to marry. Although Mr. E did not make this connection in his speech, a synchronic, associative connection may be present. At the level of the signifier this connection is the homophony between the German word *Marien* and the French word *marier*, and at the level of the signified the synchronic connection concerns the issue of marriage: the words 'marriage' and 'to marry' are connected qua meaning.

Synchrony can also be found in the logical first step of speaking. Each speech act concerns the unfolding of signifiers in time, but starts with the selection of an element from the system of language or 'treasure trove of signifiers' (Lacan, 1960, p. 682). This selection always concerns a set of alternatives, from which only one is used. Along this way, a choice is made: the speaker adheres, or alienates, to a certain lexicon to express the intention that drove him to speak. This is always a form of alienation as it binds a person to the 'alien' speech elements of a vernacular. To stress the aspect of alienation and choice in the use of language, Lacan refers to the synchrony of the language system with the term 'Other', abbreviated as 'O'.

Actually, there are a number of reasons why Lacan attributes the status of 'Other' to language. The *first* reason is that a speaker does not coincide with language. We think of ourselves as users of language, not as beings of language. This indicates that language has an external position for the speaker, which remains external even when the subject incorporates its system. *Second*, language is a cultural product that is learned and incorporated via others. Just as the mirror image is adopted via the other in the mirror stage, language is acquired in and through close relationships, whereby the figure of the other has the position of transmitting its rules. The expression 'mother tongue' reflects this relational embedment. During this transmission the infant is inscribed in a culture, a social system and a family lineage. By learning a language a child acquires a specific lexicon that will be determinant of its later relationships with others, common thought categories and elementary rules of social interaction. A *third* reason why language can be qualified as Other is the fact that it is a system that qualifies otherness. From its binary basis language classifies the world in terms of difference: two signifiers can be distinguished if their sound image is different; two signifieds can be discerned if they express different concepts. As a consequence language can be conceptualized as a system that aims to name what is 'Other'. A *fourth* reason for qualifying language as Other is the fact that people believe in language and use it as a guarantee for articulating their own existence. We humans believe that words help us build correct representations of ourselves and the world, and rarely question this presumption.

In his later work, Lacan (1975–6, p. 56) suggests that language and speech are not only Other, but even have a 'parasitical' effect on the speaker. This idea is reminiscent of theories of mental automatism, which claimed that delusions start with the experience of a parasitic element in mental life (see Chapter 1). By attributing a parasitical status to language, Lacan affirms its status as a foreign body for the speaker. It is something that has an effect on the speaker's being, largely beyond consciousness and intentional control. As a consequence, words inaugurate a deluded stance towards oneself: 'It is from language that we hold this madness that there is being' [4] (Lacan, 1976d, p. 45). By using language we fictionalize our being and live with a fictionalized account of ourselves as if we were a character in a story; it therefore creates a generalized form of madness in everyone (see Chapter 7).

Lacan's discussion of the logic of the signifier in terms of diachrony and synchrony brought him to make materialist interpretations of unconscious processes. His proposition that the unconscious is structured like a language brought him to reinterpret a number of psychological processes previously discussed by Freud. Lacan's focus on the material quality of language meant that fewer presuppositions regarding an underlying psychological agent were made. In other words, unconscious processes were not presumed to take place in a hidden space in the mind, but in the act of speech itself. For example, he argued that in operationalizing Freud's concept of 'overdetermination' we should actually examine a given signifier's embedment in the diachrony of speech, as well as the synchrony of its associative connections with other signifiers (Lacan, 1957a, p. 35). Only the signifier's connection with other signifiers gives a sufficient basis for a valid interpretation to the unconscious as a concept.

With the concepts of diachrony and synchrony the process of signification is also specified (Naveau, 2004; Van Haute, 2002). Signification is not merely an effect of linking signifiers to signifieds, but is created as an effect of syntactic processes in the signifying chain. The following figure (Figure 2.2) illustrates Lacan's understanding of how the logic of signification is generated in language (Lacan, 1957–8, 1960):

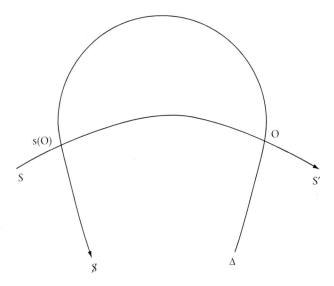

Figure 2.2 The logic of signification

In this figure, the horizontal arrow from S to S' indicates how, on the one hand, speech is always a matter of linking signifiers in a chain – a process that temporally follows diachronic logic. On the other hand, speech will be generated only if a person feels the urge to articulate an intention or need, symbolized by Δ at the basis of the returning arrow. The returning arrow indicates how this intention eventually leads to the production of *meaning* and *subjectivity*. The two intersections between the arrows are thereby crucial.

The right intersection (indicated as O) refers to the Other or 'the locus of the treasure trove of signifiers' (Lacan, 1960, p. 682) and indicates that in the production of speech, signifiers are picked up from the lexicon we have at our disposal. The idea of treasure trove thereby expresses synchrony: in the Symbolic all signifiers are simultaneously given. A speaker picks up elements from this whole and links them in a chain. By doing so the anticipation of meaning begins. Indeed, through the use of signifiers, a message is expected to arise. Yet as long as the advent of a meaning is under construction or postponed, it is suspended (Lacan, 1959, p. 446).

The left intersection refers to the moment of punctuation, in which the intention to speak eventually crystallizes in signification; in a message, indicated as s(O) in the figure above. Lacan stresses that, at a temporal level, punctuation follows a *retroactive* logic. It is only if a sufficient number of signifiers have been articulated that meaning can arise. Signifiers that are articulated later will thereby determine the final meaning of formerly uttered signifiers. For example, in the sentence 'you are my friend...no more', the first four signifiers make us antic-ipate that the message will be about a sustaining friendship, yet the last two words indicate the opposite. In this sense, as speech progresses meaning is open to change. By adding signifiers or altering punctuation, the retroactively created button ties change as well. Given the fact that meaning implies the creation of a mental image, on which people tend to focus, Lacan considers it as Imaginary. Semantics concern the imagi-nary dimension of speech, which implies that it should not be studied as such, but always situated relative to the interplay between signifiers at the level of the Symbolic.

Finally, the process of generating meaning also has the effect of pro-ducing subjectivity, indicated as $\$$ in Figure 2.2. This figure shows that whereas Lacan frequently made use of linguistic concepts, his primary aim is clinical and directed towards understanding how subjectivity is generated via the signifying chain. The signifiers articulated in the signi-fying chain mark and connote the speaker, but never denote the speaker exactly. Lacan considers the subject as an effect of this connotation and thus concludes that the subject is divided, which is expressed by the bar through S: $\$$. In terms of the process of signification, $\$$ is the result of a dialectical tension between the Symbolic and the Imaginary. At the level of the message, speech functions to build images regarding who we are. These images make up the ego, but are selective imaginary self-representations that exclude certain signifiers. The notion of the subject refers to these 'forgotten' signifiers, across which it is fundamentally scattered; hence the idea that the subject is divided (Lacan, 1957–8, 1960). In neurosis this division is experienced as internal, hence the neurotic tendency to repress, whereas in psychosis it is experienced as disconnected from one's own intentions and as coming from without.

The subject of psychosis

From his third seminar onwards, Lacan's theory on the signifying chain enables him to give body to a *materialist* and *structural* study of psy-chosis. The approach he proposes takes human discourse as its object, and examines the structure that is articulated in the use of language (Lacan, 1955–6, p. 121). Typical manifestations of psychosis, such as hallucinations and delusions, should be studied at the level of speech, and particular attention should be paid to the way the signifying chain is composed: 'It's the register of speech that creates all the richness of the phenomenology of psychosis, it's here that we see all its aspects, decompositions, refractions' (Lacan, 1955–6, p. 36). This focus is materialist since it focuses on the signifier and on peculiarities in the process of signification, and not on the content or the signifieds of psychotic ideation. Hypotheses on underlying mental processes are kept to a minimum, making room for reflection on how psychosis is expressed in language use. This materialist focus on the signifying chain should not be thought of as reductionistic; rather, it is a choice to focus on the materials of which psychoanalytical practice makes use. After all, the principal way in which a clinician gains knowledge about mental life is via a patient's speech. Hallucinations and delusions are not natural entities that can be observed, but phenomena of which a clinician acquires knowledge only when the patient talks about them: they are articulated in speech and take shape via language. Therefore, for a Lacanian analyst an individual's use of language in clinical interviews, psychoanalytical sessions or written materials is the main object of study.

More broadly, this focus on the signifier is indicative of his theory of the structure of psychosis. This is suggested in his 1959 article, where Lacan states: 'What I'm asserting here is that, in recognizing the drama of madness, reasoning is doing what it likes best, *sua res agitur*, because it is in man's relation to the signifier that this drama is situated' (Lacan, 1959, p. 478). This statement expresses the idea that psychosis primarily concerns a way of relating to the signifier that differs from the way in which people conventionally use the signifying chain. Aspects of mental dysfunction that can be deduced from a psychotic person's discourse, such as cognitive irregularities, are secondary to the underlying structure of the signifying chain. By stating that 'reasoning is doing what it likes best', Lacan suggests that rational activity addresses precisely that which makes up the drama of psychosis, a drama concerning the subject's relation to the signifier. It's with the aim of characterizing this relation to the signifier that Lacan turns to the concept of 'structure' (Lacan, 1955–6, pp. 60, 121, 310). The structure of psychosis discussed in his theory is not a presumed mode of psychological organization that is hidden in the mind. It concerns the logic of subjective functioning as expressed in the organization of the signifying chain itself. This focus on the materiality of the signifying chain implies a shift from his earlier work on psychosis. Whereas in his study of personality, Lacan was still focusing on implicit mental processes, his structural approach concentrates on the externality of language use.

However, this focus on the signifying chain does not imply that Lacan advocates a purely linguistic study of psychosis. The main difference between Lacan and his linguistic sources of inspiration is that he adds the dimension of the subject (Fink, 1995; Malone and Roberts, 2010; Milner, 2002; Parker, 2003; Pluth, 2007). Along this way Lacan gives an important twist to the linguistic theories he utilizes. Whereas the structural linguists studied language in its general form, and not in terms of speech events, Lacan studied language to the extent that it was actually uttered by a speaker and considers the dimension of the unconscious. The speaker is not an abstract figure, but a concrete person addressing someone else, like an analysant addressing an analyst. The following quote is in this context programmatic and reflects very well how he conceptualizes the subject in terms of the signifying chain: 'My definition of the signifier (there is no other) is as follows: a signifier is what represents the subject to another signifier' (Lacan, 1960, pp. 693–4).

In this statement Lacan adds an important dimension to the de Saussurean idea of the concatenation of signifiers, a dimension that also differs from the register of the referent or the *Bedeutung* (Eco, 1976). In the tradition of de Saussure, the signifier is merely an element of differentiality that obtains identity in relation to other signifiers. What Lacan adds is that the speaker's use of the signifying chain has a further effect: the differentiality of the signifier determines *human subjectivity*. In contrast to computers, where the use of language is purified and most efficient, humans cannot but articulate their own being while using language. By using speech a speaker determines his position towards himself and towards the world. Along this way the use of the signifier creates the subject.

Important to Lacan's definition of the signifier is that it does not characterize the subject as an intentional or teleological instance that gives rise to the signifier, but as the connotative effect of using signifiers. The subject doesn't produce speech; speech produces the subject.[5] In Figure 2.2 this is expressed in the position of $ at the end of the arrow of retroaction: speech is initiated via an intention, and in the end subjectivity is produced. This means that the subject is not conceptualized as a psychological entity that is articulated via speech, but as an 'emptity' resulting from references within the network of signifiers that make up someone's discourse: 'There's no other scientific definition of subjectivity than one that proceeds from the possibility of handling the signifier for purely signifying, not significant ends' (Lacan, 1955–6, p. 189). The subject is not a preverbal instance that 'uses' the signifier with the aim of narrating something, but the momentary and transitory effect of self-referential connotations in a speaker's discourse.[6] These under no circumstances form a unity, and never actually grasp the speaker's identity in definite terms: 'the subject is always a fading thing that runs under the chain of signifiers' (Lacan, 1970, p. 194). Therefore subjectivity is not a constancy or a permanency. It needs to be created time and time again by using the signifier. In Lacan's theory subjectivity even has an event-like nature: the subject arises as an event, caused by the particular composition of the signifying chain.

This view breaks with the idealist perspective characteristic of many psychodynamic theories. Idealist theories typically presume that in the mind, a soul or essence can be found that organizes psychical reality. Lacan doesn't make such an assumption and proposes a materialist approach to subjectivity, thus suggesting that what must be studied is the materiality of speech and the effects of speech on the speaker.

Clinically speaking, this theoretical starting point requires a case-oriented approach that pays attention to the fine points of speech. The only method of getting hold of the subject is a detailed study of the signifying chain from which it arises. Indeed, only by a detailed study of materials from psychoanalytical sessions or interviews, or by examining specific writings, like Schreber's autobiography, can subjectivity be touched upon. However, this should not imply that the subject is a collection of signifieds that can be pinned down. Lacan's definition of the subject suggests that changes in the chain of signifiers, like additional signifiers or different punctuations, alter the subject. The only thing that can be grasped is the logic of how the signifying chain creates the subject in a momentary way.

Some scholars and clinicians working with Lacanian theory neglect this fundamental point on the emptity and the event-like status of the subject. However, to describe the subject in terms of a psychological entity or in terms of an instance that speaks not only misses the point Lacan makes, but glosses over the radical aspect of his theory (Parker, 2003, 2010). Moreover, to focus too strongly on presumed internal mental processes can lead one to conceptualize the subject of psychosis as fundamentally different from the subject of neurosis. This is unwarranted. Lacan's reflections clearly concern the subject as such, and consequently hold true for both psychosis and neurosis (Lacan, 1955–6, p. 120, 1977). In psychosis the subject is as much an effect of the signifying chain as in neurosis; however, in both cases the subject is articulated with a different status in the signifying chain.

In 1977 Jacques-Alain Miller questioned Lacan about the issue of subjectivity in psychosis. In his reply, Lacan (1977, p. 12) simply repeated his definition from 1960: 'In paranoia the signifier represents a subject for another signifier',[7] suggesting that the psychotic subject is as 'divided' by the signifier as the neurotic subject. Similarly, he argued that the idea of the subject as a fading thing that runs under the chain of signifiers holds as true for psychosis as it does for neurosis (Lacan, 1977, p. 12). This viewpoint implies that the difference between psychosis and neurosis should not be exaggerated. In both cases an internal logic can be found in speech, and the same detailed attention should be paid to the way in which the subject is created as an effect of the signifying chain. However, differences in terms of how the signifying chain creates the subject can be expected between neurosis and psychosis.

An implication of Lacan's theory on the fading nature of the subject is that just as the signified can be characterized in terms of an incessant sliding under the signifier, so too can the subject. In this respect Lacan's idea of 'button ties' in discourse, which temporarily stop this movement, should not be solely understood in terms of how meaning is generated by using language. More important is the question of how subjectivity is pinned down via speech. The answer to this question is that the messages created by button ties in discourse attribute signifieds to the speaker. These messages temporarily stop the movement of fading and fill the emptity of the subject. They generate identity in terms of 'I am X, you are Y'; whereby X and Y are attributes that name or describe 'I' and 'you'.

To characterize aspects of fading and buttoning at the level of subjectivity Lacan often made a distinction between the 'enunciating subject' and the 'enunciated subject' (e.g. Lacan, 1958–9, lesson 3 December 1958; 1967–8, lesson 6 March 1968). The *enunciated subject* refers to the subject as it is defined and described via the actually produced signifying chain. It is the collection of different signifieds that characterize the I of the speaker. The *enunciating subject* refers to the evolving aspect of the subject. The very act of using a signifier to articulate an intention means that something always remains unsaid. Speech on the one hand presentifies the subject via language. This is what the concept of the *enunciated subject* puts forward. On the other hand, the use of certain signifiers entails the exclusion of other signifiers. For example, an analysant who speaks about his good intentions towards his child will generally focus on the communication of signifieds. By doing so he excludes those signifiers that undermine the signified he aims to convey. The concept of the *enunciating subject* concerns the non-articulated signifiers that do not fit the line of thought or the message the speaker wishes to convey. Nevertheless, excluded signifiers present themselves at unexpected moments, as manifestations of the unconscious, such as a slip of the tongue. Lacan's distinction suggests that the enunciated subject we come to know via speech never coincides with the enunciating subject, which materializes only through signifiers that crop up in discourse by surprise. A crucial problem in psychosis is that the enunciated subject remains largely undefined: rather than giving rise to subjectivity, the signifying chain is marked by a fundamental gap, and consequently the subject tends to disappear.

Conclusion

In this chapter I reviewed key concepts from Lacan's work during the 1950s. During this phase of his work he builds upon these concepts in his discussion of psychosis. In those days, notions like signifier, Other, structure, signification, and subject were radically new in psychoanalytical thinking and marked a rather innovative theoretical shift. Nowadays, these concepts have become established in the social sciences, as well as in general psychoanalytical discourse. An unfortunate side effect of such a transmission of concepts is that they have become generally accepted and thus poorly understood. As their use increases, the more provocative aspects of their implication tend to be neglected. Nevertheless, what remains both challenging and crucial is that Lacan developed and used these concepts with a materialist attitude. He put aside the idea that a more 'substantial' reality underlies the subject, or the unconscious, and focused solely on speech and language where recurrent patterns and structures can be discerned. For Lacan this should be the object of study for psychoanalysis as a science.

3
Foreclosure and Its Vicissitudes

Towards a theory on the logic of psychosis

Following his discussion on the status of the subject and the signifier, Lacan began to examine the principle of structure in psychosis. This thesis suggests that in psychosis a specific signifier, which concerns both the law and naming, is absent and as a result the structure of the Symbolic is unstable. He calls this signifier the 'Name-of-the-Father', and refers to its absence with the concept of 'foreclosure'. Both of these concepts were introduced during his critical discussion of Freud's Oedipus complex. On the one hand Lacan considered Freud's account of the Oedipus complex as interesting, since it describes a fundamental transition in human relations. On the other hand he believed it was too mythical and focused too strongly on specific neurotic fantasies, such as the little boy's murderous wishes towards his father (Deleuze and Guattari, 1972). Instead Lacan presents a formalized explanation of the shift that takes place in the Oedipus complex. He proposes that the Oedipal transition takes place via two linguistic tropes: metaphor and metonymy. Foreclosure is seen as a shift at the level of metaphor that fails to occur. An important consequence of this absent metaphorization is that metonymy in the signifying chain is rendered unstable.

Lacan's discussion of foreclosure is structural and logical. He provides a theory on the *logic* of how subjectivity is created in a social bond with others. Within this theory a number of logical steps are discerned that characterize the process of becoming a subject. These steps do not refer to actual incidents that would cause psychosis. A Lacanian psychoanalyst works with words and language, not with prospective information on human development, and is less concerned with making causal speculations with respect to arrests in mental development or problematic

50

family dynamics. In terms of Lacan's model on the logic of signification, at a particular moment a psychoanalyst might intervene on a patient's account of the past with an interpretation. These interventions function as punctuations and can have the effect of retroactively reorganizing the internal structure of the patients' speech and his subjective position towards his story. It is not aimed towards correcting the accuracy of the patient's story, even less any failures from the past.

Crucial sources of inspiration for Lacan's theory of the foreclosure of the Name-of-the-Father were Claude Lévi-Strauss, and once more Roman Jakobson. For example, from Jakobson, Lacan became interested in the distinction between metaphor and metonymy and the suggestion that these figures of speech can be applied to clinical phenomena, such as aphasia and psychosis (Lacan, 1955–6, pp. 219–24; Ragland-Sullivan, 1986). Lévi-Strauss's (1958) seminal text *Structural Anthropology* also influenced Lacan's ideas on the functioning of social groups.

Two tropes; two processes at the level of the unconscious

Metonymy and metaphor are two tropes that have been discerned in classical rhetorics, next to irony and synecdoche. Lacan (e.g. 1956a, 1957b) attributes them to the work of the first-century Roman orator Quintilian, whose book *Institutes of Oratory* contains a detailed discussion of these tropes (Quintilian, 1856). These figures of speech particularly interested Lacan because of the new light they would shed on unconscious processes, as discussed by Freud. In Lacan's interpretation metaphor and metonymy correspond with the two main processes Freud discerned at the level of the unconscious, namely condensation and displacement. Freud (1900) first discussed these processes in *The Interpretations of Dreams*. Here he discerned that when analysing dreams numerous fragments of the dreamer's thought process seemed to coalesce into one stock symbol or dream element, which he understood to reflect the unconscious mechanism of condensation. In other words, condensation takes place when numerous latent thoughts are synthesized into one single image or idea that symbolically refers to all of the latent elements (Freud, 1900, pp. 279–304). Freud also observed other dream elements that were clearly associated with anxiety provoking material, but left the dreamer unaffected or detached when recounting them. He suggested that a mechanism of displacement was at work with such dream elements. Displacement is when the libidinal charge that is attached to one idea is transferred to another idea, which consequently becomes overvalued because of the weight it carries from the repressed thought (Freud, 1900, pp. 305–9). In Lacan's interpretation of Freud's work, these modes of repression are not thought of in terms of in-depth psychological transformations, but in terms of mechanisms at the level of the signifier. For Lacan condensation and displacement can be understood in terms of the metaphoric and metonymic process of language. According to him, the unconscious should not be conceptualized in terms of something that exists in the depths of the mind, but rather as a surface phenomenon that manifests within and throughout the signifying chain.

Metonymy

Classically metonymy is defined as the substitution of the name for a thing by an attribute of it, or by something that is closely connected to it (Quintilian, 1856). Thus defined an illustration of metonymy is equating a house with a roof over one's head. Jakobson (1953, p. 61) challenged this classic interpretation and offered a more material interpretation of the idea of substitution. Rather than considering metonymy only as a trope, he thought of it as a fundamental process in language. Metonymy takes place within the diachronic linking of signifiers in a chain, where one signifier evokes another because of a thematic connection at the level of the signified. For example, in the phrase: 'I will write a letter to the newspaper'. The words 'write', 'letter' and 'newspaper' are thematically related and are connected in a relation of continuation. Lexically speaking, the verb 'to write' has a limited number of objects to which it is usually related: I can write a letter, an e-mail or a book. We also know that conventionally the word 'letter' typically refers to a mode of correspondence that has an addressee. I can write a letter to a specific person, like my daughter or sons, or to an organization, like a newspaper or a government agency. A characteristic of metonymy is that the signifieds communicated are in line with each other and provide an overall context. The context helps us understand that in this instance the word 'letter' refers to correspondence instead of a character in a word. Metonymy is present whenever signifiers are linked in chains, without producing surprise or ambiguity at the level of the signified. In terms of literary style, metonymy is purposefully used in realism and in descriptive language. Clinically speaking, Jakobson discerns problems with metonymy in forms of aphasia that are characterized by the inability to combine words in sentences.

Lacan's understanding of metonymy stays close to Jakobson's interpretation. He describes it as a mode of speech in which signifiers are combined without the interruption of ambiguous or unexpected meaning. It is the process whereby the signifying chain takes shape, and signifieds are effortlessly combined to create meaning. His logical formula to illustrate the structure of metonymy is as follows (Figure 3.1) (Lacan, 1957b, p. 428):

$$f\,(S \ldots S')S \cong S(-)s$$

Figure 3.1 Metonymy

This formula indicates that metonymy is a function of the signifier, expressed by the component $f()S$, in which signifiers are combined, expressed by the symbols S . . . .S'. As we speak, signifiers are linked in 'signifier-to-signifier' connections (Lacan, 1957b, p. 428), whereby one signifier after the other is metrically scanned and linked in a chain. This chain makes up words and sentences that change as speech progresses. In metonymy the linking of signifiers doesn't disrupt the experience of thematic continuity at the level of the signified. On the contrary, it is congruent with the maintenance of the fraction bar between the signifier (S) and the signified (s) from the basic formula of the signifier (Figure 3.2):

$$\frac{S}{s}$$

Figure 3.2 Signifier and signified

The symbol $\cong$ from the formula of metonymy (Figure 3.1) refers to congruency. The fraction bar between S and s is maintained, as symbolized by S (−) s and indicates that in the signifying chain S . . . .S' a button tie has not been established between S and s.

Thus considered metonymy describes how thematic continuity is created in sentences. In metonymy signifiers are connected in a relatively linear fashion with the aim of expressing a coherent message. This process of thematic connection reflects the mental experience of continuity. In other words, a sense of continuity is experienced not because it is out there in the world, but because we incessantly produce signifiers that are thematically linked. As a result we can experience our thoughts as an endless stream that is relatively coherent at the level of content. Conversely, the material impact of the signifier is minimized in metonymy: words are used to communicate anticipated ideas, not to create ambiguity.

However, in Lacan's theory metonymy is not just a linguistic mechanism concerning the way in which the signifying chain relates to signifieds. For Lacan, metonymy is also a structural mechanism of speech that determines the subject. In metonymic speech identity is not defined as such; the subject is not temporarily fixed by means of a button tie between S and *s*. This absence of a button tie at the level of signification implies that when metonymy is at work an allusion to the identity of the subject is present, but does not clearly define him. Through metonymy the speaking subject is connoted, without actually being defined in its identity.

By using speech a speaker automatically makes references and allusions to himself. For example, by using personal pronouns the speaker is presented in his own speech, yet these self-references do not name characteristics of the speaker. Metonymy presents the subject, but does not situate his existence: the enunciating subject is present, but the enunciated subject remains indeterminate. This is why Lacan (1960, p. 691) says that the enunciating subject is fading under the signifier. In metonymy meaning slides as the connection between signifiers progresses, and never gives a fixed anchor point to the speaker. My example 'I will write a letter to the newspaper' makes this clear. This sentence provides information about what the protagonist 'I' is doing, but leaves him undefined. Based on this sentence, the reader could make all kinds of interpretations about the protagonist: perhaps he is an easily protesting obstinate person, or someone who lives up to standards of moral citizenship. The sentence leaves all of this open to interpretation: no button tie defines the identity of the subject; subjectivity fades under the signifying chain. In metonymy an enunciating subject is at work, yet at the level of signification, no enunciated subject is produced. Metonymic speech does not attribute a clear position to the subject, and therefore it can be qualified as 'empty' (see Lacan, 1953–4).

Metaphor

In the process of metaphor this is all different. Quintilian (1856, book 8, chapter 6, verse 5) describes metaphor as a trope in which a word is transferred 'from that place in the language to which it properly belongs, to one in which there is either no proper word, or in which the metaphorical word is preferable to the proper'. The effect of this is that a new significance is added to the speech context. Jakobson (1953) explained metaphor as a process at the level of synchrony, in which one signifier is replaced by another based on similarity. Lacan picked up this idea and developed two formulas for describing the structure of metaphor. In 1957, when he also developed the formula for metonymy, he characterized metaphor as follows (Figure 3.3) (Lacan, 1957b, p. 429):

$$f\left(\frac{S'}{S}\right) S \cong S(+)s$$

Figure 3.3 Metaphor (I)

The formula indicates that metaphor is a function of the signifier, $f()S$, in which a signifier S is substituted by another signifier S'. This substitution is congruent with the creation of signification, referred to by $(+)$ s in the formula: a surplus of meaning is added to the message. Indeed, typical of the metaphoric process is that the fraction bar between the signifier and the signified is crossed; a button tie connects the signifier (S) with the signified (s). The formula indicates that by introducing another signifier (S') to a signifying chain, the signified broadens; new meaning is created extending the scope of what is said.

His second formula for describing the structure of metaphor was as follows (Figure 3.4) (Lacan, 1959, p. 464):

$$\frac{S}{\cancel{S'}} \cdot \frac{\cancel{S'}}{x} \rightarrow S\left(\frac{I}{s}\right)$$

Figure 3.4 Metaphor (II)

This notation indicates that metaphor is a process in the signifying chain, expressed by the dot that connects the two fractions in the left part of the formula, in which a signifier S replaces another signifier that was not uttered but was metonymically anticipated in the signifying chain, expressed by the barred S'. The x from the formula symbolizes metonymic anticipation of signification. The signifier S that is actually produced in a metaphor is surprising in a given speech context, and disrupts the metonymic process: at the level of the signified metaphors disrupt continuity. Metaphors create shifts in meaning at the level of signification, and add new ideas to a line of reasoning. Indeed, the effect of a metaphoric substitution between signifiers is an induction of meaning (see Lacan, 1959, p. 465). In his formula Lacan represents this 'impact of the signifier on the signified' (Lacan, 1957b, p. 428) with the following symbol, in which 'I' refers to the impact of the signifier, and *s* to the signified on which an influence is exercised (Figure 3.5):

$$\frac{I}{s}$$

Figure 3.5   Impact of the signifier on the signified

An example of the use of metaphor can be found in a passage from the New Testament in which Christ says to his pupil Peter: 'You are the rock on which I will build my church' (Matthew, 16:18). What is not said in the sentence (barred S') is that Peter has been chosen by Christ to lead the church after his death. By calling him the rock on which the church will be built, it is suggested that Peter should succeed Christ and found the movement of the church, but by speaking in terms of a rock and building, a dimension of solidity is added (induction of signified). In contrast to sand, rock provides a solid foundation: a construction built on rock will not subside.

Just like metonymy, for Lacan metaphor is not simply a linguistic trope, but a structural mode of speech along which the subject is shaped. His discussion of metaphor is not so much concerned with literary creativity, but with the question of how the speaking being is affected by language use, as depicted in his formula.

With respect to subjectivity the effect of metaphor is such that the subject, which was connoted and fading until then, is identified and denoted. At the level of the signified, a metaphor attributes predicates or characteristics to the subject, and tells us something about the identity of the person that is presented via speech. Metaphors name the enunciating subject and create an enunciated subject. This naming creates a mode of personal identity and inscribes the subject in a network of social relations. This temporarily reveals the position a person occupies in relation to others.

In our example the effect of naming can be recognized as generating subjectivity in the fact that through the metaphor Christ is defined as the builder, and Peter as the rock. These names articulate their respective positions: Christ the builder is active and powerful and he has a task that will be accomplished in the future; Peter the rock has a passive and expectant position in relation to Christ's project of building a church, but he is also the indispensable starting point of Christ's activities. Without Peter, Christ's church cannot be established. Next to defining these individual positions the metaphor also informs us about the social bond between both characters. Christ and Peter are in complementary positions and they are named in terms of a joint mission. It is only because both occupy their respective role, that the mission of creating a church can be realized.

Towards the metaphor of the Name-of-the-Father

An important move in Lacan's work consisted of applying the structure of the metaphor to Freud's mythical description of the Oedipus complex. Here he argues that the logic articulated in Freud's theory actually concerns a process of metaphorization.

In making this interpretation Lacan finds inspiration in the work of Claude Lévi-Strauss (Lacan, 1956b; Lévi-Strauss, 1949, 1958). A crucial idea outlined in Lévi-Strauss's work is that social groups, like families or tribes, function as systems, and that the logic of their functioning can be understood in terms of various combinations of signifiers. Characteristic of each social group is that it has a structure, in that its constituent members occupy specific positions and follow a typical set of exchange relations. Depending on an individual's status within the group certain exchanges are permitted, or even required, whilst others are taboo. The objects of exchange discussed by Lévi-Strauss include words, goods, food and women.

A further idea in Lévi-Strauss's work is that naming plays a crucial role in both establishing structure and regulating exchange. For example, a common name, obtained by belonging to the same family or the same totem, produces unity and determines whether a newcomer can be included in the group: names identify group membership. An additional effect of carrying a certain name is that exchange is qualified in terms of being required, permitted or forbidden. For example, the person who is qualified as the leader of a group can do things that are taboo for other group members, and vice versa. Different names attribute different positions to group members and establish status and hierarchy, whereby a set of possible or impossible exchanges is attached to each position. To understand group structures and their typical exchanges, Lévi-Strauss advocates the study of actual group functioning via observation. However, such structures and exchange patterns can also be deduced by examining myths.

In his interpretation of the Oedipus complex, Lacan follows a similar approach to that of Lévi-Strauss: Freud's model is qualified as a mythical account that illustrates an important turning point in the way the subject relates to the other (Lacan, 1960), and to fully understand it the myth's structure should be delineated in terms of interpersonal positions and exchanges. Lacan suggests that the underlying structure of the Oedipus complex actually concerns a process of metaphorization, of which naming is a crucial component. Oedipal dynamics can be adequately characterized by what he calls 'the metaphor of the Name-of-the-Father' (Lacan, 1959, p. 465) or the 'paternal metaphor' (Lacan, 1959, p. 463). As Lacan described psychosis in terms of a non-event at the level the paternal metaphor, I will discuss this metaphor in detail in the next section.

The advantage of this structural approach is that it underlines the transformation that takes place in the process of becoming a subject in logical terms, and thereby avoids imaginary speculation about scenes of love and hate that would characterize family life. Furthermore, due to its accent on formal relationships it doesn't idealize or pathologize any particular type of family constellation, nor does it prescribe normative roles to the actual members of the group. For example, a father can just as well be the carrier of the maternal desire for the child and a mother guarantee the articulation of the Name-of-the-Father. The point is that both functions are crucial in the paternal metaphor.

Desire and naming in the metaphor of the Name-of-the-Father

The logical notation Lacan (1959, p. 465) used to illustrate the structure of the metaphor of the Name-of-the-Father is as follows (Figure 3.6):

$$\frac{\text{Name-of-the-Father}}{\text{Mother's Desire}} \cdot \frac{\text{Mother's Desire}}{\text{Signified to the Subject}} \longrightarrow \text{Name-of-the-Father}\left(\frac{O}{\text{Phallus}}\right)$$

Figure 3.6   Metaphor of the Name-of-the-Father

Taking into account Lacan's general formula on the structure of metaphor, the first term to focus on is the signifier that is removed: 'Mother's Desire'. By introducing this signifier as a point of departure, Lacan suggests that the metaphor of the Name-of-the-Father builds on an already established relationship between mother and child; the child has a *signifier* for maternal desire but without the signifier of the Name-of-the-Father it cannot grasp the *signified* connected to it. In terms of Lacan's formula, the starting point of the paternal metaphor can therefore be described as follows (Figure 3.7):

$$\frac{\text{Mother's Desire}}{?}$$

Figure 3.7 Maternal desire

In this formula 'Mother's Desire' indicates that the child has a signifier for maternal desire, yet its signified is unclear, expressed by the question mark. In his fifth seminar Lacan (1957–8) indicates that the signifier of maternal desire is strictly material, and that it consists of the child's cognitive representation of the mother's appearances and disappearances. What the child knows is that at one moment mother is present and at another moment she is absent, yet the meaning of this alternation is unclear. The questions that emerge with the signifier of maternal desire, but cannot be answered by means of it, concern what it is that determines and regulates her absences, and the position the child occupies in relation to maternal desire. In Lacan's line of reasoning this lack of a signified for maternal desire is anxiety-provoking: the primitive subject is passively subjected to the other, as if it were an object, and has no concrete position of its own. He thereby proposes that the child is seized by maternal desire. In its position towards the mother, the child feels that he/she is important, yet lacks a clear concept of what motivates the mother's engagement in this unique relationship. In an allusion to Jacques Cazotte's novel *The Devil in Love*, Lacan (1956–7, p. 169) says that the basic question lurking in the child's mind is: *'che vuoi?'*/'what do you want?' This question is provoked by the acquisition of a signifier for maternal desire, which cannot be answered at this first stage of subject development (Chiesa, 2007).

Within this logic, the primordial establishment of a representation for the mother's desire is an absolute condition for later metaphorization. The paternal metaphor can only be set in motion if the child has the experience of being seized in another person's desire, without exactly knowing what it means.

In his fourth (1956–7) and fifth seminars (1957–8), as well as in his 1959 article on psychosis, Lacan indicates that a first move in interpreting the enigma of maternal desire consists of believing that what motivates the alternation between maternal presence and absence is the child's very existence. In this belief, the child has the illusion of being the central point around which the mother's desire is turning. In Lacan's (1956–7, 1958) terminology the child is the so-called 'imaginary phallus' for the mother, or the signified of her desire: if the mother's coming and going is motivated by something, it must be by the existence of the child. This belief is important for human narcissism, but typically declines when the child begins to realize that it is not alone in the world and that others attract her attention as well. This gives rise to an imaginary struggle and produces the affects of *hainamoration* and *jealouissance*, which I have already introduced in my discussion of the mirror phase: others are rivals to compete with in terms of having a privileged position in relation to maternal desire. Doubt about being the sole object of the Mother's Desire comes to the fore.

The instalment of the Name-of-the-Father brings an end to this imaginary struggle and results in the creation of a completely new interpretation of maternal desire. In the paternal metaphor, the signifier of the Name-of-the-Father substitutes that of the Mother's Desire, and leads to the creation of new signification. In the formula this substitution is illustrated as follows, to the left of the arrow (Figure 3.8):

$$\text{Name-of-the-Father} \cdot \frac{\text{Mother's Desire}}{\text{Mother's Desire}} \cdot \frac{\text{Mother's Desire}}{\text{Signified to the Subject}} \longrightarrow \text{Name-of-the-Father} \left(\frac{\text{O}}{\text{Phallus}} \right)$$

Figure 3.8 The Name-of-the-Father substitutes maternal desire

Characteristic of the Name-of-the-Father is that it *names* maternal desire, expressed by the erasure in the formula. The paternal signifier comes as a substitute for the maternal signifier and, in this process of substitution, desire is subjected to the broader context of the Symbolic, that is, to the structure and exchange of the social group. The Name-of-the-Father is the signifier of culture and taboo by means of which cultural taboos, such as the prohibition of incest, and cultural demands, such as the principle of exogamy, are imposed as the context within which the subject and Other interact. By replacing the signifier of maternal desire with the Name-of-the-Father, maternal desire loses its enigmatic quality. Henceforth it is a signifier that can be interpreted in terms of the communally accepted ways people relate to each other. The paternal signifier incorporates the maternal signifier in the Symbolic and subjects it to the law. Through the paternal signifier, the signifier of maternal desire is integrated in a normative discourse on how people should interact.

The direct effect of this naming is that a signified of desire is created, which the term 'Signified to the Subject' in the left part of the formula indicates. By bringing the paternal signifier into dialectic with the maternal signifier, the subject acquires a concept of what it is that the mother wants. Its instalment enables the subject to understand what motivates human interrelations in general, and maternal desire in particular.

Within this logic of the paternal metaphor the father is not a real or an imaginary person, as is the case in the Oedipal myth, but a symbolic function to which all group members – mother, father and child – are subjected. It provides the human being with an internalized compass of culturally and socially viable principles, and facilitates understanding of the *(m)other* as well as the behaviour of *significant others*.

In Lacan's discussion of the paternal metaphor the law is not so much described in terms of what is imposed upon the subject, as in Freud's Oedipus complex, but in terms of a symbolic framework that is imposed upon the (m)other. The formula of the paternal metaphor makes clear that the signifier of the Name-of-the-Father principally names the desire of the mother, and not the identity of the subject. Within this logic a signifier or name is attributed to the child only via a sort of cannon effect: the Name-of-the-Father names maternal desire, and by doing so the position of the child is elucidated. Through the Name-of-the-Father the child is recognized in relation to the desire of the (m)other.

What is interesting about this idea is that it inscribes the principle of recognition and naming within a *triangular logic*. However, in his first, second and third seminars, Lacan discussed this principle of recognition in a dual logic: human beings do not have an inherent or true identity, but are marked by a 'want-to-be' (Muller and Richardson, 1982, p. 22), a lack that is eventually filled with the contents of intersubjective recognition. Inspired by the texts of Hegel and by Alexandre Kojève's (1947) reading of Hegel, Lacan argued that the master/slave dialectic is most informative for mapping this logic. His position was that a master/slave relation is only created when two persons implicitly agree to take up their respective positions as 'master' and 'slave' (Vanheule et al., 2003). If they do, they enter into a symbolic pact that defines them. This mutual recognition is crucial because it determines the identity of each individual and the nature of their relation. The following figure (Figure 3.9) schematically depicts the logic of recognition between the master and slave, and shows how, by recognizing the other in a certain way (y = master), one also determines the position taken up by oneself (x = slave):

'I am your slave'

x   y

'You are my master'

Figure 3.9 Recognition between master and slave

The message 'You are my master' given by person 'x' to person 'y' (expressed by 'x → y') makes it clear, conversely, that 'x' is the slave of the other (expressed by the returning arrow). Indeed, by defining the other in a certain way, the subject receives his own message back from the other 'in an inverted form', with the conclusion 'I am your slave' (Lacan, 1954–5, p. 324). This inversion implies that 'I' and 'your' replace both the pronoun and possessive pronoun 'you' and 'my', and that the noun 'master' is replaced by its semantic opposite 'slave'. In its inverted form, the sentence 'You are my master' becomes 'I am your slave'. According to this reasoning, people determine their own identity by the way they define other people.

In the paternal metaphor the situation is different. There, a third party names 'y' and imposes a framework on 'y', based on which 'x', the subject, is defined. The Name-of-the-Father itself does not define the subject, but imposes laws onto the (m)other, and onto the social bond between subject and (m)other. Along this way certain exchange relationships are prohibited, while a repertoire of alternative exchange relationships is opened up. Due to this naming, the (m)other's actions, which minimally comprise a structure of coming and going, are no longer pure enigma and start to make sense in relation to the subject.

The Phallus and the Other in the metaphor of the Name-of-the-Father

Whereas the left part of the formula of the metaphor of the Name-of-the-Father indicates that by introducing the paternal signifier a signified for the desire of the (m)other is created, the right side indicates its consequences at the level of identification. Indeed, a further effect of installing the signifier of the Name-of-the-Father is that a space for symbolic identification is created, i.e. a type of identification that is guided by signifiers and that concerns a person's position in the group, as well as his/her position towards desire. As already indicated, the paternal law shows the child that abstract principles guide the (m)other, and that such laws also govern social exchange relationships. As a result the desire of the (m)other is no longer a riddle, but a regulated dimension that can be questioned by relating the maternal signifier to the paternal signifier. If maternal desire is subsequently questioned, the child will have to conclude that contrary to what was first believed during its identification with the imaginary phallus, it is not the only focus of maternal desire: the child will recognize that its relationship with the (m)other concerns winning the battle of jealouissance and hainamoration. By installing the paternal signifier, maternal desire will be framed in terms of patterns and laws of transaction. Apart from her maternal position the mother also occupies other roles, for example the position of wife, etc. and, in addition to her interactions with the child, she is engaged in many other exchange relationships. She might, for example, devote quite some time to work or leisure activities, activities that the child has nothing to do with. At this stage the observation that the mother's desire is not directed solely to the child does not so much give rise to rivalry, but to the question of what organizes maternal desire. The answer to this question is 'the Phallus' or the 'symbolic Phallus'.

In Lacan's (1958, 1959) theory the concept of the symbolic Phallus is a synonym for the ultimate characteristic that makes the object of maternal desire desirable. With the aim of positioning itself within the (m)other's desire, the child will detect these characteristics and identify with them. For example, in a classic nuclear family constellation the question of the symbolic Phallus will concern the relationship between the parents. In this sense, the unconscious question concerning the little boy will be: 'What is it that my father has and that makes him so interesting to my mother?'. The boy will aim to detect such characteristics and identify with traits that capture his mother's attention. What the child thus adopts are signifiers that will henceforth function as ego-ideals to the child. In Lacan's formula the outcome of the substitution of Mother's Desire by the Name-of-the-Father is represented by the right-hand part of the following formula (Figure 3.10):

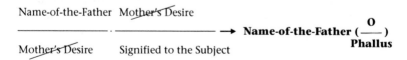

Figure 3.10 The creation of phallic signification

The last part of the formula indicates that the effect of installing the Name-of-the-Father, symbolized by →, is that the subject's way of dealing with the Other, symbolized by O in the formula, will be completely subjected to phallic logic, symbolized by the term Phallus as the denominator of the fraction O/Phallus. In this formula the Phallus is the signified to which the signifiers that make up the Other are invariably related.

In his article On a Question Prior to any Possible Treatment of Psychosis, Lacan gives quite a specific interpretation to the concept Other, defining it as 'the locus from which the question of his [the subject's] existence may arise' (Lacan, 1959, p. 459). In other words, at the level of the unconscious each speaking subject, 'psychosis or neurosis' (Lacan, 1959, p. 458), is confronted with a basic question concerning its own identity as subject. 'Who am I?' is the question all humans are unconsciously confronted with, and for which no inherent answer is readily available.

More precisely this question relates to three issues: one's 'sex', one's 'contingency in being' (Lacan, 1959, p. 459) and 'the relational signifiers of love and procreation' (Lacan, 1959, p. 461). The question of *the subject's sex* concerns whether one is a man or a woman, as well as the question of how one gives shape to sexual identity. The matter of *contingency in being* refers to the fortuity of life, and to the question what life means in the light of death. The *relational signifiers* in their turn point to the question of what it is that really connects people in love, and to the question of parenthood.

Since these questions are unconscious, they are not expressed in words as such, but principally via symptoms (Lacan 1959, pp. 457–8). By making this claim Lacan makes a case for a radical reconceptualization of the symptom. Symptoms should not be approached as markers of illness, but as phenomena through which questions on the existence of the subject are expressed, and through which a place for the subject is articulated. Indeed, diverse phenomena, including sleeplessness, panic or boredom, make sense because they articulate the questions that lie at the basis of subjectivity (Lacan, 1959, p. 457). Here, the subject is not defined as a reflective entity that asks questions, but as an entity that is created because of the fact that questions are articulated via the symptom. The question produces the subject and not the other way around. Yet far from creating a feeling of unity, these questions constitute the very reason why the subject is divided. They are questions that can never be solved definitively, and for which no inherent answer is at the human being's disposal. Hence Lacan's (1959, p. 459) suggestion that 'the question of his existence envelops the subject, props him up, invades him, and even tears him apart from every angle'.

Indeed, in his work from the 1950s, Lacan principally approaches the question of subjectivity in terms of the effect of questions on the existence of the subject. Here, such questions are thought to be inherent to human life and expressed clinically in symptoms, rather than in self-conscious questions. What Lacan did not address at this stage, but picked up in the 1960s, concerns the question of what the subject was before it started to be a subject. Obviously Lacan preferred to stay with a materialist operationalization of the subject in terms of linguistic processes, leaving the preverbal status of the subject largely out of consideration.

Lacan's formula of the paternal metaphor indicates that at the level of the unconscious answers to questions of the existence of the subject cannot be found. It is precisely the incorporation of the Name-of-the-Father that provides a framework to address them. In other words, the Name-of-the-Father provides a symbolic structure whereby answers to these questions can be constructed. In principle, this is done via symbolic identification. People answer questions of their own existence by adopting phallic traits – characteristics they assume make them desirable to others. This is what the last part of Lacan's formula expresses: by installing the Name-of-the-Father, the Phallus becomes the common denominator to all questions on the subject at the level of the Other.

However, in making this point Lacan has a rather precise idea of the Phallus as a signifier that is ever lacking. The Phallus should not be interpreted as a phantasmatic or imaginary object, and even less as a symbol for the sexual organ, but in terms of desire (Lacan, 1958). In his view the confrontation with the Other quite brutally opens the dimension of desire in the subject. At first this dimension is puzzling, but with the Name-of-the-Father this confrontation produces the assumption that something must be causing desire. Phallus is the conceptual name Lacan gives to this presumed cause; the Phallus is the signifier the speaking subject searches for in pursuit of that which causes desire. At the same time Lacan (1958) defines the Phallus as a negativity: it is the signifier people search for in a Sisyphus-like way, but never find. This doesn't mean that their search is fruitless. As people search for what it is that determines desire, identification with signifiers or traits detected in the other takes place – signifiers that are seen as indications of that which causes desire. These symbolic identifications mark subjectivity. They make up the arsenal of signifiers that will be mobilized when questions of existence come to the fore. These signifiers can be thought of as phallic to the extent that they stand in for the ever unknown Phallus.

The foreclosure of the Name-of-the-Father in psychosis

In neurosis the signifier of the Name-of-the-Father replaces the signifier of maternal desire, such that a dialectical identity is inaugurated. Incompatible identifications are disagreeable to the unity-seeking ego and are repressed (Nobus, 2000; Ver Eecke, 2006; Verhaeghe, 2004). In psychosis the situation is different: for one reason or another the signifier of the Name-of-the-Father remains absent. Lacan states: 'At the point at which the Name-of-the-Father is summoned...a pure and simple hole may thus answer in the Other' (1959, pp. 465–6). To refer to the absence of the Name-of-the-Father Lacan introduces the concept of *foreclosure* (Grigg, 2008; Lacan, 1955–6, pp. 321, 1959, p. 465; Maleval, 2000). The result of such foreclosure is that the paternal metaphor is not set in motion.

Lacan defines foreclosure as the opposite of what Freud calls '*Bejahung*' or affirmation. For Freud the concept *Bejahung* refers to the so-called judgement of existence. This is the process whereby a young child makes a decision concerning whether something exists or not: 'it asserts or disputes that a presentation has an existence in reality' (Freud, 1925, p. 236). Freud situates what he calls a drive-related 'primitive perception' at the basis of this judgement of existence. This refers to a mode of hallucinatory perception that is determined by libidinal wish-fulfilment and less concerned with creating a presentation of external reality. Judgement of existence encroaches upon such primitive perception and decisions are made about whether perceptions correspond to external realities or not. Affirmation means that such a perception is qualified as something that exists in reality. The effect of *Bejahung* is that the primitive perception is transformed into a representation, and more broadly that a representation-based mental life is created (Hyppolite, 1953). If, by contrast, drive related perceptions are disputed, and considered to be non-existent in reality, no mental representation is created.

After having touched upon it in his first seminar, Lacan further discussed the concept of *Bejahung* in his third seminar. There he puts forward that via the judgement of existence 'the subject constructs himself a world and, above all, that he situates himself within it, that is, that he manages to be more or less what he has admitted that he was – a man when he finds himself to be of masculine sex, or conversely, a woman' (Lacan, 1955–6, p. 83).

In this sense, *Bejahung* does not concern mental life in general, but only specific aspects of it. It is more specifically related to questions concerning the existence of the subject, which make up the unconscious.

The effect of *Bejahung* is that questions of existence can be addressed via the signifier, offering the subject the ability to occupy a position as a subject in the world. With his discussion of the paternal metaphor in mind, it is not too difficult to see how Lacan concludes that the *non-Bejahung* or foreclosure in psychosis concerns the Name-of-the-Father (Lacan, 1959, p. 470). With the incorporation of the paternal signifier, questions on the existence of the subject at the level of the unconscious can be addressed in phallic terms. However, foreclosure of the Name-of-the-Father undermines such subjective development.

Yet, before making the specific link between foreclosure/*non-Bejahung* and the Name-of-the-Father in 1959, Lacan had already used the concept *Verwerfung* or rejection to refer to the problem of *non-Bejahung* (see Lacan 1953–4, 1955–6, 1957a). At this stage he did not specifically link *non-Bejahung* to the signifier of the Name-of-the-Father. This is illustrated in his discussion of the Wolf Man (Freud, 1918; Lacan, 1955–6). Freud suggests that in the case of the Wolf Man castration was rejected, in that no mental representation of castration was introduced and as a result castration could only be experienced in a hallucinatory way. Such a hallucinatory experience of castration was evidenced in the Wolf Man's recollection that once while playing with a knife he cut his finger, which was left hanging on by just a piece of skin. In his discussion of this case at the start of his third seminar, Lacan (1955–6, p. 13) argued that the Wolf Man's problem actually consisted of a rejection of castration, meaning that castration failed to be acknowledged in the Symbolic. In other words, *Bejahung* did not take place and as a consequence the signifier of castration was not installed. The result, he says, is that the theme of castration 're-emerges in the real' via a hallucination (Lacan, 1955–6, p. 13). Later Lacan stopped using rejection as a synonym for *non-Bejahung*. Rejection wrongly suggests that a presentation was previously accepted but subsequently expelled and therefore that there was once *Bejahung*. To avoid such confusion Lacan prefers to use the term foreclosure towards the end of his third seminar as a more straightforward reference to *non-Bejahung* (Lacan, 1955–6, p. 321).

What is interesting about Lacan's use of the concept of foreclosure is that it actually brought him to take a distance from Freud's ideas on projection and rejection in psychosis. As already indicated in Chapter 1, Freud (1911) first preferred the notion of projection to characterize the basic mode of defence in psychosis. Lacan (1955–6, 1959) was highly critical of this idea. He deemed it useless because of its non-specificity in relation to psychosis. After all, projection can just as well be recognized in neurotic fantasies as in psychotic delusions. In addition, he argued that the idea of projection sets clinicians on the track of *imaginary speculation*, which is counterproductive as it draws attention away from the study of how the signifier is organized in chains. To maintain a focus on the Symbolic, foreclosure is a better conceptual point of departure.

Furthermore, by using the concept of foreclosure in the place of *non-Bejahung*, Lacan made an interesting choice. The concept is not a typical psychological term and following Lacan's own theory we can qualify his use of the term as metaphorical. Foreclosure is a term that is actually derived from a legal framework: it designates a situation in which a homeowner is unable to make interest payments on a mortgage, as a result of which the lender may seize and sell the property. It is defined as 'to take back property that was bought with borrowed money because the money was not being paid back as formally agreed' (Cambridge Advanced Learner's Dictionary, 2008, p. 559). By his metaphorical use of this concept Lacan refers to the fundamental problem of *ownership* in psychosis. Whereas the instalment of the paternal metaphor introduces the individual to the social order, and via identification even makes him a 'co-owner' of its conventions, such evolution is absent in psychosis and as a result the individual remains an outsider.

Consequences of foreclosure

As indicated above, the mechanism of metaphor implies that the fading subject is named. Metaphors induce new meanings at the level of the signified, and introduce the enunciated subject. In terms of the paternal metaphor this implies that meaning can be attributed to the desire of the (m)other and that questions on the existence of the subject can be addressed in phallic terms. The paternal metaphor determines the identity of the desiring (m)other and allows a person to respond to the (m)other's desire with phallic identifications. Indeed, the idea of installing the signifier of the Name-of-the-Father implies that cultural conventions function as a background whereby questions of desire and identity make sense.

In psychosis the absence of the paternal metaphor implies that the subject is not named in relation to maternal desire; in relation to questions of existence a gaping hole remains. Due to the foreclosure of the Name-of-the-Father questions of existence that are posed at the level of the unconscious – 'Who am I?' and 'What do you want from me?' – cannot be addressed in a conventional manner. The issues that typically lead to the articulation of the subject do not obtain an answer, which destabilizes the experience of identity. Indeed, in psychosis the socio-cultural set of answers incarnated by the Name-of-the-Father fails to function as a basis for the individual to articulate a position as a subject in relation to others.

This implies that the desire of the (m)other remains fundamentally enigmatic. In psychosis the 'code of convention' that is needed to navigate the enigma of what the other wants is absent. The result is a fundamental difficulty in making sense of the other's intentions, and, as theorists of mind also suggest (Brüne, 2005), a difficulty in 'reading' the other's mind. In Lacan's formula of the paternal metaphor foreclosure implies that it remains unclear what the term 'Mother's Desire' signifies to the subject. A consequence of this is that making accurate interpretations of other people's intentions and drawing conclusions about how to manage the desire of the other is most complicated and distressing. A characteristic of foreclosure is that no 'phallic' conclusions can be drawn about the desire of the other. In psychosis, the confrontation with the other produces confusion, as do intimate relationships. Close interpersonal demands provoke perplexity to the extent that little sense can be made of the other's intentions. The closer the (m)other's desire comes, the more confusion and intimidation experienced.

This inability to find a secure position in relation to others also affects the way the individual feels about the social group, like for example the family. While group interaction is not impossible, foreclosure typically implies that a sense of interrelatedness and common concern is lacking. No matter which position the person actually occupies within the group, foreclosure leaves the subject with the feeling of being an outsider with a fundamental sense of not belonging.

A second consequence of the foreclosed Name-of-the-Father is that the question of personal identity – 'Who am I?' – remains unanswered. Foreclosure leaves 'black holes' at the level of a person's identity: for example, sexual identity, which typically makes up human subjectivity, cannot be addressed by articulating who one is in the context of conventional discourse. This is because in the Symbolic a framework where such conventions can be articulated has not been installed. At the level of the unconscious, questions concerning subjective identity can insist, but the psychotic subject cannot deploy conventional signifiers to manage them. As a result the subject remains unarticulated. Whereas metaphors usually name the enunciating subject of speech and create an enunciated subject, foreclosure undermines the experience of identity.

Indeed, with respect to personal identity the foreclosure of the Name-of-the-Father implies that a framework for addressing questions of existence remains lacking. The result is that there is little to hold on to vis-à-vis one's identity as a man or a woman, how to deal with love and sexuality, how to give shape to intergenerational relationships, or the purpose of life in the light of death. A consequence of the absence of the paternal metaphor is that these questions cannot be addressed in phallic terms, that is, in terms of what renders a person desirable in relation to others. In psychosis the question 'Who am I?' does not lead to reflection on how one can and should relate to others. As a result of foreclosure, questions on the existence of the subject reveal what Lacan calls 'the Real', that is, the realm of the radically non-signified. Questions of the identity provoke an inability to answer with signifiers and even bring the signifying chain to a dead end. In psychosis confrontations with existential questions have a perplexing effect on the subject: they don't bring about the appearance of the subject by means of references between signifiers, but actually provoke its disappearance.

The peculiar status of the unconscious in psychosis

Although Lacan situates the same questions at the basis of the unconscious in both neurosis and psychosis – 'Who am I?' and 'What do you want from me?' – he argues that the unconscious has a different status in both structures.

In neurosis, these questions are approached via incorporated normative answers, which Lacan explains by referring to the signifier of the Name-of-the-Father. By installing this signifier as a reference for addressing desire, questions on the identity of the subject take shape and prompt answers via the signifying chain. Given the fact that such answers are only constructions, they give rise to conflict. Neurotic symptoms and formations of the unconscious, like dreams, are crystallization points where such conflicts, and their repression, are expressed. In the psychoanalytic treatment of neurosis the analysant can make sense of his/her symptoms and dreams and explore what the symptom reveals: symptoms and formations of the unconscious are rebuses whereby warded-off truths about the subject are expressed.

In psychosis the situation is different in that what is at stake has nothing to do with repression. Foreclosure, writes Lacan (1959, p. 465) refers to 'a function of the unconscious that is distinct from the repressed'. As indicated above, foreclosure means that questions of existence cannot be approached by taking a position in relation to conventional discourse. This means that in the confrontation with existential questions, signifiers are not available to articulate the subject. Lacan (1959,

p. 465) says that 'at the point at which the Name-of-the-Father is summoned', that is, when an appeal is made to position oneself in relation to a question of existence, 'a pure and simple hole' answers in the Other. In psychosis, the subject lacks a symbolic compass at the level of the Other, due to which subjectivity remains undefined in its confrontation with the questions of existence. Given the fact that no metaphoric effect takes place, the enunciated subject is not defined and the identity of the subject is not created. Indeed, typical for psychosis is that *the subject fails to be articulated in terms of desire in relation to the Other*. Lacan articulates this by saying that the hole at the level of the Other gives rise to 'a corresponding hole in the place of phallic signification' (Lacan, 1959, p. 466). Contrary to neurosis, questions on the existence of the subject are not addressed in terms of what makes a person desirable in relation to others. Such confrontations shake the foundations of the subject.

Furthermore, in psychosis elements from the unconscious are not experienced as coming from within – as in neurosis, where symptoms express warded-off truths – but as strange messages that come from without. Due to the absence of *Bejahung*, themes of the subject's existence do not enter into the law of the Symbolic, but emerge in the Real as puzzling and overwhelming problems that seize the subject from the outside. This is what Lacan indicates in his statement that 'what is refused in the symbolic order re-emerges in the real' (Lacan, 1955–6, p. 13), and in his suggestion that in psychosis 'the nonsymbolized reappears in the real' (Lacan, 1955–6, p. 86). Manifestations of the unconscious are experienced as external realities: strange messages that cannot be framed in terms of one's own broader mental life.

In his discussion of the Schreber case study, Lacan (1959, p. 472) gives an example of how the external status of the unconscious is expressed clinically. In the incubation period before the outbreak of his second illness period Schreber, in a state of daydreaming, had the fantasy that it would be beautiful to be a woman submitting to the act of copulation. This fantasy, which concerns his sexual position as a man or a woman, was not qualified as a product of his own imagination – the type of judgement that would give rise to repression – but as a strange communication that was revealed to him, and that could not be put aside. Lacan argues that this reaction makes clear that productions of the unconscious are experienced as divinatory messages that come from without. At first Schreber is perplexed and shocked by the message: he cannot understand where it comes from or what it means. Later the same theme is elaborated in the delusion and brings Schreber to the conclusion that he is in the process of becoming the wife of God.

In contrast to what happens in neurosis, productions of the unconscious in psychosis are not fictional messages that can be deciphered via free associations. Indeed, Lacan (1955–6, p. 132) argued that in psychosis the subject is only a witness of the unconscious: 'The psychotic is a martyr of the unconscious, giving this term *martyr* its meaning, which is to be a witness'. By indicating that the psychotic is a martyr or a witness, he emphasises that the subject does not feel implicated in the production of formations of the unconscious. In psychosis formations of the unconscious force themselves upon the speaking subject; they cannot be understood as something that is defensively self-generated, or expressions of hidden desires. Therefore, Lacan (1955–6, p. 143) concludes that in psychosis 'the unconscious is present but not functioning'. The subject cannot think of himself as being immanent to productions of the unconscious. Either these productions are dismissed as being impenetrable or they are experienced as revelations of an external truth. In the latter case the experience of truth concerns the relation of an agency that is external to the subject (God, the devil, the central bank, Darth Vader ...), and not the relation of a subject to himself, as in neurosis. In Schreber's reaction to his sexual fantasy both positions can be retrieved. First he experiences his daydream as unfathomable; later he interprets it as a message that reveals the position he should occupy in relation to God.

Clinically speaking, the external status of the unconscious implies that treatment with psychosis will not focus on deciphering symptoms like delusions or hallucinations via free association (Apollon et al., 2000; Fink, 2007; Maleval, 2000; Svolos, 2001). In psychosis the analyst offers a place where a testimony *can* be given on the way in which the subject is affected by the externally manifested unconscious. This is done, not just in order to become 'secretaries to the insane' (Lacan, 1955–6, p. 206), but with the purpose of restoring a place for the subject. The analyst aims at installing a place where the Real of the psychotic experience can be enclosed by means of the Symbolic and the Imaginary. Psychoanalysis creates a space for signifying articulation, starting from which a subject, which we assume is an effect of the references between signifiers, can be produced.

Furthermore, a Lacanian analyst will aim at limiting confrontations with the two questions presumed to be at the basis of symptoms and formations of the unconscious: 'Who am I?' and 'What do you want from me?'. Logically speaking, psychotic symptoms and productions of the unconscious are responses to these questions. They reflect a confrontation with a perplexing question of subjectivity. In line with their external status to the patient these symptoms and productions cannot be explored in terms of warded-off truths. Therefore, clinical work will not be directed towards producing free association, but at detecting the identity-related issues that symptoms address. For example, signifiers appearing in delusions and hallucinations typically allude to specific existential issues that prove to be intolerable to the patient, and the analyst's task consists of discerning them. Through conversations with a psychotic patient the analyst will aim to help him/her avoid such brutal confrontations with questions of identity and also support the patient's solutions in managing them.

Compensation of foreclosure via conformist imaginary identifications

An idea accompanying Lacan's thesis on the foreclosure of the Name-of-the-Father is that metaphoric processes that determine the subject are fundamentally unstable. However, a further idea he develops is that this instability can be partly repaired through certain modes of compensation, which then fill the hole opened up by unconscious questions on the existence of the subject. In the 1950s Lacan discusses two modes of compensation: the creation of a delusional metaphor (Lacan, 1959, p. 481), which I examine in Chapter 5, and conformist imaginary identifications (Lacan, 1955–6, pp. 192–3, 204–5).

Conformist imaginary identifications are characterized by blindly adopting lifestyles and habitual modes of behaviour from others. In his third seminar Lacan (1955–6, pp. 192–193) discusses these identifications in terms of the 'as if mechanism' described by Hélène Deutsch (1942) in relation to cases of schizophrenia. He explains it as 'a mechanism of imaginary compensation ... for the absent Oedipus complex' (Lacan, 1955–6, p. 193). Deutsch's proposition was that *as-if* identifications constitute ways of living and thinking that are simply copied from other individuals or groups. Such identifications appear remarkable for their lack of affectivity, their uncritical nature and their lack of subjective implication. However, Lacan suggests that such identifications should not be disparaged; indeed, in a case of foreclosure such conformist identifications have a stabilizing function. *As-if* behaviour is functional in that it allows a person to take up a social role in relation to others without questioning the position he/she actually occupies. It provides a person with ideas on what one has to do to be a man, woman, father, mother ... and therefore sutures the gap foreclosure leaves at the core of subjectivity (Lacan 1955–6, p. 205).

Moreover, Lacan's (1955–6, p. 193) notion of 'imaginary compensation' should not be understood in terms of *Gestalt*-psychological processes, which might be implied by the construct of the Imaginary with its resonance of the mirror stage. In Lacan's discussion, imaginary compensation above all refers to the process of acquiring a *signified* that responds to questions on the existence of the subject. For example, when questioned at the level of one's identity as a mother, imaginary identification provides a person with a concept of what it is that mothers do. Indeed, the concept of imaginary compensation indicates that subjective identity doesn't exclusively arise as an effect of the paternal metaphor. Alternatively, a signified of how life should be lived can also be acquired by adopting the habits of others. Through imitating the behaviour of others, and adhering to a strict routine in daily life, questions of identity can be avoided. In that case, life is lived by following *social life narratives*, i.e. scripts on how life should be lived in relation to others. Imaginary identification with social life narratives means that a person exclusively thinks of himself in terms of the narrative. This precludes the question of whether one is doing the right thing and gives an individual the feeling that the things he does are self-evident. Imaginary identification sidesteps dialectical conflict about identity.

Social life narratives can be found almost everywhere: cultural products ranging from religions and ideologies to sitcoms, novels, commercial advertising and celebrities; all provide scenarios of how one should behave in relation to others. Such narratives can also be found in groups, where all members are potential role models that demonstrate how one should behave and relate. What is typical of compensatory imaginary identifications is that social life narratives are used as univocal prescriptions, and not as thoughts or opinions that are dialectically related to other thoughts or opinions. They provide a template based on which a person models his ego. In other words, identification with a narrative can be understood as conformist, not due to the content of the narrative, but the style with which it is adopted. In such conformist identification a given narrative is entirely and uncritically adopted. It is accepted with a remarkable black-and-white rigidity and dealt with as the only possible option for positioning oneself as a man, woman, husband, wife… In symbolic identification elements from discourse are selected, but not wholly absorbed, hence the psychological conflict experienced when identifications are made with elements from contradicting discourses. In imaginary identification, however, narratives are adopted as a whole.

Such imaginary identification occurs both in neurosis and in psychosis, but plays a different role in both cases. In neurosis imaginary identifications have a desire-related function, and aim at questioning or provoking a certain type of relationship with others (Verhaeghe, 1999). In psychosis this masquerade and pretence is not what *as-if* identification is about; the façade is the only thing there is and it functions as an ultimate attempt to hold on to shared reality.

At the level of content, social life narratives that serve as the basis for conformist imaginary identification can be most diverse. They might consist of conservative mainstream ideas, as well as more subversive ways of living that are valued only in subcultures. Identification with mainstream ideas typically gives rise to a socially acceptable, but colourless way of behaving. Billiet (1996, pp. 54–5) illustrates this with the clinical example of a woman who positions herself in her family in terms of the ideal housewife. Alternatively, subcultures might provide a person with socially deviant patterns of relating to others that nevertheless help him/her find a feeling of identity. Lacan (1955–6, pp. 204–5) illustrates this by referring to the case of a psychopathic criminal who uncritically adopts the law of criminal gangs without experiencing moral conflict about the life he leads. By following the rules of the gang and demonstrating virility through violent behaviour, he can compensate for an experience of ailing masculinity, for example. In this case 'alienation is radical' says Lacan (1955–6, p. 205), and a direct consequence of 'the nihilation of the signifier'. This means that when the signifier of the Name-of-the-Father is foreclosed, identification with social life narratives can have a repairing function to the extent that they provide a person with a fixed set of rules to follow in relation to others, hence the idea of *radical* alienation.

In my interpretation Lacan's conceptual distinction between the enunciating subject and the enunciated subject sheds an interesting light on conformist imaginary identifications. After all, these attract attention because of the absence of an enunciating subject in the process of signification. In neurosis, the process of signification builds upon signifiers. In confrontations with questions of subjective identity, neurotic speech falls back on symbolic identifications, through which a message on the identity of the subject takes shape. Here the paternal metaphor has led to a series of phallic identifications with signifiers that define the subject in terms of desire in relation to the Other. When an interpellation is made to articulate the identity of the subject, a set of signifiers is produced. The message made up by these signifiers is the enunciated subject. This process of articulation also implies that other conflicting signifiers and identifications are excluded. Something about the subject remains unsaid, which is how the enunciating subject takes shape. Both the enunciated and enunciating subject are two poles in a dialectical tension. In conformist imaginary identifications by contrast, the enunciated subject is not articulated by mobilizing phallic identifications. In this context when interpellations are made to articulate the subject, identity will be derived by articulating the subject in terms of the signifieds from a social life narrative. Social life narratives provide a framework in reference to which an 'I' can be defined. They provide the possibility of acquiring an ideal reality and an ideal ego, in terms of which daily life can be managed. This way of defining an enunciated subject does not leave a remainder at the level of the signifier; there is nothing that remains unsaid, hence my suggestion that no enunciating subject is created. However, this does not mean that imaginary identification is a perfect solution for the absence of subjective anchoring in the signifier of the Name-of-the-Father. In his discussion of ordinary psychosis, Miller (2009, p. 157) points out that whereas conformist identifications make it possible for the subject to define itself, a dimension of emptiness can be frequently observed at the verge of such identifications. A feeling of subjectivity can only be enunciated by conforming to external standards. Without the support of such stereotypical discourse, the identity of the speaker is not generated, hence the feeling of emptiness that often accompanies such identifications.

Psychotic decompensation

These ideas on the imaginary compensation of foreclosure make clear that Lacan did not equate psychosis with a typical set of symptoms, characteristic of the psychiatric paradigm. Instead, psychosis was understood as a mode of relating to oneself and to the world, characterized by an inability to signify desire and subjective existence through a set of incorporated answers: the Symbolic provides no anchor in the process of dialectically articulating the subject's position, hence Lacan's notion of the external status of the unconscious. An important question to be asked in this context is how a discrete mode of psychotic functioning turns into a manifest psychotic episode.

With his concept of the Name-of-the-Father, Lacan answers this question by reconsidering his ideas on the triggering of a psychotic episode. Whereas in the 1930s and 1940s he approached the question of the onset of psychosis (*déclenchement*) with a theory of specific and non-specific causes (see Chapter 1), in the 1950s he reconsiders the triggering of psychotic episodes exclusively through his concept of foreclosure.

As we saw, in his third seminar Lacan (1955–6, pp. 205, 250) suggests that psychotic decompensation often occurs incidentally: at the moment a person is required to speak, or take a position in relation to questions of existence. If the Name-of-the-Father is foreclosed, the subject is brutally confronted with the absence of the necessary Symbolic scaffolding: identity cannot be addressed via a set of dialectically functioning answers. The effect of such confrontation is complete destabilization: a place for the subject can no longer be articulated, and the signifying chain starts breaking up. This is how Lacan explains the appearance of hallucinations and delusions (see Chapters 4 and 5). Contrary to the first phase of his work, Lacan no longer focuses on psychological or biological triggers of psychosis, instead paying attention to the destabilizing effect of specific life events in terms of the individual's ability to articulate a subjective position via the signifier, or more specifically the way in which a person can frame the event by means of the Symbolic. Lacan (1955–6, p. 306) illustrates this line of reasoning with a case presentation. In this case of a West Indian man, decompensation occurred the moment his partner tells him that she is pregnant. The confrontation with the prospect of fatherhood destabilizes him, which is indicated by the paternity-related theme of the hallucinations he subsequently experienced.

In On a Question Prior to Any Possible Treatment of Psychosis Lacan (1959) makes an additional step in this line of reasoning. He argues that a confrontation with a Real other precedes the onset of a psychotic episode. Within this logic, an other is 'Real' to the extent that his/her actions cannot be framed by means of the Symbolic or the Imaginary: conventional ideas on exchange relationships and social positions in a group do not provide the symbolic framework whereby sense can be made of the other's actions. This leads to a clear sense that the other is unpredictable. If the other's actions cannot be framed by taking oneself as an imaginary reference point, the effect of estrangement is complete.

In this context, Lacan (1959, p. 481) writes: 'But how can the Name-of-the-Father be summoned by the subject to the only place from which it could have come into being for him and in which it has never been? By nothing other than a real father'. He also notes that the notion of the Real father should not be interpreted in terms of a person's actual father: the Real father is not the biological or psychological father, but the 'One-father' or 'A-father' [*Un-père*] (Lacan, 1959, p. 481). Lacan is somewhat sparing in his explanation of the concept 'One-father' or 'A-father'. It is possible that he is not only framing this concept of father in opposition to the Symbolic father and the Name-of-the-Father; the figure of the Real father may also refer to the primordial father of Freud's text Totem and Taboo (Freud, 1913; Lacan, 1963).

In Totem and Taboo Freud describes a number of steps in the evolution of social organization in tribal societies, which he links to mental functioning in neurosis. Freud outlines how exchange relationships between members of the group in tribal societies were gradually subjected to cultural laws and taboos. Prior to this it was the law of the jungle that guided the interactions between humans, and the primordial father physically imposed his power in a way that was convenient to him. Eventually, however, members of the tribe began to impose restraints on each other's actions. Totems symbolized these laws and indicate how abstract principles guide people's interactions.

In my interpretation Lacan's theory of the destabilizing effect of the encounter with A-father is connected to Freud's line of reasoning in Totem and Taboo. Just as the primordial father's actions were overwhelming before the law was installed – they could not yet be judged in terms of the law since the law was not yet there – the Real father incarnates a puzzling aspect of functioning that cannot be framed by means of the Name-of-the-Father. Lacan states that for the Real father to have such a destabilizing effect, he 'must still come to that place to which the subject could not summon him before' (1959, p. 481).

In his discussion of the onset of psychotic episodes, Lacan (1959, p. 481) suggests that the encounter with A-father only has a triggering effect if this Real father situates himself 'in a tertiary position in any relationship that has its base in the imaginary couple *a-a'*. Lacan (1959, p. 462) explained this idea of the imaginary couple *a-a'* earlier in that text. The component '*a*' is an abbreviation of the French word *autre* and refers to the imaginary other. The element '*a*' refers to the ego. By using the notation '*a*' Lacan stresses that the ego is nothing but an internalized reflection of the other: all signifieds a person can attribute to himself are acquired via others or via (sub-)culturally prevailing ideas on how life should be lived. By referring to the tertiary position of the Real father Lacan indicates that a radical questioning of the subject's adopted social life narratives can be found at the basis of psychotic decompensation. Whereas conformist imaginary identification compensates for the problem of foreclosure, the figure of A-father destabilizes the acquired solution and puts the absence of a signifier to the fore. This has a dramatic effect at the level of subjectivity: without the material support of the signifier, the subject cannot be articulated in relation to the subjective core that the Real father touches.

Conclusion

Pivotal to Lacan's discussion of psychosis in the 1950s is the idea of the foreclosure of the Name-of-the-Father. The starting point of it is a reinterpretation of the Oedipus complex in terms of a language-based metaphorical transition, which leads to a relationship between subject and Other that builds on desire. At first the desire of the (m)other is enigmatic, because it is only expressed via signifiers the subject cannot comprehend. When in a second step an additional signifier, the Name-of-the-Father, enters the field this enigma is clarified: the puzzling signifiers the (m)other first conveyed can be interpreted in terms of social laws and taboos, which creates a context for the articulation of the subject in terms of desire. Importantly, Lacan also indicates that at the level of the unconscious, the subject is confronted with questions about its own existence. The point of who the subject is as a living mortal, as a sexual being and as a relational creature is not established at birth, but must be constructed via language. In this context the Name-of-the-Father is the subject's key reference: through a dialectical relationship with this signifier identity is constructed. However, in psychosis this second step is lacking says Lacan: no Name-of-the-Father is available for articulating the identity of the subject. At the level of the unconscious such absence implies that signifiers pointing to questions concerning the subject's existence cannot be experienced as coming from within. Therefore, Lacan qualified the subject in psychosis as a martyr of the unconscious, a passive witness of strange messages that come from without. A further consequence of the foreclosure of the Name-of-the-Father is that metaphoric processes that determine the subject are fundamentally unstable. This instability is not necessarily dramatic since it can be partly repaired through certain modes of compensation, of which imaginary identification with social life seems to be most prominent. However, radical questioning of a subject's adopted social life narratives, has dramatic effects and is seen as the basis of psychotic decompensation.

In my interpretation the strength of this foreclosure theory lies in Lacan's proposition that psychosis should not be understood as a synonym for psychotic disorder, as defined in psychiatry. This implies that psychosis should not be marked by positive symptoms, such as hallucinations and delusions. It can, but not always. What is crucial is that his theory provides a framework to reflect on ways in which subjectivity takes shape. This framework exceeds the examination of psychosis in terms of typical symptoms, and focuses on the subject–Other relation, which is considered to be a better basis for orienting clinical practice. Indeed, this conceptual reflection led Lacan to formulate some general principles about the treatment of psychosis. Whereas some see psychosis as a counter-indication for psychoanalytic treatment, Lacan, like Melanie Klein, argued that psychoanalysis offers a framework for treating psychosis. He thereby suggests that psychoanalysts should help psychotic patients deal with the effects of foreclosure. Concrete guidelines for treating psychosis, by contrast, cannot be found in his work. Later on, many analysts working with Lacanian theory tried to make these treatment principles more explicit, but then again, only interaction with each singular patient can be used as a guide for concrete interventions.

4
A Novel Approach to Hallucinations

A hallucination is (not) a perception without an object

In the previous chapter we saw how Lacan makes a connection between the onset of psychosis and hallucinatory experiences. When the Name-of-the-Father is foreclosed, situations in which the subject is expected to take a personal position in relation to questions of existence have a radically destabilizing effect. One outcome of such destabilization is the experience of hallucinations. In psychosis, hallucinations are the expression of a radical disturbance in the signifying chain (Miller, 2007a, 2007b; Vanheule, 2011). While hallucinations can also appear in neurosis, there they are the expression of a return of repressed material, and not of foreclosure (Maleval, 1991).

Historically, hallucinations were first delineated as a distinct mental phenomenon by the French psychiatrist Jean-Etienne Esquirol, who defined them as follows: 'A man who has the intimate conviction of an actually perceived sensation, while no external object apt for provoking this sensation is within his field of perception, is in a state of hallucination'[1] (Esquirol, 1838, p. 80). While this definition aroused quite some debate (Berrios, 1996), a point of agreement amongst many authors was that a hallucination is a perceptual experience in the absence of a relevant external stimulus. Lacan's friend and intellectual opponent Henri Ey, for example, characterized hallucinations as 'perceptions without an object to be perceived'[2] (Ey, 1973a, p. 50). In more recent studies, hallucinations have been defined as 'any perceptual experience in the absence of external stimuli' (Allen et al., 2008, p. 176), or as 'a sensory experience which occurs in the absence of corresponding external stimulation of the relevant sensory organ, which has a sufficient sense of reality to resemble a veridical perception, over which the subject does not feel s/he has direct and voluntary control, and which occurs in the awake state' (David, 2004, p. 110). As we can see, these definitions focus on sensory perceptual experience, and underline the unreality of hallucinatory perceptions. Despite some changes in the wording, it is obvious that these definitions are remarkably similar to Esquirol's original definition of hallucinations.

Lacan (1959), by contrast, abandoned the idea of disordered perception and suggested that what is at stake concerns the relation between the subject and the signifier, hence his proposition that hallucinations should not be studied in terms of their variability at the sensory level. In other words, hallucinations should not be studied in terms of a distinction between visual, auditory and motor phenomena, but in terms of how the process of signification is organized. From Lacan's point of view, hallucinations are above all *verbal* and it is at the level of the patient's speech that they should be explored.

A crucial source of inspiration for Lacan (1959) in this context was Merleau-Ponty's 1945 book on the Phenomenology of Perception (Kusnierek, 2008; Miller, 2001). Lacan rarely cited this work, but clearly borrowed from Merleau-Ponty's critique of empiricist and intellectualist theories of hallucinations. In Merleau-Ponty's view, both theories are naïve. Moreover, any study of hallucinations should adhere to a phenomenological method of understanding. Empiricist theories try to explain hallucinations in the same way as they explain perception and focus on the way in which sensory information is processed. Merleau-Ponty (1945, p. 391) argued that within this perspective, a 'hallucination is an event in the chain of events running from the stimulus to the state of consciousness'. However, since patients typically make distinctions between perceptions and hallucinations, such an approach is considered as inadequate. Intellectualist theories, on the other hand, study hallucinations in terms of cognitive processes. According to Merleau-Ponty (1945, p. 390) the basic idea underlying intellectualist theories is that 'since the hallucination is not a sensory content, there seems nothing for it but to regard it as a judgement, an interpretation or a belief'. Again he argues that this viewpoint is problematic: typically patients do not think that their hallucinations correspond to an external reality that can be objectively discerned, and they are aware that their experience is a private reality. Indeed, the opinions patients seem to have about their hallucinations are not as erroneous as often thought.

The alternative approach Merleau-Ponty advocates focuses on personalized comprehension: 'When the victim of hallucinations declares that he sees and hears, we must not believe him, since he also declares the opposite; what we must do is understand him' (Merleau-Ponty, 1945, pp. 392–3). Such understanding can only be realized by entering into a dialogue with the hallucinating person and by attempting to comprehend the patient's living environment, as this is the context within which the hallucination is produced. We must follow the patient's descriptions about his experiences in detail, make explicit our own experience and 'understand one through the other' (Merleau-Ponty, 1945, p. 393).

In *On a Question Prior to Any Possible Treatment of Psychosis*, Lacan (1959) takes up Merleau-Ponty's critique of empiricist and intellectualist theories of hallucination. A common limitation to both theories is that they don't go beyond scholastic ideas of perception, which Lacan accentuates by using classical scholastic terminology in his discussion of the psychiatric model of hallucinations. More concretely, Lacan indicates that most theories of hallucinations build on the idea that our *sensoria* extract information from objects in the extra-mental material world, and based on this information the perceiving subject (the *'percipiens'*, 'he who is seeing') builds a synthetic image of the world (the *'perceptum'*, 'what is seen'). Lacan (1959) indicates that this linear causal model is faithful to Thomas Aquinas's theory on perception and cognition, which indeed follows a similar path (Stump, 2003). It assumes that when senses are stimulated by an extra-mental object, the *percipiens* is prompted to create a *perceptum*. Schematically, this can be presented as follows (Figure 4.1):

Figure 4.1   Scholastic model of perception

Within the scholastic paradigm, a hallucination is seen as a *'perceptum* without an object' (Lacan, 1959, p. 446); there is no extra-mental object giving rise to sensorial processing, but a mental image is nevertheless produced. Lacan suggests that this basic idea leads to the formulation of typical questions on the nature of hallucinations. On the one hand, it gives rise to a study of disorders at the level of the sensorial processing, which Merleau-Ponty had characterized as an empiricist approach. On the other hand, it leads to a dazzling search for pathogenic processes in the *percipiens*, processes that are responsible for the production of erroneous *percepta*, which Merleau-Ponty had characterized as an intellectualist approach.

Starting from these theories, research strongly focuses on the brain mechanisms accompanying hallucinations. This research interest certainly prevailed at the time Lacan was elaborating his theory on psychosis, and has since that time remained somewhat dominant. de Clérambault (1942) and Ey (1934, 1973a, 1973b), for example, believed that in order to establish a good understanding of hallucinations cerebral mechanisms should be closely examined. More recent research of this kind is characterized by a similar but ever more detailed search for underlying brain dysfunction (Allen et al., 2008; Tracy and Shergill, 2006). However, Lacan didn't express much interest in such approaches. In his 1959 article he ironically refers to scholastically based theories as a kind of 'cuisine' that is preoccupied with 'preparing brains', and not with the subjective effect hallucinations have on the person (Lacan, 1959, p. 445). In this sense, they were not thought to be very useful for the psychoanalytic treatment of psychosis.

At a more detailed level, Lacan (1959) considered the empiricist focus on sensorial processes as simply irrelevant. According to him the sensorial quality of hallucinations simply doesn't matter. Congenitally profoundly deaf people, who by definition have never processed auditory sensorial information, can indeed experience auditory verbal hallucinations (see also: Atkinson, 2006). This would not be possible if a prerequisite for verbal hallucinations is an active auditory register, which is not the case in deaf people. Lacan rules this out and concludes that the act of hearing should not be understood in terms of the sensory registers involved, but in terms of a meaning-generating process.

Theories with an intellectualist focus are equally problematic, as they presume that, above all, the *percipiens* is an instance that synthesizes incoming sensorial information and actively builds perceptions. For Lacan the *percipiens* is only unifying to the extent that a person makes use of the dimension of the Imaginary. This means that it is only to the extent that he creates *Gestalts* or consistent mental representations and images that a *percipiens* shapes his own *perceptum*. The Imaginary enables a person to develop delineated and coherent experiences, and to create a sense of reality. However, this unifying tendency reflects only one dimension of the way in which a person relates to the world. Conversely, Lacan suggests that special attention should be paid to how a person is affected by his own hallucinations. In line with Merleau-Ponty (1945), Lacan (1959) stresses that at an idiographic level, an open-minded clinician will usually observe that hallucinating patients do not experience their hallucinations as being consistent with other aspects of their mental life. This casts doubt on the rationale of emphasizing the patient's own synthetic activity. Hallucinations, by contrast, tend to pose a problem for the patient and evoke an experience of perplexity. Lacan (1959, p. 447) suggests that if one listens attentively, and does not allow oneself to get blinded by theoretical presumptions on pathological processes in the patient, one will typically observe a number of 'paradoxes to which he [the hallucinating subject] falls victim in this singular perception'.

By making this claim Lacan subverts the question of how a hallucinating *percipiens* produces erroneous *percepta*, and turns it into a question of how the hallucinated *perceptum* affects the *percipiens*. The latter is what really matters to him; a hallucinating person does not coincide with his hallucinations, but is subjected to them: the hallucination 'renders equivocal the supposedly unifying percipiens' (Lacan, 1959, p. 447). A conclusion we can draw from this is that a hallucination should not so much be seen as a *perceptum* without an object, but as a *perceptum* that has a paradoxical or even dividing effect on the *percipiens*. Schematically, this idea of subjective division can be presented as follows (Figure 4.2):

Percipiens   Perceptum

Figure 4.2   Effect of the *perceptum* on the *percipiens*

Lacan suggests that qua *perceptum* hallucinations have an internal logic or organization, which cannot be deduced from the external world alone. Merleau-Ponty (1945) makes a similar point and argues that, as a consequence, we should aim at understanding what hallucinations mean in terms of how a person makes sense of the world and of his own position in the world. Lacan (1959), by contrast, suggests that we should be careful about using 'understanding' as a clinical tool. The problem he discerns in the methodological use of understanding is that it draws too strongly from the clinician's ego and imagination, and therefore obfuscates what is at stake for the hallucinating person. The alternative approach Lacan proposes is to study the inner structure of the *perceptum* in terms of the signifier. Hallucinations are events that occur in the production of a signifying chain, and thus they should be examined in terms of the process of signification. Hallucinations disrupt classic processes of meaning generation and therefore also affect the way in which the subject is constituted via speech.

A hallucination is an unchained signifier responding to a rupture in the signifying chain

To explore the subjective effect of hallucinations, and more broadly to map the structure of the hallucinatory experience, Lacan (1955–6, 1959) uses the case of a paranoid woman interviewed in 1955 during one of his clinical case presentations. The case concerns a young woman who was hospitalized together with her mother, with whom she had a shared delusion. In this delusion the conviction of being intruded upon and being threatened was pivotal. During the case presentation Lacan questioned this conviction and invited the patient to explain her situation in detail. One of the problems she mentioned was that she and her mother had been insulted by their neighbours, and this was the complaint upon which Lacan focused. At first, contacts with these neighbours – a woman and her lover – were kindly received. The neighbour was a friend; she frequently visited the patient and her mother at their home and they got on well. However, at a certain point both mother and daughter began to experience these visits as intrusive: 'She would always come and knock at their door while they were in the toilet or just as they were dining or reading', which motivated them to take a distance from her (Lacan, 1955–6, p. 50). Although the patient was reluctant to document her conviction with examples, she does give Lacan the anecdote that one day, as she crossed the hallway of their apartment building, she was offended by her neighbour's lover. What we know about this lover is that he was a married man having an affair, and that our patient thought of him as someone of loose morals (Lacan, 1955–6, p. 48). Upon meeting him in the hallway she had a hallucination of hearing the offensive term 'sow'.

To the patient, the term 'sow' illustrated the meaning of the insults she and her mother had had to endure, yet Lacan noticed that she was quite reluctant to utter this heavily laden word. The young lady was not only scandalized, but also confused and perplexed by what she had heard. She did not know exactly what to make of it, and consequently had difficulty talking about it. This is the experience Lacan referred to when he indicated that a hallucination has a paradoxical effect on the *percipiens*; it is a *perceptum* that a patient cannot bring into coherence with her other experiences.

What is more, for Lacan this experience of paradox primarily refers to a radical interruption in mental life. In this context, Lacan (1959,

p. 449) qualifies a hallucination as an 'irruption in the Real'. By making this claim he is emphasizing that, for the patient, a hallucination comes out of the blue; it is an encounter with an unimaginable element that imposes itself from without. A hallucination is Real to the extent that it is 'a sudden emergence of total strangeness' (Lacan, 1955–6, p. 86).

Referring to his theory on the logic of signification, Lacan (1959, pp. 447, 485) more specifically argues that the hallucinated *perceptum* is basically an 'unchained signifier', a signifier that escapes the logic of concatenation. Whereas speech is basically characterized by the linking of signifiers in series, a hallucination constitutes a sudden interruption in the signifying chain: beyond the speaker's intention, a strange element is introduced. This element can be situated at the level of the patient's unconscious, but remarkably, it cannot be read as a message that leads to a questioning of her own subjectivity. Instead it is an immense signifier she cannot deal with. This has a dramatic effect at the level of meaning and subjectivity. In terms of the schema that was introduced in Chapter 2 on the logic of signification, the unchained signifier of a hallucination fundamentally disrupts the message speech produces as well as the conclusions a speaker can draw from his own thoughts.

The case of this young paranoid woman can thereby illustrate what is at stake for the subject. As 'sow' is an unchained signifier, Lacan suggests that any relevant intervention should try to locate this signifier in the context of the signifying chain from which it emerged. In other words, a hallucinated signifier is unchained only in relation to the context of signifiers from which it diverges. To understand the logic of why it suddenly appears, this context needs to be studied. Therefore, in his clinical interview Lacan asked his patient what she herself had said to her neighbour that day in the hallway. This type of intervention is diachronic and aims at situating the hallucination in the actual circumstances that led to its production. The intervention was not in vain, argues Lacan (1959, p. 448), 'for she conceded with a smile that, upon seeing the man, she had murmured the following words which, if she is to be believed here, gave no cause for offence: 'I've just been to the pork butcher's...'

According to Lacan, the phrase 'I've just been to the pork butcher's...' is very important as it is in the context of this signifying chain that the hallucination 'sow' must be situated. In commenting upon this expression, he focuses on the structure of its composition and concludes that the sentence is allusive and incomplete. The phrase is allusive as the patient has problems in specifying what it means, and why exactly she said this to the man. Lacan further stresses that, grammatically speaking, the sentence is also allusive, and this is more fundamental. As it is her own utterance it introduces her as the subject of the phrase, reflected by the pronoun 'I'. On the other hand the predicate 'have just been to the pork butcher's' fails to provide her with a meaningful position towards this particular man with his particular reputation in the corridor. The sentence gives a description of what she has been doing in daily life, but it does not adequately signify who she is and what she is living through. At the level of the message it does not define an enunciated subject. The sentence is incomplete as it is suddenly ruptured, which Lacan indicates by adding an ellipsis at the end of it. The speech accompanying the encounter in the corridor introduces her as a woman in relation to a man who is engaged in a type of enjoyment that is foreign to her, but fails to articulate a position in relation to him.

In Lacan's terminology from 1959 the man can be considered as Real, in that she cannot understand or grasp him in terms of her own image or any incorporated normative ideas on how men are, or should be. What is typical of such an encounter with a Real person is that it calls into question one's 'existence as a subject' (Lacan, 1959, p. 460). It raises the question of who she is as a woman in relation to men and touches upon the issue of what it is that ties a man and a woman. The patient's description of the encounter in the corridor shows that at precisely the moment of confrontation with the question of her existence as a subject, punctuation on her identity is deferred. In terms of the logic of signification, this implies that the anticipatory suspension, which is inherent to the use of the signifier, remains unsolved. Lacan (1955–6) suggests that this typically provokes a feeling of enigma and tension, since an enunciated subject fails to emerge. The formulated sentence does not adequately signify the intention that drove this woman to address herself to the man, and illustrates her failure to take up a desiring position in relation to the man she meets.

With Lacan's later terminology from the 1960s, which will be discussed in Chapter 6, I suggest considering this man not only as Real, but also as a figure who incarnates *jouissance*. That is to say, his presence not only perplexes her at the level of the signifier, but above all embodies a libidinal charge that she cannot grasp. This man confronts her with several drive-related problems, which the signifiers she ordinarily uses to denote her subjective existence are unable to resolve. Within this perspective the tension the situation raises is not just the expression of failed signification. It bears witness of a confrontation with the thrust of the drive from which the signifier breaks.

Lacan argues that the hallucinatory appearance of the signifier 'sow' solves this tension and retroactively binds the suspension that marks the predicate 'I've just been to the pork butcher's...'. The sudden manifestation of the hallucinated signifier installs the punctuation that was thus far deferred and results in the generation of a meaning. The modifying noun 'sow' will henceforth signify the identity of the 'I' that was first introduced as the subject of the phrase, and lead to the creation of an enunciated subject. The message thus obtained is that 'I' is equated with 'sow', which leads the woman to the conclusion that she has been insulted. In this speech context, 'sow' functions like a judgment. It is a final concluding signifier about the subject, and does not open up the dimension of the enunciating subject. The hallucinated signifier provides an ultimate verdict, and does not function as an intermediate stop in the process of articulating the subject.

In terms of the logic of signification Lacan further (1959) notes that the longer the process of punctuation takes to come to an end, the stronger the degree of certitude about the finally obtained message will be. This is what Lacan expresses with his statement that the hallucinated signifier takes on 'a reality proportionate to the time, which is perfectly observable in experience, involved in its subjective attribution' (Lacan, 1959, p. 447). The longer the perplexity caused by the rupture in the signifying chain persists, the stronger the experience will be that the final signifier enunciates the identity of the subject.

The status of hallucinations in relation to foreclosure

Lacan's suggestion that hallucinations reveal signifiers in response to an underlying rupture in the signifying chain is interesting in that it invites us to de-pathologize hallucinations. Rather than a symptom in the medical sense of the word, a hallucination functions as an attempt to repair an underlying problem, which is the rupture in the signifying chain. Along this way, Lacan connects with Freud (1911, p. 77), who argued that hallucinations are attempts at recovery, typical in dementia praecox.

Moreover, in his further analysis of the rupture at the basis of hallucinations, Lacan broadens the discussion by including his concept of foreclosure. With this concept, hallucinations are considered as a reaction to the two questions that lay at the basis of one's subjective identity: 'Who am I?' and 'What do you want from me?'. In case of foreclosure there is no previously incorporated symbolic framework to support the subject when he/she is confronted with such questions and expected to articulate a position of his own. In other words, when the signifier of the Name-of-the-Father is foreclosed questions on subjectivity are in the Real and have a perplexing effect on the subject. Confrontations with such questions do not lead to a positioning of the subject via the signifier of the Name-of-the-Father and phallic signification, but to a rupture in the signifying chain. The hallucination itself is a reaction to this rupture. The unchained signifier that comes to the fore in hallucinations sutures the gap that was opened up by the question of subjectivity, thus repairing it.

Lacan's case presentation of the paranoid woman seems to illustrate his hypothesis that the basic question of the relation between man and woman was unmanageable for her. Evidence of this can be found not only in the fact that the presence of an adulterous man had a destabilizing effect on her, but more broadly in the context of this patient's life. Lacan (1959, p. 448) indicates that this woman was married and had recently left her husband. She took this decision rather suddenly and fled from their house in the countryside. She was convinced that he and her in-laws were planning to kill her and carve her to pieces. Similar to the situation with her neighbour's lover in the corridor, the question of the relation between man and woman radically destabilized the patient in her married life.

The general formulation Lacan gives to questions on the existence of the subject leaves room for reflection on how such questions take shape for each individual. In psychosis such questions are insurmountable at the level of the signifier. However, in spite of this theory of hallucinations, it is not possible to know beforehand whether or which event may evoke questions of the subject's identity and thus provoke a psychotic hallucination. Disruption will take place only when the enunciated subject cannot be articulated via copy-cat solutions with social life narratives, and when a person is summoned to articulate his own position.

Variability in questions on the existence of the subject is illustrated, for example, by the West Indian man Lacan (1955–6, p. 306) interviewed during one of his case presentations. Lacan described this man as having led an extraordinarily heroic life. However, one day he was confronted with the issue of paternity, which completely destabilized him. The man had a relationship with a woman who announced to him that she was going to have a baby. Although it was not clear whether he was the biological father, within days he began to experience a hallucination that the Biblical figure Elisabeth sent him the message: 'You are Saint Thomas'. Lacan argues that apart from the uncertainty regarding his responsibility for this pregnancy, his partner's announcement presented him with the matter of paternity and the message he actually received was: 'You are going to be a father'. Obviously the matter of occupying the position of father baffled him, and left him without any reference point in the Symbolic; as a result, his identity remained non-signified. In the hallucination, allusions to the problem of paternity come to the fore. Indeed, it is quite remarkable that the voice of Elisabeth emerged as the messenger, as she was also informed quite late in life that she was going to have a child; Elisabeth thus defines him as the incredulous Thomas (Lacan, 1955–6, p. 306), Christ's apostle, who was most hesitant about the Messianic truth. The hallucinated message punctuates his identity. It doesn't define him as a paternal figure, but as the eternal hesitator who couldn't believe that God the Father had sent his son to earth.

The case of Schreber: message phenomena and code phenomena in hallucinations

A further crucial reference for Lacan (1955–6, 1959) in his structural discussion of hallucinations is the autobiographical book by Daniel Paul Schreber (1903), which Freud (1911) also studied. Through his theory on the logic of signification, Lacan (1959) discerns two characteristic types of hallucination in Schreber's text: message phenomena and code phenomena.

On the one hand he recognizes hallucinations that have a similar structure to those detected in the case of the paranoid woman: hallucinations in which deferred punctuation is pivotal. A key reference in this context is the passage from Schreber's autobiography (1903, pp. 198–9), in which he describes how unfinished sentences and fragmented ideas are exerted on him from without, via the 'rays' that connect him with God. For example, Schreber hallucinates the expression 'Now I shall' and feels compelled to complete the fragment with the answer 'resign myself to being stupid'. Lacan (1959) considers these unfinished sentences as indicative of interruptions in the process of generating meaning, and qualifies them as *message phenomena*: due to ruptures in the chain of signifiers, a message that defines an enunciated subject is not created. In Schreber's case, the sentence 'now I shall' introduces him as the subject, yet all predicates that would further define him remain lacking.

In one respect, the interrupted messages described in Schreber's autobiography differ from the hallucinatory experiences of the woman from

Lacan's case presentation. Schreber hears the first part of the sentence and complements it with his own supplementary signifiers, whereas the hallucinating woman utters the first part of the sentence and then hears the complement. However, at the level of structure both hallucinations have a number of characteristics in common. In both cases the interrupted sentence fails to convey a message but leads to the movement of anticipating meaning. In both cases this interruption leads to a situation of enigma and suspension of meaning for the subject. Lacan (1959) also concludes that, similar to his own patient, the unfinished sentences are interrupted at the point at which the subject is introduced, but not yet defined. The unfinished sentence contains a *protasis* that introduces the subject, but suspends its definition, which would be contained in the *apodosis*. In other words, the *apodosis* which would complement the sentence by attributing qualities to the subject is lacking. As a result the production of the message is disturbed, which Lacan refers to as message phenomena.

As the message typically breaks off at the moment the subject is introduced via a personal pronoun, Lacan indicates that 'each sentence is interrupted at the point at which the group of words that one might call 'index terms' ends, the latter being those designated by their function in the signifier ... as shifters' (Lacan, 1959, p. 452). Strictly speaking this statement is incorrect. Schreber himself (1903, p. 198) reports *protases*, such as 'this of course was' and 'lacking now is', in which no personal pronoun appears (and which Lacan doesn't cite). From a clinical point of view, the idea that hallucinations of this type always introduce the subject via a personal pronoun is not tenable. The proof of the contrary can easily be found in testimonies of psychotic patients. Yet, what Schreber's unfinished sentences do introduce in each case is the subject of the sentence in the *grammatical* sense of the word. Unfinished sentences typically nominate the grammatical subject, or allude to it, without further defining its characteristics. In terms of the logic of signification, the effect on the subject can be thought of as indirect. As previously indicated, all signification has the effect of generating subjectivity since the articulated signifiers connote speaker and listener. When the process of signification itself is interrupted, as is the case in the unfinished sentences, this connotation will be deferred. At the level of the message this will produce a suspension: no identity-generating punctuation takes place, and as a result the person involved in the speech act remains essentially undefined in relation to the Other.

On the other hand, Lacan also discerns *code phenomena* in the hallucinations Schreber describes. These refer to fundamental changes in the set of signifiers used by the subject. Through his hallucinations Schreber acquires a new set of signifiers, such as 'nerve-contact' or 'soul-murder' (Schreber, 1903, pp. 23, 34), which are added to the conventional lexicon of which he makes use. These words have no conventional meaning, and make part of the so-called 'basic language': the vernacular in which God addresses Schreber (1903, p. 26). Lacan (1959, p. 450) indicates that in terms of the process of signification, such words reflect a change at the level of the Other, or at the level of the code: 'Code phenomena are specified in locutions that are neological in both their form (new compound words, though the compounding here takes place in accordance with the rules of the patient's mother tongue) and usage'. Through hallucinations, words with a radically private meaning can be conveyed; such words have no intelligible meaning outside the context of a psychotic person's speech and designate an essential aspect of the person's experience. Neologisms name aspects of experience that, due to the foreclosure of the Name-of-the-Father, cannot be named in conventional ways. The neologism 'nerve-contact', for example (Schreber, 1903, p. 23), is constructed to specifically name the physical contact Schreber believes he has with God. Another example is the utterance 'wretch' (Schreber, 1903, p. 131), which God expressed to Schreber one night. This word has a conventional meaning, and might therefore designate that he is a miserable or despicable person. However, in Schreber's explanation the expression 'wretch' does not have such meaning, and above all denotes 'a human being destined to be destroyed by God and to feel God's power and wrath' (Schreber, 1903, p. 131). An interpretation of the word in terms of conventional meanings is inappropriate. Such interpretation imposes the perspective of the listener onto the speaker, and obfuscates the status of the word in terms of the signifying chain. Hence the idea that in our clinical work understanding in terms of convention should be minimized, while contextual understanding should be maximized.

Furthermore, Lacan (1955–6, p. 225) indicates that at the level of the signified a range in meaningfulness can be discerned in code phenomena: 'The register in which the onset of psychosis is played out is located between those two poles – the word of revelation, which opens up a new dimension and gives a feeling of ineffable understanding, which corresponds to nothing previously experienced, and on the other hand the refrain, the same old song'. Indeed, on the one hand hallucinating persons can be impressed by the genius or the importance of what is revealed. This is for example the case with Schreber's word 'wretch', which is a miraculous communication from God that makes a strong impression: 'My impression was not one of alarm and fear, but largely one of admiration for the magnificent and the sublime; the effect on my nerves was therefore beneficial despite the insults contained in some of the *words*' (Schreber, 1903, p. 131). On the other hand it might be that hallucinated signifiers are experienced as absurd and nonsensical. An example of a meaningless hallucinated signifier from Schreber's Memoirs (1903, p. 191) is the expression 'damned fellow'. Schreber heard this expression over and over again from miraculously created birds. These birds are '*remnants* (single nerves) *of souls of human beings who had become blessed*' (Schreber, 1903, p. 130), but are no more intelligent than natural birds. They continuously utter phrases in a parrot-like way, and Schreber concludes that not too much attention should be paid to these.

Conclusion

In a general reflection on the position of psychoanalysis in our culture, in 1954 Lacan argued that Freud provoked a revolution in man's relation to himself (Lacan, 1954–5, p. 13). With this idea he stressed that Freud established an original method for studying unconscious processes in neurotic symptoms and behaviours, and that he formulated an innovative theory, claiming that our actions are principally determined by unconscious dynamics. In Lacan's study of hallucinations in the 1950s he extrapolated Freud's method and ideas to the domain of psychosis. Lacan suggested that psychosis should be studied via detailed investigations of minute psychotic experiences, just as Freud argued that neurosis should be studied via meticulous examinations of specific symptoms. On the other hand he differed from Freud, stating that attention should not be directed towards modes of defence against drive impulses. Instead, language use should be studied and attention should be paid to the way in which existential questions and foreclosure are expressed in speech about psychotic experiences. For Lacan it didn't make sense to examine psychotic experiences in terms of their deviance from reality. What matters is how a fundamental difficulty in articulating one's position as a subject is expressed.

By following this path, Lacan's approach also deviates from the standard psychiatric paradigm. For him, hallucinations are not indicators of random noise in the mind. They are events that reflect a subjectively relevant incident that the person cannot manage. Whereas in the field of psychiatry hallucinations are usually studied with a focus on erroneous sensory perceptions, Lacan suggests studying the structure inherent to the hallucinatory experience. In pursuit of such detailed examination of psychotic experiences Lacan does not follow the path of phenomenological exploration, as advocated by Merleau-Ponty, but focuses on the materiality of the signifying chain and on the way in which the subject is affected by disrupted concatenation. In Lacan's view a hallucination is an unchained signifier: it is a signifier that appears from without and cannot be reconciled with other beliefs a person maintains about himself and the world. He thereby indicates that studying a person's speech about his/her hallucinatory experiences will reveal the specific existential questions that lay at their basis. Hallucinated signifiers allude to issues pertaining to identity that perplex and overwhelm the subject as they cannot be assumed by means of the Symbolic. They bear witness of a rupture in the signifying chain, and of suspension in the articulation of an enunciated subject. Moreover, in terms of the process of signification Lacan discerns two typical disruptions relative to common speech. On the one hand, sense-making can be suspended by the appearance of interruptions in the signifying chain (message phenomena). On the other hand the process of signification can be disrupted by the appearance of speech elements that do not fit within the set of signifiers a person usually uses to express himself (code phenomena). In both cases the concatenation of signifiers is suspended, which brings the articulation of the subject to a halt.

5
Delusions Scrutinized

Is a delusion a faulty thought or belief?

This chapter explores how Lacan characterizes delusions qua speech event. I will show how his method has a number of advantages over the content-based approaches, typical of most psychiatric studies of psychosis. Attention will be paid to metonymic disturbances situated at the basis of delusions, and their destabilizing effect at the level of subjectivity. I will examine Lacan's notion of how foreclosure can be repaired by adopting a delusional metaphor that compensates for the absent paternal metaphor. I will argue that rather than providing a cure for psychosis, the creation of a delusional metaphor enables the subject to obtain symbolic consistency. With the aid of a delusional metaphor, questions on the existence of the subject no longer provoke debilitating perplexity, but lead to the creation of an alternative identity. However, before discussing metonymic disturbances and the delusional metaphor I first outline the way delusions are typically approached in psychiatry.

In psychiatry delusions are traditionally regarded as a pathogenic symptom. They are seen as a signal of a psychotic condition to the extent of being almost synonymous with it. Since the nineteenth century delusions have been defined in terms of morbid beliefs or erroneous ideas that do not correspond to reality. Berrios (1996, p. 126) argues that various other characteristics, like 'conviction, unshakeability, bizarreness, cultural dislocation, and lack of insight', have since then been considered as additional criteria. However, these criteria are not enough for a diagnosis since they cannot be delineated clearly from related concepts, such as superstitions, obsessions or beliefs. Therefore, in defining and diagnosing delusions psychiatry relies mainly on *thought contents* (Berrios, 1996). For example, Munro (1999, p. 50) suggests that in delusional thinking 'thought form is relatively normal but the abnormal thought content predominates and is associated with profound illogicality'. A content-based perspective also pervades the Diagnostic and Statistical Manual of Mental Disorders (DSM-IV-TR; American Psychiatric Association, 2000), in which delusions are described as 'distortions in thought content' or 'erroneous beliefs that usually involve a misinterpretation of perceptions or experiences' (American Psychiatric Association, 2000, p. 299). In these descriptions, the term 'erroneous' refers to a radical divergence from what is seen as acceptable by most in a given socioeconomic and cultural context. A belief or thought is erroneous if it clearly deviates from commonly held beliefs and if 'the belief is held despite clear contradicting evidence regarding its veracity' (American Psychiatric Association, 2000, p. 299). Within this logic a person like Daniël Paul Schreber is deluded because he persistently believes in phenomena and events that, realistically speaking, are impossible, e.g. the idea that the end of the world actually took place, or that nerve contacts link him to divine powers (Schreber, 1903, pp. 20–1).

Deeply convinced that a number of fundamental problems are inherent in content-oriented approaches, Lacan argued that in studying delusions one should focus on the structural characteristics of discourse, and not its content, let alone an assumed underlying illness entity. Rather than examining delusions in terms of beliefs or thought contents, he argued for a materialist study of delusions in terms of how speech is organized.

Typical for a content-based approach to delusions is that it builds on comparing personally held convictions with what is commonly thought to be valid reality, i.e. to an accepted standard of what is supposedly *true* about the world. Such a comparison typically lies at the basis of a psychiatric evaluation of abnormality. However, evaluations of this kind are fundamentally flawed in a number of ways. First of all, thought content is strongly influenced by social and cultural factors and what is thought to be true changes from one context to another. It is therefore often very difficult to determine a priori what is or is not delusional; ideas that are acceptable in one (sub)cultural context might sound unusual in another, and vice versa (Butler and Braff, 1991). Moreover, thought content is strongly influenced by the spirit of the time. Convictions that were valid centuries ago are not seen as valid today, and vice versa. As a consequence, a content-based approach to delusions must always fall back on the diagnostician's ideas about the world and his ability to make decisions about the extent to which another person's ideas diverge from reality. The absence of objective indicators for such assessments means that the sanity of the assessor functions as the ultimate guarantee for gauging the insanity of the other. His understanding of reality, and of the other's divergence from what is realistically possible, make up the foundation of classic psychiatric evaluation (Lacan, 1959; Verhaeghe, 2004).

Lacan's fundamental problem with such an approach is not only that it relies too strongly on the diagnostician's world view, but that there is nothing orienting at all about the clinical activity of deliberate understanding (Lacan, 1955–6, pp. 6–7, 1959, pp. 448, 480). In criticizing the idea that clinicians should try to understand their patients, Lacan focuses on the work of German psychiatrist Karl Jaspers, which he discussed in his doctoral thesis. Central to Jaspers' approach is the suggestion that whereas most mental phenomena are rationally and empathically understandable for psychologists, delusions are not. Non-understandability and incorrigibility are his key criteria for qualifying ideas as delusional (Jaspers, 1959, pp. 408–11). According to Lacan these criteria are contestable, since they produce only an impression of similarity or dissimilarity to the ideas and beliefs that the diagnostician holds true: Jaspers' approach concludes at the observation of deviance and veils the enigma with which the deluding patient confronts us. In Lacan's view, deliberate understanding obfuscates the problem of psychosis, since it distracts attention from the logic reflected in a patient's ideation and from the structure that is articulated in what the patient says. He therefore argues for deliberate *non*-understanding (Lacan, 1959, p. 448), that is, *not* approaching the patient's narrative in terms of whether its content is plausible. In my interpretation, with his structural concepts, such as the chain of signifiers, foreclosure of the Name-of-the-Father and the notion of the subject, Lacan demonstrates that a delusion is primarily a *speech event*, which is why he studies delusions in terms of ruptures in the conventional use of speech.

Freud's work was pioneering in this respect. Rather than focusing on thought content he aimed at studying associated mental processes. In his work, delusions are not approached as markers of insanity, but as indicators of a fundamental disruption in mental life. In his analysis of Schreber's (1903) *Memoirs*, Freud argues that a delusion should not be mistaken for a 'pathological product' of psychosis (Freud, 1911, p. 71) or 'for the disease itself' (Freud, 1911, p. 77). He states that if a patient presents with a delusion, the psychoanalyst must above all explore the subjective conditions that gave rise to the delusion, as well as the internal logic or mechanism of the delusion (Freud, 1911, p. 18). Similar to Carl Gustav Jung, he qualified a delusion as a typically paranoid attempt at recovery and as 'a process of reconstruction' (Freud, 1911, p. 71). Indeed, Freud understands the function of delusions in terms of a process of mental reorganization: at the basis of a psychotic outbreak a dramatic mental decomposition can be found and a delusion is an adaptive reaction to this problem of disintegration. More specifically, Freud says that whereas libido becomes radically detached from objects during the first stage of a psychotic episode, this is repaired by a delusional system. Delusions defend the subject against radical breakdown, they function in the processing of unconscious mental representations and help restore a person's object relations. The central defence mechanism Freud (1911, p. 66) discerns is projection. He describes projection as the mechanism through which 'an internal perception is suppressed, and, instead, its content, after undergoing a certain kind of distortion, enters consciousness in the form of an external perception'. In other words, by means of a process of distortion and externalization, a delusion masters the mental representations and experiences that could not be processed otherwise.

Whereas in the 1930s and 1940s Lacan was enthusiastic about the idea of projection (see Chapter 1), this was no longer the case within his structural paradigm. Indeed, in the 1950s Lacan harshly criticized the concept of projection, and argued that psychoanalysts who recognize projection in a patient's delusions are actually forcing their own assumptions onto the case (Lacan, 1959, p. 448). In making this criticism he does not refer to his own earlier work, but to the theories of Anglo-Saxon authors such as Katan and Macalpine, who worked with this Freudian concept (Lacan, 1959, pp. 453–7). Likewise, in the 1950s Lacan argued for a careful interpretation of Freud's idea that delusions have a recovering or curing function. Whereas in his doctoral thesis he was enthusiastic about auto-therapeutic forces in paranoia, his position gradually became more modest. For example, during his third seminar Lacan asks the following question with respect to Schreber's delusion of progressing feminization (i.e. Schreber believed that he was in the process of becoming the wife of God): 'May we speak of a process of compensation, or even of cure, as some people would not hesitate to do, on the pretext that when his delusion stabilizes the subject presents a calmer state than at its appearance? Is he cured or not? It's a question worth raising, but I think it can only be wrong to speak of a cure here' (Lacan, 1955–6, p. 86). In asking this question, and in suggesting that the idea of cure is too specific an interpretation, Lacan argues against overvaluing the therapeutic role of delusions. His own position is that delusions do not inherently provide stability. Only to the extent that a delusion creates an anchor, based on which the process of signification is stabilized, can it be thought of as a stabilizing factor in mental life. In that case, an element of the delusion, called the delusional metaphor, functions as an alternative for the absent Name-of-the-Father, and provides a framework based on which the subject can again be signified. However, before addressing the idea of the delusional metaphor here, I will first discuss the problem underlying the delusional metaphor; a rupture at the level of metonymy.

From mental automatism to ruptures in the structure of metonymy

As already discussed in Chapter 3, foreclosure of the paternal metaphor implies that the metaphoric and metonymic processes that determine the subject are unstable. Metonymic processes are not punctuated by a central organizing metaphoric principle, as a result of which questions on the existence of the subject remain undetermined. Lacan suggests that this problem at the level of metaphor and metonymy can be clinically observed, not so much in the language a person uses, but in the way a speaker signifies his own being via speech. As a result of foreclosure, the subject's relation to speech bears witness of a number of 'structural transformations' (Lacan, 1955–6, p. 60, 1959, p. 479). These transformations should not be thought of as dramatic or obvious. Rather than stressing radical differences, Lacan says that in psychosis the speaker finds himself '*a little bit* at odds with, askew in relation to the signifier' (Lacan, 1955–6, p. 322, my italics). In this sense, neither strangeness nor eccentricity should be used as markers of psychosis; what is more decisive is the way in which signification takes place. In contrast to psychiatric theories on this matter, which can be found in the works of Bleuler (1911) and Kraepelin (1913, 1920), Lacan does not focus on changes in language or linguistic disorders. What is at stake in Lacan's theory is the question of how subjectivity is affected by the structure of the signifying chain. As I interpret Lacan's writing, he describes two distinct forms of disruption of the metonymic sequence in the chain of signifiers: either a dialectically inert or static gap can occur or so-called autonyms (invented words) are inserted that cannot be integrated into the chain. In both cases, the dynamic flow of speech comes to a halt, which has a profound effect on subjectivity.

In discussing these ruptures in the process of metonymy, Lacan refers to what de Clérambault called 'mental automatism' or 'passivity syndrome' (de Clérambault, 1942; see also Lacan, 1932, pp. 126–38;

Sauvagnat, 2000). By these terms de Clérambault referred to a fundamental disruption in thought processes made up of both positive and negative elementary phenomena.

The positive elementary phenomena mainly consist of the sudden appearance of unexpected parasitic ideas, nonsensical words or thought echoes that provoke an experience of contradiction and estrangement. These phenomena bear witness to a disturbed relation between the thinker and his thoughts. What becomes lost is ownership ('this thought is mine') and agency ('I thought this thought'). The negative elementary phenomena consist of experiences of sudden blockages or inhibitions and the abrupt disappearance of thoughts. These phenomena typically produce diffuse feelings of perplexity or estrangement.

de Clérambault (1942) gradually broadened these ideas to include phenomena outside the domain of cognition. To the concept of mental automatism he added 'affective problems', such as sudden outbreaks of anxiety and perplexing somatic and motor phenomena, including overwhelming fatigue or strange bodily experiences. Furthermore, in de Clérambault's line of reasoning, delusions are to be understood as a person's intellectual and affective reaction to elementary phenomena that disrupt mental life. Mental automatism makes up the primal psychotic event, and delusions are psychological reactions to it. Within this logic delusions are epiphenomena. In some cases they do come to the fore as a reaction to the mental state created by the passivity syndrome, yet this is not always the case. At other times mental automatism can be observed, while delusions remain absent.

According to Lacan (1966c), de Clérambault's discussion of mental automatism is most interesting as it is structural *avant la lettre*. What he appreciates is that de Clérambault stays close to the patient's subjective text and aims to grasp the underlying logic of the elementary phenomenon, which consists of a perplexing and sudden change in mental life. However, contrary to his teacher, he does not consider it as a mechanical phenomenon that is determined by brain disturbances: 'This is totally inadequate. It's much more promising to think of it in terms of the internal structure of language' (Lacan, 1955–6, p. 250). Lacan builds on de Clérambault's work, but only adopts ideas that he can integrate into a language-oriented approach.

Lacan further disagrees with de Clérambault in that he doesn't understand delusions in terms of a hypothetical psychological reaction to an elementary phenomenon: 'A delusion isn't deduced' he says (Lacan, 1955–6, p. 19). In his view, elementary phenomena and delusions merge into one another and are organized in the same way. Both turn around a speech element that is closed to all dialectical composition, that is, a component of discourse that is 'inaccessible, inert, and stagnant with respect to any dialectic' (Lacan, 1955–6, p. 22). In other words, in mental automatism and delusions a strange component that cannot be framed within the patient's mental life reveals itself in his discourse: a radical and baffling transformation manifests in language. This dialectic inertia is clearly distinct from the referential process that characterizes the signifier. In structural linguistics, a signifier is defined by its reference to other signifiers; signifiers derive their status through a process of metonymy (Lacan, 1957b). The dialectal inertia of speech elements in elementary phenomena and delusions, by contrast, bring continuous signifier to signifier connections to a halt, and rupture the process of metonymy.

In his work, de Clérambault (1942) makes a distinction between positive and negative elementary phenomena. Whereas Lacan does not explicitly pick up this distinction, I believe the distinction is relevant for our discussion. In terms of positive elementary phenomena, the rupture in metonymy can take the form of *dialectically inert signifying elements* that insist in discourse. For negative elementary phenomena, the rupture can take the form of a *dialectically inert break in discourse*. Both phenomena reflect a curious relation to the signifier. Lacan suggests that metonymic phenomena in psychosis point to a relation of exteriority: 'If the neurotic inhabits language, the psychotic is inhabited, possessed, by language' (Lacan, 1955–6, p. 250). Indeed, the metonymic processes I will discuss indicate how language can obtain a peculiar mode of autonomy, which disrupts the process of signification. Changes in the chain of signifiers occur suddenly and independent from the speaker's intentions. These perplex the speaker and undermine his experience of identity.

Furthermore, next to his idea on the structural similarity between elementary phenomena and delusions, Lacan marks a clear moment at which the pre-delusional state turns into a proper delusion. The turning point he stresses is the moment a person starts to attribute the cause of the changes he experiences in himself and the world to an external force (Trichet, 2011). Lacan makes this point while commenting on a paper from Katan (1950), where a young man's psychotic outbreak is discussed. It is not the bizarreness of a person's experience that is decisive of the transition into a delusion, but the moment a so-called 'inmixing of subjects' comes to the fore (Lacan, 1955–6, p. 193), that is, the moment self-other boundaries start fading away and an active exploitation by another body is experienced. 'The essential point', says of speech, signifier and signified are connected via button ties in discourse, a radical split between signifier and signified manifests itself in this experience of ineffability. The person intuitively feels that at the level of the signified important changes are taking place, which cannot be grasped via habitual ways of speaking and thinking. Indeed, the system of language itself often starts to be experienced as a puzzling body of signs that pervades the world. Lacan argues that this sense of bewilderment can be observed during clinical interviews. In conversations with individuals in a pre-delusional state, a clinician can have the feeling 'that the subject has come to the edge of a hole' (Lacan, 1955–6, p. 202). This experience is significant, and should be taken literally: in terms of the logic of signification the link between an intention to say something and language as a means to do so fades away, and as a result the metonymic concatenation of signifiers comes to an end. This interruption in metonymy is dialectically inert, in that once the breaking point has been reached, speech cannot be relaunched.

An illustration of such interruption in metonymy can be found in Schreber's autobiography, when he indicates that in some instances God withdraws and he loses 'the capacity to say one single word' (Schreber, 1903, p. 187). All that is left at such moments of 'thinking nothing' (Schreber, 1903, pp. 22, 55, 187, 204), when the voices he usually hears become silent, are feelings of confusion, pain and despair, and a number of so-called miraculous phenomena come to the fore. Schreber (1903, p. 188) documents these miraculous phenomena as follows:

'when I give myself up to thinking nothing, the following phenomena which are interrelated occur almost at once (at first sight):

(1) Noises around me, mostly consisting in violent outbursts among the lunatics who of course form the majority of those around me.
(2) In my own person the advent of the bellowing-miracle when my muscles serving the processes of respiration are set in motion by the lower God (Ariman) in such a way that I am forced to emit bellowing noises, unless I try very hard to suppress them; sometimes this bellowing recurs so frequently and so quickly that it becomes almost unbearable and at night makes it impossible to remain in bed.
(3) The winds arise, however not uninfluenced by the existing state of the weather; but short blasts of wind coinciding with pauses in my thinking are quite unmistakable.
(4) The cries of 'help' of those of God's nerves separated from the total mass, sound the more woeful the farther away God has withdrawn

from me, and the greater therefore the distance which those nerves have to travel, obviously in a state of some anxiety'.

In 1956 Lacan (1955–6, p. 140) calls these phenomena 'connotations of a linguistic order', that is, experiences in which non-signifying aspects of speech come to the fore. More specifically, he says that the bellowing miracle opens up 'an absolutely a-signifying vocal function' of speech, and that the other phenomena are outbreaks of meaning in which nonsensical signifieds come to the fore. Lacan (1959, p. 468) argues that in these experiences a kind of 'halo effect' of the signifier can be found. What happens is that the signifier has 'fallen silent in the subject' (Lacan, 1959, p. 468), and this produces a number of echoes at the level of signification: the expression of signifiers stops, but resonances of signifying articulation can still be observed: vocalization perseveres through bellowing, and at the level of the message the production of meaning comes to a halt. Indeed, Schreber's miraculous experiences still present him with elementary fragments of meaning, yet these are nothing but remainder phenomena, which illustrate that the metonymy of the signifier actually came to a halt. Later, with his theory of the object *a* (see Chapter 6), the above phenomena can be interpreted as indicators of the non-extraction of the object *a* (see: Lacan, 1959, p. 487, footnote 14; Miller, 1979).

With respect to ruptures in metonymy, Lacan suggests that the associated experience of confusion never appears unexpectedly. Sudden confrontations with a gap in the chain of signifiers should be understood in the light of foreclosure. Signifiers typically fade away when an appeal is made to the subject 'from where there is no signifier' (Lacan, 1955–6, p. 202), or when an interpellation is made of 'an essential signifier that is unable to be received' (Lacan, 1955–6, p. 306); that is, when a signifier the subject cannot integrate is brought to the fore. Indeed, due to the absence of *Bejahung*, a number of questions concerning the existence of the subject simply cannot be addressed. Within this logic, the (pre-)delusional experience of stupefaction is a direct manifestation of foreclosure: there is no signifier at a person's disposal to cope with an issue in life, and thus nothing can be constructed around it. All that remains is a deep wordlessness in the speaker.

Such interruption in metonymy does not leave the subject unaffected. On the contrary, the logical consequence of a confrontation with foreclosure at the level of the signifier is a radical experience of deficiency at the level of the signified and a radical suspension in the experience of subjectivity. The enunciating subject is erased and, due to the absence of signifying articulation, the subject cannot be enunciated via button ties in the chain of signifiers. What ruptured metonymy produces is the experience that identity fades away. For example, Schreber (1903, p. 187) states that when God withdraws and the voices can no longer be heard, his own thinking stops and 'a feeling as if I were moving among walking corpses' is produced. This experience indicates that the moment signifying articulation comes to a halt Schreber's environment suddenly loses meaning. Suddenly people no longer seem to be people, and personally he feels that he is in a state of 'complete stupidity' or 'dementia' (Schreber, 1903, pp. 187, 220). This suggests that the experience of consistency, which accompanies metonymic articulation, has actually fallen away. Radical estrangement from himself and his surroundings is all that is left.

In On a Question Prior to the Treatment of Psychosis, Lacan situates such an experience of subjective disappearance and estrangement at the beginning of Schreber's second illness episode, suggesting that before the delusional metaphor was constructed 'the subject had died' (Lacan, 1959, p. 473). At that time Schreber was hospitalized in the clinic of Dr. Flechsig. He was convinced that his doctor was plotting against him and that a so-called 'soul-murder' had been attempted on him (Schreber, 1903, p. 34). On the one hand he relates this attempted soul-murder to historical connections between his own family and Flechsig's, but above all, soul-murder refers to the conspiracy Flechsig and God held against him. The clue of this conspiracy is that once his mental illness is recognized, and his reason is destroyed, Schreber will be unmanned: his body will be transformed into a female, he will be sexually abused and, in the end, he will be 'simply 'forsaken', in other words left to rot' (Schreber, 1903, p. 63). This plan shocks Schreber. It is an offence that radically goes against what he calls 'the Order of the World' (Schreber, 1903, p. 124). Whereas before the idea of a conspiracy took shape, Schreber could still experience regularity with respect to his own position in the world, now the experience of order abruptly falls apart. Suddenly his usual perspective of the world no longer seems valid. At the level of the signified this non-articulation of the subject of the signifier also leads to fragmented experiences of identity, which are quite common in psychosis. For example, Schreber indicates that for a while he was living in a vague zone between life and death: 'I lived for years in doubt as to whether I was really still on earth or whether on some other celestial body' (Schreber, 1903, p. 81); he had the impression that he was wandering around like the living dead; and he believed that he was afflicted by the plague and that his body was actually disintegrating.

Given Schreber's conviction of being 'forsaken' and his experience of decay, Lacan argues that the notion of soul-murder refers to a disturbance 'at the inmost juncture of the subject's sense of life' (Lacan, 1959, p. 466). It indicates how parallel to the rupture in metonymy, vitality fades: an element that has to do with desire and with the experience of oneself as a living human being disappears. This cannot but be lived through as a personal drama. Conceptually speaking, such a disturbance is a consequence of the deficient paternal metaphor. It indicates how the hole at the level of the Other gives rise to what Lacan (1959, pp. 466, 481) calls a corresponding hole at the level of the signified.

In discussing Schreber's confrontation with this point of foreclosure, Lacan notes that it activates the dynamics of what he later calls *hainamoration* (see Chapter 1). In the Symbolic register no clear position can be occupied by the subject, who in turn begins to function within an Imaginary register. Schreber undergoes a 'topographical regression' to the mirror stage (Lacan, 1959, p. 473): two instances become opposed to one another and the notion of a struggle for life and death predominates. In the light of the first era in Lacan's work on psychosis, this idea of a predominating lethal imaginary relationship is not new. However, by introducing the concept of *topographical* regression, which is clearly distinct from the idea of a developmental regression or arrest, Lacan adds a new element to this line of reasoning. What matters in the event of topographical regression is that a certain mode of relating to the other comes to the fore, caused by a failure at the level of the signifier.

Interestingly Schreber describes a number of ways he deals with the ruptures in metonymy that are expressed in God's withdrawal and in his experiences of thinking nothing. Lacan does not discuss this, but they are worth noting since they consist of actively using scansion at moments of rupture in metonymy. The examples Schreber gives include 'counting aloud', which he notes is very boring for any length of time; 'reciting poems' and 'swearing aloud' (Schreber, 1903, pp. 204, 301). Schreber (1903, p. 203) indicates that these are modes of 'defence' against the tests that supernatural powers force upon him. The result of such scansion is that metonymy is restored, albeit in a minimal way. Schreber's coping techniques fill the unbearable silence. They sooth the experience of being torn apart, create a feeling of mental consistency and provide a link with conventional activities. Nevertheless, they do not signify his subjectivity.

Autonyms or the insistence of dialectically inert speech elements

Parallel to what de Clérambault called positive elementary phenomena, metonymy can be ruptured by the appearance of insisting speech elements that are also dialectically inert. In such cases 'certain words take on a special emphasis, a density that sometimes manifests itself in the very form of the signifier, giving it this frankly neologistic character that is so striking in the creations of paranoia' (Lacan, 1955–6, p. 32). Whereas in classic psychiatry a neologism refers to the creation of novel words that don't exist in common language, Lacan argues that it is more specifically people's *use* of language that should be taken into account. In On a Question Prior to Any Treatment of Psychosis he emphasizes that, in the neologistic character of certain words, what matters is not so much the question as to whether they are lexically new, but the fact that they are 'autonymous' or self-referential (Lacan, 1959, p. 450). Lacan characterizes them as 'lead in the net' (Lacan, 1955–6, p. 33), as immobile 'erotized' elements in the network of the subject's discourse (Lacan, 1955–6, pp. 54–5). In other words, neologisms are a peculiar type of signifier, which present themselves as isolated elements that do not enter the referential process with other signifiers. Lacan concludes that they are the hallmark of delusions (Lacan, 1955–6, pp. 33–4). However, following the structural linguistic definition of the signifier, one wonders whether these autonyms are really signifiers. Given their exclusion from contextual reference, the logical conclusion is that they are not. This is precisely what comes to the fore in his eleventh seminar, where Lacan indicates that psychotic speech is marked by so-called 'holophrased' speech elements. This means that in psychotic discourse some phrases or signifiers are excluded from dialectical reference and therefore seem to condense complete phrases (Lacan, 1964, p. 237).

Of the various descriptions Lacan gives of dialectically inert phrases and signifiers in psychotic discourse, their characterization as autonyms or as autonymous speech elements seems most adequate. The term neologism carries the ambiguity of suggesting that it always concerns the creation of a new word; and the term holophrase wrongly suggests that more speech is hidden behind the dialectically inert element. Crucial to psychosis is precisely the inability to contextualize or elucidate certain experiences. Whereas a signifier is defined in its reference to another signifier, formally noted as S → S', an autonym is defined by its exclusion from this reference process. The self-referential nature of autonyms and their exclusion from the signifying chain can be presented as follows (Figure 5.1):

Figure 5.1 Autonym

The idea of exclusion is interesting as it grasps the idea that, as an element that suddenly appears, the psychotic autonym always initially evokes surprise in the person who utters it. Autonyms do not refer to existing signifiers and ideas, but open up a new, perplexing field of signification that might initially provoke anxiety. Lacan (1955–6, p. 38) says that the psychotic can 'bear witness' to such speech elements, but always in terms of an imposed and invading reality. An autonym is not the result of a creative move by a speaker in language, but a word or sentence that was revealed (Lacan, 1955–6, p. 85).

An example of such autonym is the phrase 'nerve-contact' from Schreber's *Memoirs* (1903, p. 23). As such this word is not that strange; it refers to the neurological idea of how a nerve is tied to another nerve or to a muscle. Yet in Schreber's book 'nerve-contact' refers to a reality that was miraculously brought to light, and concerns the way in which God relates to humans. Schreber argues that whereas humans are made up of a body with nerves, which contain the soul, God is made up of only an infinite bundle of nerves. The idea of 'nerve-contact' means that God communicates 'fertilizing thoughts and ideas about the beyond' to human beings (Schreber, 1903, pp. 23–4), and such communication takes place through 'divine rays'. These rays materialize the divine nerve, and following a parabolic trajectory they enter Schreber's cranium through the occiput (Lacan, 1959, p. 468; Schreber, 1903, pp. 275–6). In this fantastic description Schreber doesn't disclose any insight or belief. What he communicates is not a conclusion that was reached after an elaborate thought process, and no act of faith can be found at its basis. Conversely, Schreber's explanation of the phrase 'nerve-contact' provides us with a description of a reality that, to his own complete surprise, was revealed to him: 'I have come infinitely closer to the truth than human beings who have not received divine revelation' (Schreber, 1903, p. 16). The fact that he explicitly frames it as an element that did not arise from his own beliefs or reflections, but something that was imposed upon him, indicates that we can qualify it as an autonymous speech element.

At the level of speech pragmatics the appearance of autonyms is clearly discernible in Schreber's book, which was explicitly written as a testimony. However, their appearance can be rather subtle. Lacan

suggests that in early phases of delusional development in particular, people can be very reluctant to reveal autonyms (see Lacan,
1955–6, p. 256, 1959, p. 448), presumably due to the perplexity they
evoke.

Listeners usually experience psychotic autonyms as enigmatic, allusive or ironical. Their appearance disturbs the process of anticipation
in the generation of meaning, and evokes confusion. In attending to
someone else, a listener typically expects continuation at the level of the
signified. Autonyms interrupt this continuation, and even cast doubt on
the notion that sense can be made of the other's speech at all. In this
respect, autonyms differ from metaphors. As indicated in Chapter 3, a
metaphor is an unexpected signifier that induces sense in a given speech
context. Its effect is poetic insofar as it opens up a new dimension in
the signified of a speech act: 'There is poetry whenever writing introduces us to a world other than our own and also makes it our own,
making present a being, a certain fundamental relationship' (Lacan,
1955–6, p. 78). An autonym by contrast doesn't add a subtle meaning
to discourse, but destabilizes it. A similarity with metaphor is that it is
also unexpected, yet, contrary to a metaphor it doesn't induce sense.
Autonyms rather have a ridiculing effect on the meaning a listener was
anticipating. They damage the imaginary expectation that a signified
will be shared, and therefore violate the code of exchange in the social
bond. Indeed, an encounter with autonyms leaves the listener with an
impression of non-communality. In the field of phenomenological psychiatry, Lacan's contemporary Hendicus Rümke (1960) described this
kind of impression with the concepts 'schizophrenia experience' and
'praecox experience' (Verhaeghe, 2004). Pivotal to such experience is a
feeling of estrangement caused by the patient's peculiar use of certain
words or phrases.

Interestingly, however, as a delusion is elaborated, a change in the
condition of autonymous speech elements can be observed. Whereas at
first they are experienced as 'intimate exteriorities', as communications
from without that touch upon the intimacy of a person's being, their
status changes to that of what I call 'exterior intimacies', in that they
gradually start to be the intimate poles around which discourse is organized. Indeed, typical for the initial manifestation of autonyms is that
they are startling phrases that cannot be situated in a person's usual
experience of the world. Schreber's *Memoirs* illustrate this well. He indicates that the divine powers revealed a variety of peculiar expressions
to him such as 'soul-murder' or 'nerve-contact', which were previously
completely foreign. Schreber writes that these phrases concerned him

Lacan, 'is that the delusion began the moment the initiative came from the Other' (Lacan, 1955–6, p. 193). Indeed, the turning point he situates between pre-delusional experiences of estrangement and the development of proper delusions is the moment an external intelligence is held responsible for actively manipulating one's thoughts and actions. The delusion ensues when a person experiences himself as a puppet that, beyond all personal control, is played by a puppeteer.

In terms of Schreber's case this means that his delusion starts at the moment of his second hospitalization in the clinic of Dr. Flechsig, when he concludes that this doctor is manipulating him. In an open letter to Dr. Flechsig, Schreber (1903, p. 8) writes that the first impetus of his nervous illness consisted of: 'influences on my nervous system emanating from your nervous system'. Schreber believed that his doctor was involved in a conspiracy with supernatural powers, and that a plot was devised against him. He quite specifically dated this experience 'March or April 1894' (Schreber, 1903, p. 63). As time progressed Flechsig gradually dropped out of the picture, and God was held responsible for the strange things that were happening to him: '*He Himself* must have determined the whole policy pursued against me' (Schreber, 1903, p. 235). What changes through time is the leading figure to which the initiative is attributed, but what remains constant is that an external intelligence is held responsible for the changes he lived through. In this context it should be further noted that Schreber's God is quite a specific figure. Schreber (1903, p. 61) notes that God is actually composed of two personages: a 'lower God', named Ariman, and an 'upper God', named Ormuzd. The two of them play different roles but both inflict all kinds of changes from without. For example, Ariman produces 'the miracle of unmanning', while Ormuzd has 'the power of restoring manliness' (Schreber, 1903, p. 61).

A dialectically inert hole in the network of signifiers

The first way in which a rupture in metonymy can come to the fore is a radical break in discourse: suddenly, the individual has the experience of having no words or speech at his disposal to explain what is happening to him/her. Something 'ineffable' that is 'beyond words' stupefies the person, and leaves him/her with an overwhelming feeling of perplexity. Lacan (1955–6, p. 194) underscores this observation from de Clérambault and other classic psychiatrists, and argues that such experience is common in psychosis: 'At the heart of psychoses there is a dead end, perplexity concerning the signifier'. Whereas in regular uses concerning the existence of the subject cannot be addressed. Autonyms have a reconstituting function in relation to these questions, and cover up the gap exposed by questions on the existence of the subject. Within this logic an autonym is an 'automatic' answer to an appeal concerning the themes of sexual identity, contingency of being and close relationships, which the person fails to address. It is an answer that is not generated by an enunciating subject, but is nevertheless revealed in the chain of signifiers. By their appearance in the signifying chain autonyms again start articulating subjectivity. In this respect, Lacan (1955–6, p. 307) says that when a person is unable to respond to questions on the existence of the subject, 'The only way to react that can reattach him to the humanization he is tending to lose is to make himself permanently present in this slender commentary on the stream of life that constitutes the text of mental automatism'. Autonymous speech elements of mental automatism provide a basis from which the enunciated subject can again be formulated.

Schreber, the man of metaphor

The central idea Lacan puts forward in his discussion of Schreber is that, in the process of elaborating a delusion, he created a delusional metaphor that compensated for the absence of the Name-of-the-Father. As I will explain, this alternative metaphor reinstated a place for the subject, and restored order in a world of chaos. First I highlight Lacan's ideas on the outbreak of psychosis in the case of Schreber; next I examine how the delusional metaphor compensates for the lack of an anchor in the Symbolic.

In discussing the structure of Schreber's psychotic experiences, Lacan suggests that confrontations with issues pertaining to fatherhood were problematic. It was not so much that he experienced a number of disappointments, as indicated in his reflection that he and his wife failed to have children of their own (Schreber, 1903, p. 46). Nor was it the success of being promoted to presidency of the High Court in Dresden, which overwhelmed him with stress (Schreber, 1903, p. 46), granting him a fatherly position in society (Lacan, 1959, p. 484). What is important is that through such events he was confronted with the absence of an anchor in the Symbolic. Lacan (1959, p. 484) argues that Schreber missed 'the signifier of paternity'. This made him vulnerable to events in which paternity was at stake and the foreclosed signifier was summoned. Such events were Real and provoked his disappearance as a subject, rather than giving rise to signifying articulation.

In terms of his formula on the metaphor of the Name-of-the-Father, Lacan argues that the Symbolic function of the Father was zeroed-out[1] and, as a result, desire with respect to paternity could not be signified. He was simply unable to establish an identity in relation to questions of fatherhood. Paternity was like a black hole in the universe of the Symbolic. As long as this black hole could be avoided, order was present in the Symbolic. However, as soon as it was touched upon, order and imaginary consistency disappeared. Conceptually speaking, Lacan concludes that parallel to foreclosure the phallic function was missing[2]: with the lack of a signifier concerning paternity, Schreber could not establish a coherent sense of himself as a desiring subject in relation to concrete events in life where paternity was addressed. On the contrary, such events were not mediated through the Symbolic, triggering a psychotic experience.

In my interpretation the result of such an encounter with the black hole of foreclosure is that *the Other goes mad*: suddenly the Symbolic loses its internal organization, which obliterates the structure in language. Indeed, a fundamental idea in Lacan's structural theory of psychosis is that *the Symbolic is dis-ordered,* in that the primordial problem is not a disturbance at the level of the subject, but disorder at the level of the Other. This is reflected in Lacan's idea that foreclosure concerns an element at the level of the Other and in his discussion of how a delusion is organized. Within the context of a delusion the subject's capacity to cope with a disregulated Other is seriously put to the test. In this discussion Lacan suggests the possibility of the subject's capacity to restore some order to the deranged Other. The Other of the symbolic order may have gone awry, but a solution to deal with this madness can still be invented.

With respect to the case of Schreber, Lacan (1959, p. 468) outlines three instances that bear witness of dis-order in the Symbolic: when language starts to speak alone via hallucinations; through the appearance of autonymous speech elements, strange creatures begin to populate his world and, in a most peculiar way, God starts to intervene in Schreber's life[3].

Of these elements, Schreber's delusional relationship with God should be further discussed, not least because Schreber's God is quite a remarkable character. Whereas in the Judeo-Christian tradition God is a symbolic father figure, through which people have trust in human fate and make sense of life, Schreber's God is notable for incarnating the opposite position. Schreber is shocked by the way God entered his life and believes that his experiences with the divine were so touching that they might add a new perspective on religious matters (Schreber, 1903, pp. 7, 16–18). What is striking about his religious ideas is that he holds on to a number of novel conceptions of the divine, e.g. the idea that God is actually made up of a 'lower God (Ariman)' and an 'upper God (Ormuzd)', or the idea that heaven is divided in 'forecourts', 'posterior realms' and 'anterior realms' (Schreber, 1903, p. 30). Yet his religious views illustrate that, above all, the divine cannot be trusted. His God is a largely unpredictable, often shocking, and sometimes ridiculous figure. Hence Lacan's suggestion that his actions bear witness to foreclosure: divine principles that give Schreber some sense of the world are simply absent from his *Memoirs*. In this respect his chronicle strongly differs from reports by mystics. None of his encounters with God gave rise to the kind of experiences that religious mystics like St. John of the Cross bore witness to, such as joy, unity or peacefulness (Lacan, 1955–6, p. 77, 1959, p. 479). His God is not a 'Thou' that can be treated with awe, but a brutal force that interferes with Schreber's life in a most exasperating manner. Lacan (1959, p. 479) therefore concludes that Schreber's relationship with God can be characterized as a relation of 'mixture rather than as a union of being with being'. Indeed, Schreber's God is the villain conductor of a perfidious policy, with whom compromises must be made, and not the safe haven that religiously minded people typically long for.

However, Lacan (1959, p. 481) suggests that Schreber efficiently countered the dis-order of the Symbolic, and thanks to the creation of a delusional metaphor he managed to stabilize the relation between signifier and signified. This metaphor replaces the absent paternal metaphor and provides an anchor in discourse, based on which the subject's identity ('who am I?') and the desire of the (m)Other ('what do you want from me?') can be signified. Central to this delusional metaphor is a signifier at the level of the foreclosed Name-of-the-Father, which replaces another signifier at the level of the desire of the (m)other. As a result of this substitution, the Other is subject to a general organizing principle.

Lacan (1959, p. 481) introduced the concept of the delusional metaphor at the end of On a Question Prior to the Treatment of Psychosis, as he made the following conclusion on the organization of Schreber's delusion: 'It is the lack of the Name-of-the-Father in that place which, by the hole that it opens up in the signified, sets off a cascade of reworkings of the signifier from which the growing disaster of the imaginary proceeds, until the level is reached at which signifier and signified stabilize in a delusional metaphor'. How the process of metaphorization would exactly take place is not discussed in this essay, and he did not elaborate the construct in his later work. However, based on the discussion that precedes the introduction of the concept, I suggest presenting the working of the delusional metaphor as follows.

The centrally organizing signifier of Schreber's delusional metaphor is *entmannen/Entmannung* ('to unman/unmanning' or 'to emasculate/ emasculation')[4] Starting from this signifier, which can be called a *delusional signifier*, he assesses God's enigmatic comings and goings, and the supernatural manipulations to which he is subjected. Whereas the starting point of a delusion consists of the vague sensation and elementary observation that one is seized by an external force, the delusional metaphor provides another signifier that places this first signifier in chain. Usually this chain eventually takes the shape of an explanatory theory in which the mad Other's intentions are explained. Indeed, via the idea of emasculation, Schreber makes up his mind about the conspiracy in which Flechsig and God are involved, which makes their actions somewhat comprehensible. Lacan suggests that the ideas to which this signifier gives rise stop the gap in the Imaginary that foreclosure created: 'For in the field of the imaginary, a gap had recently opened up for him in response to the absence of the symbolic metaphor, a gap that could only find a way to be eliminated in the carrying out of *Entmannung* (emasculation)' (Lacan, 1959, p. 470).

Quite early in his *Memoirs*, Schreber defined emasculation as an indisputable plan that describes the course of events in the universe. He qualifies it as 'the tendency innate in the Order of the World, according to which a human being ("a seer of spirits") must under certain circumstances be "unmanned" (transformed into a woman) once he has entered into indissoluble contact with divine nerves' (Schreber, 1903, p. 53). Throughout the book Schreber hangs onto this principle, and regularly adds new details. He describes it as an irrefutable principle that will once take place in full glory.[5] It is the *axiom* starting from which he reads the laws of the world, hence the idea that it replaces the foreclosed signifier of the Name-of-the-Father.

As indicated above, the principle of unmanning enables Schreber to develop a theory about the way in which Fleschig and God entered into 'nerve-contact' with him. He qualifies their plot to commit a 'soul-murder' on him as a mockery of the principle of unmanning: Schreber will be subjected to 'sexual misuse', his body will be 'prostituted like that of a female harlot', and in the end he will be 'left to rot' (Schreber, 1903, pp. 63, 96). By engaging in such intrigue God and Flechsig are 'misconstruing the above-described fundamental tendency of the Order of the

World' (Schreber, 1903, p. 63). As a consequence the idea of unmanning first filled Schreber with disgust: here God goes against the 'Order of the World'. Schreber indicates that in this respect he feels subjected to God's 'voluptuousness': female 'nerves of voluptuousness' are implanted in his body in great masses, and the danger of being sexually abused is lurking everywhere (Schreber, 1903, p. 124). In order to cope with such shameless sensuality, Schreber defends himself against 'every feminine impulse' he experiences and against all situations in which abuse might come to the fore (Schreber, 1903, p. 125).

Characteristic of this first step in the delusional metaphor is that two signifiers are placed in dialectical opposition: Schreber's 'axiom of emasculation' is opposed to God's 'voluptuous plot'. Formulated conceptually, I conclude that in this dialectical relationship the *delusional signifier* is opposed to what I suggest calling the *signifier of the Other's madness*. In this context it could be further argued that the signifier of the Other's madness only takes shape by being opposed to a delusional signifier. Prior to this opposition there is simply is no *signifier* for the Other's madness. Before the transition towards the signifier is made, this madness is only a Real intuition, which is nameless and perplexing.

At the level of the subject this transition has an important effect: through the dialectical relationship in which the instigator's intentions are balanced against the axiom of emasculation Schreber assures a place for himself. The axiom safeguards him against the conspiracy, and provides him with a position where he can condemn what is happening: 'From this apparently so unequal battle between one weak human being and God Himself, I emerge, albeit not without bitter sufferings and derivations, victorious, because the Order of the World is on my side' (Schreber, 1903, p. 67). The principle of emasculation enables him to consider the world from the perspective of a law, which is exactly parallel to what the Name-of-the-Father effectuates in the paternal metaphor.

The next step in the process of metaphorization consists of a dialectical *Aufhebung*, in which the delusional signifier starts to re-signify God's plot. Schreber thereby indicates that God's lecherous idea of unmanning is not necessarily a problem, and that 'a solution of the conflict in consonance with the Order of the World' is possible (Schreber, 1903, p. 121). The solution he has in mind implies that God's voluptuous plan can be subjected to the axiom of emasculation. Schreber's name for this solution is '*Versöhnung*', a term Lacan (1959, p. 472) indicates refers to 'reconciliation', i.e. a way out of the clash between opposing tendencies, as well as 'sacrifice', i.e. giving up something. The idea of *Versöhnung* that

Schreber has in mind is that in further pursuing the axiom of emasculation, he will in fact become God's wife, and through the intercourse that takes place between him and God he will lay at the basis of a new humanity that will repopulate the universe. In terms of the process of metaphorization, *Versöhnung* is the new signified to which the dialectical *Aufhebung* between the delusional signifier and the signifier the Other's madness gives rise.

Essential to this *Versöhnung* is that it first of all bears witness of a submission of God's voluptuous plot to an even broader plan. The metaphor re-signifies God's sexual intentions, which no longer have a purely voluptuous aim; they do not aim to simply abuse Schreber but to impregnate him 'for the purpose of creating new human beings' (Schreber, 1903, p. 164). In this case, the first outcome of the delusional metaphor is that it offers *a treatment of the mad Other* with which Schreber was confronted. Via the *Versöhnung* his God is submitted to a law. From then on God can no longer escape the axiom of emasculation.

The second result of the delusional metaphor is that it re-signifies the subject. The change Schreber makes can be characterized as a transition from the position of 'the whore' to the position of 'the Madonna'.[6] The position of 'the whore' was occupied as long as God pursued his voluptuous plot. Schreber (1903, p. 96) indicates that God only sees him as a 'harlot', and that the plot revolves around sexual exploitation. With the execution of *Versöhnung* this changes. Schreber decides to sacrifice his masculinity and concludes that it is his destiny to become God's wife, which brings about peace of mind. Given the fact that in an earlier comment on the Immaculate Conception of the Virgin Mary, Schreber (1903, p. 17) stated that 'God, as a Being endowed with human sexual organs, had intercourse with the woman from whose womb Jesus Christ came forth', his new position can be qualified as that of the Madonna. Lacan (1959, p. 471) suggests that by occupying this new position, Schreber identifies with a phallic position towards God. Henceforward he *is* the link between the Lord and the Order of the World that was missing until then.

Parallel to assuming this position of the Madonna, Schreber begins to cultivate the image of himself as a woman. Whereas before the *Versöhnung* Schreber was confused about signs of feminization that seemed to mark his body, the delusional metaphor results in a full assumption of it: 'Since then I have wholeheartedly inscribed the cultivation of femininity on my banner, and I will continue to do so as far as consideration of my environment allows, whatever other people who are ignorant of the supernatural reasons may think of me' (Schreber,

1903, p. 164). In Lacan's (1959, p. 474) interpretation this cultivation of femininity is important; it restored Schreber's experience of subjective consistency at the level of the Imaginary.

Schematically the operation effectuated by Schreber's delusional metaphor can be presented as follows (Figure 5.2):

$$\frac{\text{Axiom of emasculation}}{\text{God's voluptuous plot}} \cdot \frac{\text{God's voluptuous plot}}{\text{Signified to the Schreber}} \longrightarrow \frac{\text{Axiom of}}{\text{emasculation}} \left(\frac{O}{\text{Versöhnung}}\right)$$

Figure 5.2 Schreber's delusional metaphor

This schema indicates that the axiom of emasculation replaces the signifier of God's voluptuous plot. As a result of this transition the idea of *Versöhnung* came to the fore. On the one hand *Versöhnung* provides a signified to Schreber: he will become God's wife. On the other hand *Versöhnung* is the denominator in the light of which all actions of the Other are henceforward considered.

Schreber the resilient

In his discussion of Schreber's way of coping with the outbreak of psychotic episodes, Lacan (1959, p. 469) mentions two more factors that, next to the creation of a delusional metaphor, made up Schreber's resilience: he sought to document his private experiences and conclusions through his *Memoirs*, and he continued to find a position qua partner in his relationship with his wife. Both of these factors imply that he remains somewhat embedded in a social bond, which provides structure based on which the subject can be articulated.

The first additional factor making up Schreber's resilience is the fact that he did 'not hesitate...to use the word' (Lacan, 1959, p. 469), and that he addressed himself to an audience in order to disclose what he lived through. While Schreber didn't start writing his *Memoirs* with the idea of publishing them, he gradually came to believe that what had happened to him had a broader societal value, and deserved publication: 'I believe that expert examination of my body and observation of my personal fate during my lifetime would be of value both for science and the knowledge of religious truths' (Schreber, 1903, p. 3). In terms of Lacan's ideas on interpersonal recognition, which is discussed in Chapter 3, this kind of dedication is not trivial. What Schreber intentionally communicates is that his autobiography is dedicated to humanity and that we are his audience. The message sent back to him in an inverted form is that his personal experiences matter since they can be expressed in the literary genre of a memoir, and that qua identity, he is the author. Indeed, not only by writing a book, but by also publishing it, Schreber inscribes himself in a cultural mode of personal expression, in which a socially valued subjective position towards others is occupied.

The second factor Lacan connects to Schreber's resilience is that he maintained his relationship with his wife. Schreber (1903, p. 165) indicates that while it must have been impossible for his wife to understand his 'trends of thought fully', their relationship stood the test of his psychotic episodes: his wife continued to show devoted love for him (Schreber, 1903, p. 119), and he retained his 'former love in full' (Schreber, 1903, p. 165). In discussing this conjugal relationship Lacan (1959, p. 478) stresses the stabilizing role of friendship. Schreber doesn't present his wife as a figure who in some way or another challenged his identity as a subject, but as a partner who faithfully stood by his side. By holding on to this relationship Schreber maintained an ordinary common sense-like connection with reality, in which a non-delusional way of relating to the other stands to the fore. What is disrupted in Schreber's relation to the world is his relation to the Other, where a number of 'anomalies' come to the fore (Lacan, 1959, p. 478). Yet this kind of disruption can coexist quite well with an ordinary way of relating to semblables. Lacan stresses that by clinging to this relationship the imaginary consistency of Schreber's ego was maintained.[7] No matter what transformations Schreber lived through, continuity at the level of his identity as a husband enabled him to stand his ground.

Conclusion

With Lacan's concept of foreclosure a new perspective on delusions can be articulated that breaks from Freud's theory as well as the psychiatric focus on pathological processes. Whereas from a medical perspective delusions are typically seen as indications of psychosis and barriers to recovery that should be eliminated, Lacan argues that delusions make sense at the level of the individual. They are speech events with an internal logic that can change across time, whereby the person qua subject is at stake. This variability can be characterized with the concepts of metonymy and metaphor, where three steps can be discerned. Firstly, when metonymy is ruptured in response to a confrontation with a radical hole in the network of signifiers the subject loses its material basis. The continuity of the signifying chain fades away and the subject is threatened by the possibility of disappearance. Secondly, autonyms give scansion to this hole and thus can be thought of as elementary self-regulating responses. They are initially experienced as 'intimate exteriorities' or communications from without that touch upon the intimacy of a person's being. Gradually, however, their status changes to that of 'exterior intimacies', in that they start to be the intimate poles around which discourse is organized. In terms of their impact on the subject, autonyms cannot be qualified as beliefs or erroneous thoughts, a basis from which an enunciated subject can once again be formulated. In a third step, delusions can give rise to a process of metaphorization, in which the mad Other that confronts the subject is subdued by a law, and thus a new means of articulating the subject with respect to identity can come to the fore. Lacan suggests that the construction of a delusional metaphor stabilizes the relation between signifier and signified, and that it compensates for the absence of an anchor via the metaphor of the Name-of-the-Father.

Compared with Freud's approach, Lacan's discussion of delusions is striking due to the various theoretical coordinates he presents. Projection is not seen as a useful starting point and is replaced by the idea that a delusion can be qualified as a way of articulating the subject with respect to questions of existence when a support in the Symbolic is lacking. In its elementary form, a delusion reflects the conclusion that one's thoughts and actions are actively manipulated by an external force. This attribution does not safeguard the subject against disintegration, which is why a delusion is not considered to be stabilizing. Stability can be obtained by creating a delusional metaphor and by embedding the subject in a social bond. A delusional metaphor stabilizes the delusion from within. Through a central signifier it names the motives of the mad Other, which produces order in the Symbolic, and designates an identity for the subject. Moreover, by embedding the subject in a social bond a delusion can be stabilized from without. Inherently a delusion is a private undertaking. Lacan stresses that if the delusional metaphor itself can be introduced in cultural contexts, or if bonds of friendships can be maintained next to the delusion, a structure for articulating the subject is provided.

However, this does not imply that the construction of a delusion is always stabilizing, and that therapeutically we should aim to cultivate the elaboration of a delusional metaphor. Many delusional patients never come to the point of discerning an encompassing law for interpreting the behaviour of the figures in the delusion or their own position in the world. Exploring their delusion tends to reinforce the experience of a mad Other, which is why later Lacanian analysts, such as Jean-Claude Maleval (2000), suggest that next to the possibility of elaborating a delusional metaphor other modes of mastering elementary phenomena should be discerned.

Moreover, it should be noted that in Schreber's case the delusional metaphor did not prove to be stable over time. Later on in his life Schreber experienced a third illness episode, in which experiences that could not be mastered with the delusional metaphor came to the fore (Maleval, 2000). The concept of the delusional metaphor offers one way of understanding delusions, but should not be seen as the ultimate model. In my interpretation, Lacan's suggestion that writing for an audience and holding on to friendship added to Schreber's resilience further indicates that obtaining stability is not exclusively due to the elaboration of a delusional metaphor.

Instead of thinking of the delusional metaphor as a paradigm for interpreting all delusions, I suggest taking Lacan's detailed study of Schreber's *Memoirs* as an example. With his discussion of how subjectivity is organized in terms of concrete signifiers, Lacan demonstrates that the method psychoanalysts should follow consists of a thorough examination of the patient's speech, paying particular attention to the role played by questions of existence at the level of the unconscious and to the way in which the individual deals with his mad Other. Such a methodical approach is paramount to understanding how concrete therapeutic intervention should be organized.

Part III

Third Era: The Age of the Object *a*

6
The Object *a* and Jouissance in Psychosis

Lacan's shift in the 1960s

After having focused on the signifier for many years, Lacan makes an important shift in the early 1960s. Problems that he first approached with strict attention to the logic of the signifier are now addressed in terms of the *limits of the Symbolic*. The new idea he embraces is that some aspects of being cannot be grasped via language and that the registers of libido and drive cannot simply be reduced to the Symbolic. Whereas in the 1950s Lacan argued that the drive is expressed via the signifying chain, by the 1960s he concludes that aspects of the drive resist representation and cannot be articulated in the signifying chain.

In this period of Lacan's work he not only began to add new concepts to his lexicon, but the degree of abstraction in his work increased. Prior to the 1960s, Lacan strongly focused on other authors' work, formulating ideas that were based on detailed commentaries of their texts. Yet from that decade on this changes. References to other authors are present, but to move forward conceptually, he is no longer preoccupied with generating dialogue with other psychoanalysts or psychiatrists. Lacan gradually pursues an own, innovative line of thinking, and as a result his seminars and written texts become increasingly difficult for those not familiar with his work. This increased level of abstraction will also be evident in this chapter and in the next.

Two key concepts Lacan used to address the domain of subjectivity that can be found at the limit of the Symbolic are 'jouissance' and the 'object *a*'.[1] As Lacan (1970, p. 194) indicates, the French term *jouissance* cannot be easily translated into English, which is why it is usually left in its original form. 'Enjoyment' would be its literal translation, but this term is inadequate because of the connotation of pleasure it entails. For

Lacan jouissance denotes a mode of satisfaction or drive gratification beyond pleasure. Because it primarily plays at the level of our corporeal experience, Lacan places jouissance in dialectical opposition to the signifying chain. The object *a* refers to what remains of the mythical partial object by using language.

With the concepts of jouissance and the object *a*, Lacan somewhat reorients his discussions of psychosis. In the years after Seminar III (Lacan, 1955–6) and his article On a Question Prior to any Possible Treatment of Psychosis (Lacan, 1959), and before Seminar XXIII on Joyce, Lacan (1975–6) commented only marginally on psychosis. However, his sporadic comments indicate that, as a consequence of the foreclosure of the Name-of-the-Father, the object *a* and jouissance have a particular status in psychosis.

This chapter gives an overview of the concepts of jouissance and the object *a*. First I explore these concepts in detail as they are the building blocks of the later sections of this chapter. Next, starting from Lacan's statement that there is no so-called 'Other of the Other', i.e. that no signifier can guarantee the consistency of the Symbolic, I again review his concept of the Name-of-the-Father. I argue that, in the 1960s, Lacan gives a different interpretation to the Name-of-the-Father, which has important implications for how foreclosure should henceforth be interpreted. Subsequently I discuss how Lacan conceptualizes the object *a* in psychosis, focusing on the difference between paranoia and schizophrenia. To conclude, Lacan's (1965) discussion of Marguerite Duras's (1964) novel *The Ravishing of Lol V. Stein* is reviewed. His discussion of the fictional case of Lola Valerie Stein can be interpreted as an illustration of how stabilization can be obtained in psychosis, without relying on the signifier. Given the fact that Lacan's comments on psychosis are spread over different texts and seminars, the ideas presented in this chapter reflect my own reading and interpretation of his comments.

Jouissance and the object a

By including the concepts object *a* and jouissance in his work, Lacan formulates a theory of what he calls the 'the Real', that is, the aspect of being that fails to be articulated in terms of the Symbolic (Shepherdson, 2008; Verhaeghe, 2001). Following Alain Badiou (1982, 2009, 2010), it could be argued that from the 1960s onwards Lacan makes a strict distinction between *being* and *existence,* which he defines as two *dialectically opposed categories*. Whereas existence refers to the articulation of the subject in the Symbolic, being is Real.

In the 1950s, Lacan did not make this distinction. Being and 'living' were seen as Imaginary phenomena determined by the Symbolic (Lacan, 1959, p. 461), which Lacan believed was the only register on which psychoanalysis should concentrate. Existence, in its turn, referred to the position of the subject and was directly situated in the Symbolic, which implies that existence was thought to determine being. In the 1960s, by contrast, being is reconceptualized as the antipode of existence. In this view, existence still concerns the articulation of the subject in the Symbolic, but being is henceforth qualified as Real (Miller, 1999). Turning points in this respect are Seminar IX (Lacan, 1961–2), in which the limits of the Symbolic are explored with a strong focus on logic and topology, and Seminar X (Lacan, 1962–3), in which anxiety is studied (Miller, 2004a). In these seminars Lacan opposes the *subject of the signifier* to the so-called *'subject of jouissance'*[2] (Lacan, 1962–3, pp. 203–4). The subject of the signifier refers to subjectivity that arises as an effect of concatenating signifiers. This subject 'exists', to the extent that its position and identity in the world are articulated via the Other. The subject of jouissance, by contrast, refers to the libidinous corporeality of being. It designates a state of being that is not (yet) determined by the signifier. The subject of jouissance 'is', but does not exist. It designates the human being qua Thing, before it is differentiated by means of the signifier. Its identity and its position in the world are not articulated.

Importantly Lacan conceptualizes the relationship between the Other and the subject of jouissance in dialectical terms. This means that in the tension between jouissance and Other an *Aufhebung* or upheaval is realized, which gives rise to a new component of subjectivity: the object *a*. The object *a* is a component of libidinous corporeality that is created by using signifiers, but that is not represented by means of the signifier. It is an element of being that persists in the subject of the signifier, but is not transformed into Symbolic existence.

To elaborate his ideas on the object, *a* Lacan principally uses a logical approach: in 1961–2 he starts from surface topology, and in 1962–3 from a quasi-arithmetical explanation. What is important in this context is that he didn't adhere to a developmental psychological perspective. Similar to his reinterpretation of the Oedipus complex in metaphorical terms (Lacan, 1959), Lacan believes that, in the process that gives rise to the object *a*, the *dialectical transition* should be studied. Speculation about associated interpersonal and developmental dynamics is deemed irrelevant. This is apparent in Lacan's reaction to a guest lecture by the psychoanalyst Piera Aulagnier in his 1961–2 seminar (lesson 2, May 1962), where she discussed the relation to the partial object in normality, neurosis, perversion and psychosis. Aulagnier argued that an individual's relation to partial objects reflects a past history, which can best be framed in terms of interactional dynamics between a child and its parents. Both in his direct comments on Aulagnier's lecture and in the later seminars, Lacan does not follow her developmental logic. Instead, he focuses on the logical status of the object and on the dialectical structure in which it can be situated, not on presumed causal mechanisms.

The central terms Lacan puts forward in his dialectical model are the *Other* and the *subject of jouissance*. The Other still refers to the 'locus' or 'the treasure trove' of signifiers (Lacan, 1962–3, pp. 37, 189), through which the subject is articulated. The subject of jouissance refers to 'the hypothetical subject at the origin of this dialectic [with the Other]'[3] (Lacan, 1962–3, p. 135). It is 'the still non-existing subject, that has to situate itself as determined by the signifier'[4] (Lacan, 1962–3, p. 37). Lacan characterizes the subject of jouissance as 'the mythical subject which is the sensible phase of the living being: this fathomless thing capable of experiencing something between birth and death, capable of covering the whole spectrum of pain and pleasure in a word' (Lacan, 1970, p. 194). Further exploring the concept he adds: 'If the living being is something at all thinkable, it will be above all as subject of the *jouissance*; but this psychological law that we call the pleasure principle (and which is only the principle of displeasure) is very soon to create a barrier to all *jouissance*. If I am enjoying myself a little too much, I begin to feel pain and I moderate my pleasures. The organism seems made to avoid too much *jouissance*' (Lacan, 1970, pp. 194–5).[5]

These dense characterizations of the subject of jouissance reveal three principal ideas on the nature of being. First, Lacan suggests that the subject of jouissance denotes the corporeal side of being, and that it makes up the dialectical counterpart of the signifier. Without such counterpart in the living organism, the subject of the signifier would simply not exist. Second, Lacan's description makes clear that the subject of jouissance qua living organism should not be thought of as a smoothly operating machine. He does not describe it as a mythical unity that is marked by primordial satisfaction, but as a 'fathomless thing'. By calling the human organism a 'thing', he stresses that humans do not coincide with their corporeality – it is by no accident that we commonly say that we *have* a body; not that we *are* one (Lacan, 1976d). The idea that the body is 'fathomless' in its turn stresses that our corporeal being is enigmatic and Real: computers and machines can be programmed, yet the human body largely escapes such Symbolic direction. Third,

Lacan's characterization indicates that the body qua living organism should be thought of as 'sensible', and 'capable of experiencing something'. This sensibility is far removed from the phenomenological idea of experience, or from the psychological concept of emotion. The type of experience Lacan attributes to the Real body is *jouissance*. Jouissance concerns the way the body is affected by the thrust of the drive, and indicates that beyond the experience of pleasure a mode of gratification is found in excitation and agitation. The substance of the body is marked by fleshy urges, which continually disrupt the imaginary experience of unity and the smooth articulation of signifiers. The jouissance of the body is an excess that cannot but be experienced as overwhelming (Lacan, 1966–7, lesson 24, May 1967). In this respect we are subjects of jouissance, to the extent that we are *subjected* to jouissance, that is, to the extent that we don't control the forces that move our being qua living organism. Furthermore, Lacan adds that the pleasure principle, as described by Freud (1915, 1920)[6], is a barrier to jouissance. The jouissance of the body is too unlimited to be endurable, and the pleasure principle, which actually avoids displeasure, functions as a regulatory system through which excessive excitation is avoided.

The division of the Other and its consequences

To understand the transformation that is produced in the dialectical tension between the Other and the subject of jouissance, Lacan (1962–3, pp. 37, 135) proposes a quasi-arithmetical explanation in Seminar X, and introduces the following scheme[7] (Figure 6.1):

$$
\begin{array}{c|c}
O & S \\
\hline
\text{\$} & \varnothing \\
a &
\end{array}
$$

Figure 6.1 The matheme of the division of the Other

This quasi-arithmetical scheme, which I will call the matheme of the division of the Other, is 'homologous' to the arithmetic representation of division, in its European notation (Lacan, 1962–3, p. 135). It expresses that a dialectical tension between the Other (O) and the subject of jouissance (S) is the basis of the process via which the divided subject ($) comes into existence. Indeed, in this formula, Lacan first of all defines two fields: the field of the Other, situated to the left of the matheme, and the field of the subject, situated to the right. In terms of mental experiences, the elements situated in the field of the Other are experienced as belonging to the external world, whereas the materials that are situated in the field of the subject are experienced as internal.

However, by presenting the relation between S and O in such arithmetic terms, Lacan not only depicts a dialectical relationship, but more particularly suggests that O *is divided by S:* the Other, or the Symbolic, is the point of reference, upon which the primitive subject, or the Real, is imposed.

The fact that O is presented as the element that will be divided makes clear that Lacan still brings into play the primacy of the Other: O is the system through which bodily jouissance is transformed. The idea this conveys is that humans give a place to the jouissance of their body by making use of language. In this respect he said that 'the subject has to constitute itself at the place of the Other under the primary species of the signifier'[8](Lacan, 1962–3, p. 189), and that 'it is along the path of the Other that the subject has to realize itself'[9] (Lacan, 1962–3, p. 203). These statements indicate that the existence of the subject can only take shape by articulating one's being in terms of the Other. By doing so the primitive subject of jouissance is partly incorporated into language, which is what the concept of the divided subject ($\mathcal{S}$) expresses: some aspects of subjectivity can be articulated via language, but this articulation is not complete, which is what the bar through $\mathcal{S}$ indicates.

A second element, next to $\mathcal{S}$, that Lacan considers to be an effect of the division of O by S, is Ø. Qua concept Ø is the symbol Lacan calls 'the barred Other'[10] (Lacan 1962–3, p. 136), and stands for the signifying chain that is articulated via speech. What is more, Lacan suggests that this chain makes up the unconscious: 'What is on my side now [at the side of the subject after the division], is that which constitutes me as unconscious, namely Ø the Other in so far as I do not reach it'[11] (Lacan, 1962–3, p. 37). This idea is not really surprising since prior to the 1960s Lacan (1959, p. 459) already qualified the unconscious as 'the Other's discourse', meaning that it is a stream of signifiers that, beyond any intention of the ego, is expressed in human functioning. The idea that Ø reflects 'the Other in so far as I do not reach it' points to the impossibility of a final compatibility between S and O, which is new in his work from the 1960s. The idea is that no matter how much speech is produced about S, some aspects of jouissance cannot be articulated via the Other. This idea brings Lacan to the conclusion that in our use of language, 'The whole existence of the Other suspends on a guarantee that is lacking, hence the barred Other'[12] (Lacan 1962–3, p. 136). The only thing the Other provides to the living being is a medium by means of which a subject can be articulated. What it does not offer is a standard against which this articulation can be tested, nor does O supply a set of ultimate signifiers through which S can be fully named. The bar drawn on Ø indicates that irrespective of how much signifying articulation takes place, something remains unsaid. There is no final signifier that can hook up the true signification of speech. No so-called 'Other of the Other' gives consistency to the signifiers that are actually articulated as a result of this division.[13]

The object *a*

The third element that the division of O by S creates is the object *a*, symbolized by *a* in the scheme. Lacan (1962–3, p. 189) describes it as follows: 'The *a* is what remains irreducible in the total operation of the advent of the subject to the locus of the Other... it is precisely that which represents the S in its irreducible real status'.[14] Indeed, in the operation of articulating S via O, something will continue to resist. No matter how elaborate the flow of signifiers is, some aspects of the subject of jouissance will remain unarticulated. The object *a* refers to the element of the living being that cannot be inserted into the order of the Symbolic; a component of flesh and blood that remains inert in relation to the signifier. Lacan (1961–2, session, 27 June 1962) concludes that it is 'being in so far as it is essentially missing in the text of the world'.[15] The fact that Lacan defines the object *a* as the *remainder* of the division between O and S, indicates that the basic dialectical situation is a crucial starting point for interpreting the concept. The object *a* refers to jouissance that is created by using language and is therefore strictly correlative to the Symbolic: if there were no attempt to signify S by means of O, *a* would not be created.

Although primarily introduced as a concept, Lacan strongly emphasizes that the object *a* is clinically relevant. Diverse complex phenomena ranging from desire in neurosis to persecution in psychosis reflect the position of the subject towards the object *a*. In operationalizing the object *a* Lacan starts from Freud's idea that the libidinous drive is expressed in specific erogenous zones, and from Melanie Klein's and Donald Winnicott's theory on the partial object which says that object relations don't necessarily focus on people, but can just as well be concentrated on body parts such as a mother's breast (Kirshner, 2005; Lacan, 1975; Vanier, 2011). In line with Freud, Lacan argues that the object *a* is manifested in specific registers of the drive, which in their turn are connected to specific erogenous zones. Without claiming that his list is exhaustive (Lacan, 1960), he states that manifestations of the object *a* can be found in the oral, anal, scopic and invocative registers.

To understand the precise manifestation of the object *a* in these registers of the drive, I suggest making a clear distinction between the object *a* and the partial object. Following Lacan, the partial object denotes the object of jouissance to which the erogenous zone relates apart from language. The relation to this object plays at the corporeal level, and is accompanied by a mode of gratification that concerns the stimulation of an erogenous zone with an adequate physical object. At a more detailed level it can be argued that at the oral level the mouth is the erogenous zone, and the partial object it relates to is the nipple; at the anal level the anus is the zone where the drive manifests, and the corresponding object is the scybalum; at the scopic level the eye is the erogenous zone and the corresponding object is the image; and at the invocative level the ear is the erogenous zone and the object it relates to is sound (Dolar, 2006; Lacan, 1962–63, 1963, 1964; Lysy, 2008; Miller, 2004a; Stasse, 2008).[16] These objects are not clearly differentiated from the subject, such that at moments of libidinous activity the subject coincides with the excitation or jouissance the object provokes (Vinciguerra, 2010). Hence Lacan's idea that the primordial subject is a subject of jouissance.

The object *a*, in its turn, is what remains of the partial object upon its transformation by using language. Given Lacan's assumption that the subject is already determined by language before birth, such that a child can even become the carrier of repressed signifiers from its parents (Lacan, 1959, 1969), it can be concluded that the partial object is only a hypothetical notion. At all times language mediates the human relationship to the objectal world, which means that we never have a strictly corporeal relationship to it. This transformative effect of language primarily consists of fictionalization. By using language we don't relate to Real things in the world, but to Symbolically determined representations of the world. However, this fictionalization is not complete. Human beings typically think that beyond words, they are in touch with reality. This is what the object *a* expresses. Humans assume that beyond the wall of words and images by which the Other is made up, the dimension of being can be found, which fascinates them. In this context Lacan stresses that contrary to the partial object, the object *a* is not a tangible object, but a pastiche that covers up the Real of being (Santiago, 2009).

Parallel to the idea that partial objects relate to specific erogenous zones, Lacan says that manifestations of the object *a* are related to specific registers of the drive. In the oral, anal, scopic and invocative registers in particular, manifestations of the objects *a* can be found. Lacan (1960, 1962–3) states that in the invocative register the object *a* takes the shape of the *voice*, and that in the scopic register it manifests itself as the *gaze*. However, in his discussion about the object *a* in the anal and the oral registers Lacan is less precise. It is frequently argued in Lacanian literature that the nipple/breast and the scybalum/excrement are the oral and anal objects *a*, respectively. In my interpretation this is wrong, as these are the partial objects to which the subject of jouissance relates. Building on Lacan's earlier work (Lacan, 1957–8, 1958–9) and comments from the 1960s (Lacan, 1960, 1962–3, 1964; Stasse, 2008), I suggest that in the oral register the object *a* can be found in the dimension of *nothingness around which each act of taking-in is gravitating*, whereas in the anal register the object *a* takes the shape of *giving nothing*. Schematically I suggest presenting these partial objects and their corresponding objects *a* as follows (Figure 6.2):

Drive	Partial object	Object *a*
Oral	Nipple	Taking in nothing
Anal	Scybalum	Giving nothing
Scopic	Image	Gaze
Invocative	Sound	Voice

Figure 6.2 Partial objects and corresponding objects *a*

Interestingly, in the matheme of the division of the Other, Lacan situates the object *a* in the field of the Other. This indicates that, in *neurosis*, the object *a* is attributed to the figure of the Other. It specifies that the neurotic seeks to find a bit of jouissance, or a kernel of being, beyond the Other's words. Lacan placed this missing aspect of being in relation to the Other's desire (Miller, 2004a). The idea is that before the division of O, the subject is enigmatic: S is not articulated in signifying terms, and is therefore an unknown entity. As signifiers are articulated, the status of the subject changes: in the dialectical tension between S and O the subject is expressed in terms of Ø and via retroactive buttoning ties in speech its identity is addressed. Yet, parallel to this articulation of the subject, O becomes more opaque and obscure. The more signifiers used from O, the clearer it becomes that the Other is nothing but a collection of signifiers for which a guarantee of being is lacking. The underlying idea is that while in the process of signification the Other functions as a treasure trove of signifiers, from which elements can be borrowed, it cannot 'answer for the value of its treasure' (Lacan, 1960, p. 693). There is no subset of signifiers in the Symbolic to provide a guarantee of the adequacy or truthfulness of all other signifiers. Hence his suggestion that there is no Other of the Other.

Furthermore, Lacan suggests that confrontations with the lack in the Other provoke anxiety. Such confrontations make it brutally clear that there is no final answer for the enigmatic dimension of jouissance in the subject, which unsettles the initial trust in the Other. The neurotic copes with this unsettling observation by linking the enigma of what the Other wants to the object *a*, fostering the belief that the object *a* expresses the desire of the Other (Hoornaert, 2008; Lacan, 1960, 1962–3, 1963). In neurosis the object *a* functions as a patch that covers the enigmatic lack in the Other and, as a mechanism that sets desire in motion; it mediates the relation between subject and Other. By attributing the object *a* to the Other, attention in neurosis shifts away from the puzzling remainder of jouissance that concerns the subject. This attribution follows an externalizing defensive strategy: elements of jouissance that cannot be framed by means of the Symbolic are ejected from the subject and, via projection, they become a focus of attention in the Other qua interpersonal figure. Such externalization is defensive since it helps the neurotic *not* face the incomprehensible enigma of his own functioning. Lacan (1962–3, 1963) argues that this reduces the experience of anxiety, which is mobilized when elements of enigmatic jouissance are detected within the subject.[17]

Within this view the object *a* not only has a connecting role in relation to the Other, in that it is a point of reference for interpreting the Other's desire, it also functions as a cause in relation to the subject of the signifier: the moment the subject of the signifier has the impression of being in touch with the objectal dimension in the Other, desire grows stronger. In this respect Lacan says that the object *a* occupies the place of the so-called '*plus-de-jouir*' or 'surplus of jouissance' (Lacan, 1968–9). This means to say that by concentrating on the object *a* in the Other the neurotic aims to recuperate some of the jouissance that is lost through the use of language.[18] The neurotic's belief is that by focusing on the virtual object in the Other, an experience of gratification will finally be reached.

In a footnote of On a Question Prior to Any Possible Treatment of Psychosis, which was only added upon the publication of his *Écrits* in 1966, Lacan emphasizes this organizing role of the object *a* in neurosis and says that it 'props up the field of reality' (Lacan, 1959, p. 487).

Since in neurosis the object *a* is 'extracted' or 'separated' from the body, and attributed to O, the subject can believe that the Other is not just a mechanical entity or a deeply incomprehensible dark force, but a desiring being, just like himself. The importance of such an 'extraction of object *a*' cannot be underestimated (Lacan, 1959, pp. 487, 1961–2, session 30, May 1962; Miller, 1979). Its function resides in delimiting the lack in the Other, and in disambiguating the position of the subject: 'by the extraction of object *a*' neurotic reality takes shape (Lacan, 1959, p. 487).[19]

An example of how the object *a* functions in neurosis can be found in everyday conversations, where the dimension of the voice plays an important role. On the one hand conversations have a communicative function, which is largely based on *language use*: people take materials from established discourse, build ideas and exchange messages. On the other hand conversations also have an affective side, which is reflected in people's *use of speech*: beyond their content conversations tire or excite, attract or repel, which indicates that apart from what is enunciated, the enunciation itself affects the people involved. The act of enunciation thereby reveals that speakers are not mechanistic entities, but living beings who are immanent to what they say. The voice qua object *a* points to this immanence of the living being in speech.

The Names-of-the-Father

As he elaborated his ideas on the division of the Other, Lacan also refined his concept of the Name-of-the-Father, and gave a more humble status to the paternal signifier. Whereas prior to the 1960s Lacan (1957–8, p. 192) maintained that the Name-of-the-Father functions as an 'Other of the Other', that is, as the ultimate point of reference in the Symbolic on which all other signifiers rest, in the 1960s he argued the opposite. He then argued that there is no Other of the Other and that both in neurosis and psychosis an ultimate point of reference is lacking. Henceforth, the Symbolic is thought of as an open system, to which new elements can always be added, without ever reaching consistency (Verhaeghe, 2009).

However, rejecting the Other of the Other does not imply that Lacan left behind the concept of the Name-of-the-Father. Starting from the idea that no signifier functions as a universal support in the Symbolic, he redefined the paternal signifier, arguing that it is a local and partial solution for the lack in the Other. Within this view *the Name-of-the-Father is not intrinsically unique but a uniquely used signifier*, which is different from what he suggested in his previous work. In the 1950s Lacan proposed that the Name-of-the-Father is a kind of super signifier: it is the benchmark for all other signifiers and it incarnates the dimension of the law in the Symbolic (Lacan, 1959). A problem with this line of reasoning is that it doesn't explain how a single signifier can actually represent the law. Theoretically this viewpoint is not tenable. It contradicts the structuralist idea that signifiers have no inherent meaning, and it goes against the assumption that only references between signifiers produce signification. By stressing that the Name-of-the-Father is not intrinsically unique but a uniquely used signifier, Lacan solves this problem. His novel idea in the 1960s is that a signifier can obtain a law-like status for the subject if it is articulated by a master figure upon making an authoritative claim: 'No authoritative statement has any other guarantee here than its very enunciation' (Lacan, 1960, p. 688). Within this view the Name-of-the-Father is not covered by a higher truth. Its credibility is purely an effect of speech pragmatics: it is only to the extent that a person has faith in a Father figure or master figure that his rules and explanations function as a law whereby sense can be made of desire. Within this view there is no such thing as *the* paternal signifier. Indeed, starting from the last session of Seminar X (Lacan, 1962–3), and in a session of an interrupted Seminar on of the Name-of-the-Father, Lacan (1963) modifies his old position on the paternal function. From then on many *Names*-of-the-Father are presumed to exist (Lacan, 1963): paternal signifiers are not universal guarantees, but locally accepted Symbolic elements used as a benchmark for making sense of the world.[20]

This pluralizing of the Name-of-the-Father also has an effect on how psychosis, which continues to be studied in terms of foreclosure, is henceforth understood. Whereas his model of the 1950s emphasized that due to an absent *Bejahung* a crucial signifier is lacking, his reflections from the 1960s imply that in psychosis *an act of faith has not taken place*. Henceforth, neurosis and psychosis are not presumed to be dissimilar in terms of how the Symbolic is materially composed, but in terms of how the Symbolic is used, whereby the difference between both resides in the instalment or the non-instalment of a belief in the Other as a guarantee. Whereas neurosis is characterized by belief, believing is not an issue in psychosis (Lacan, 1964). Marked by a fundamentally sceptical and distant attitude, the Other's rules and explanations are not taken as a benchmark for addressing questions of existence.

An important consequence of Lacan's accent on the status of faith and belief in the Other as a guarantee for truth is that it implies a shift away from a deficit model of psychosis. No matter how strongly Lacan argued that psychosis should not be studied in terms of inherent defects, and that the dimension of the subject should be valued, his concept of foreclosure still implied that compared to neurosis a signifier is lacking. Given that the signifier is considered as the building block of subjectivity, this still suggests that psychosis is marked by a fundamental flaw. His view in the 1960s is different in that it emphasizes the difference between neurosis and psychosis in such a way that this non-instalment of a belief in the Other as a guarantee for truth has both positive and negative sides. Characterized negatively, foreclosure of faith in the Other implies that the Other is not the kind of safe haven in which the neurotic trusts; characterized positively it implies that the psychotic remains relatively protected from being duped by a naïve dependence on the Other (Miller, 1993, 2002a).

Importantly, parallel to focusing on the differential status of belief in neurosis and psychosis, and shifting away from the material deficit model, Lacan also began to challenge the idea that psychosis would be a more 'severe' condition than neurosis. Both are just different 'subject structures', or different logics by means of which sense is made of the world, and nothing more. In both structures normality is possible, just like in both structures the subject can suffer (Lacan, 1961–2): 'the neurotic, just like the pervert and the psychotic, are nothing but figures of the normal structure'[21] (Lacan, 1961–2, session 13, June 1962).

Jouissance and the object a in psychosis

As he elaborated his theory on the dialectical relation between the Other and jouissance, Lacan also formulated ideas on the object *a* in psychosis. His main proposition was that while in neurosis reality takes shape by separating the object *a* from the body and situating it in the field of the Other, such extraction does not take place in psychosis (Lacan, 1961–2, session 30, May 1962). This determines the way in which subjectivity and reality take shape. Contrary to the neurotic, who uses the object *a* in the Other as a benchmark for comprehending questions of desire, the subject in psychosis is plagued by a non-separated object. Indeed, in psychosis the object *a* is not an external element that fuels desire in the subject, but a strange internal element the subject has to manage. To characterize this Lacan says that the subject in psychosis 'has its cause in its own pocket' (Lacan, 1967), which is to say that it is confronted with an overwhelming non-signified excitation that manifests itself from within. This excess excitation threatens to efface the subject's footing in the signifier, and in this respect makes up the *structural cause* of how the subject takes shape. Thus considered the non-extraction of the object *a* can be thought of as correlative to foreclosure. Whereas the concept of foreclosure indicates that the Name-of-the-Father does not function as a support for articulating the subject's *existence*, the idea of the non-extracted object *a* suggests that *being* also poses a problem. At a vital level, people living through a psychosis typically feel that their sentiment of life has changed. A strange force, which manifests itself as an experiential fact that cannot easily be named, seizes the subject.

In terms of Lacan's (1962–3) matheme on the division of the Other, it could be argued that due to foreclosure the transformation of the subject of jouissance has a different outcome in psychosis than in neurosis: in psychosis the unconscious (Ø) is situated in the field of the Other, while the object *a* is located within the subject. Note that, compared with Lacan's work from the 1950s, the idea that in psychosis the unconscious is external is not new: it is an idea he maintained throughout his later work. For example, in Seminar XII he emphasizes that while the neurotic knows that productions of the unconscious, such as dreams, relate to thoughts with which he is preoccupied, the psychotic knows that such productions bear witness of immixtures from without (1964–5, session 7, April 1965).

In discussing the non-extraction of the object *a* in psychosis, Lacan differentiates between two modes of psychotic functioning: paranoia and schizophrenia. These are not considered to be subtypes of psychosis with unique and overlapping symptoms, but two clinical structures, meaning two ways of relating to a non-extracted object *a*, in which the categories of the Other and jouissance have a different status in relation to the subject. For example, whereas Schreber's case reveals both paranoid and schizophrenic elements, the case of Aimée more specifically illustrates a paranoid structure.

Paranoia

Lacan's basic statement concerning paranoia is that the *subject identifies with the object of jouissance of the Other*: beyond any reason the paranoiac 'knows' that another person, or more abstractly a force, has 'got it in for him'. This 'paranoid knowledge' is not based on learning, but on revelation (Lacan, 1966b, p. 215): while sometimes there is confusion about what exactly is happening to him or her, the paranoid person *observes clear signs* that the Other is driven by a malevolent plan, of which he or she as a person is the victim. The Symbolic is invaded by a maddening force of which the subject is the mere object, and does not function as a guarantee whereby subjective identity can be articulated.

Parallel to what he maintained in the 1950s, in the 1960s Lacan holds on to the idea that such paranoid logic comes to the fore in relation to foreclosure: paranoid ideation is triggered when the absence of a Name-of-the-Father is laid bare with respect to a question of personal identity. This typically takes place in the face of life events. However, by declaring that paranoia consists of 'identifying jouissance in this place of the Other as such'[22] (Lacan, 1966b, p. 215), a new element is added to his thinking. The idea that the Other is marked by jouissance stresses that the immixing activities of the Other are libidinously charged. The intrusions experienced in paranoia have a shocking and puzzling effect, not only because they go against conventional views of the world, but above all because of the obscene and mad pleasure by which the Other proves to be driven.

In terms of the non-separation of the objectal dimension, it could be argued that in paranoia par excellence, the subject finds itself in the position of having the object *a* in his own pocket. The object *a* is not experienced as a virtual element, as in neurosis, but as a tangible reality that bears witness to the thieving intentions of the Other in the actuality of a person's life. People living through paranoia describe the object *a* as a concrete actuality, and as the ultimate proof that a jouissance-seeking Other wrongfully makes use of them. Whereas in neurosis the object *a* is a *presumed* element of being in the Other which fascinates the subject, in paranoia the jouissance emanating from the Other is experienced as being directed towards an element in one's own *actual* being: the Other hunts for the essence of one's own being, which is why all intrusions have such a devastating effect. Indeed, in paranoia the gaze, the voice, the gift and the nothingness around which the act of taking in gravitates are palpable experiential dimensions that disturb the individual's experience of the world. Common clinical manifestations of the object *a* in the scopic and invocative registers include the gaze that is felt as seeing through one's mind (Žižek, 1993), or a commanding voice that intrudes with jouissance-laden comments. In the anal register the gift is typically experienced in terms of manipulations from without that put something into the body or into the mind. In the oral register the object *a* is frequently experienced in terms of taking away a vital element that attaches the individual to life. For example, in Schreber's case, this oral dimension comes to the fore in the experience of 'soul-murder': God steals an aspect of Schreber's sense of life and leaves him like a living dead in a collapsing world.

In Schreber's case the identification of jouissance in the domain of the Other can be more broadly found in the fearful conviction that Flechsig and God will abuse him in all possible ways, dump him and leave him to rot. Lacan (1966b, p. 214) summarizes this position by stating that 'God or the Other takes advantage of/enjoys his [Schreber's] passivated being',[23] and points to the relationship of 'mortifying erotomania' in which he is trapped (Lacan, 1966b, p. 217). At first this passive position throws Schreber into a deep sense of hopelessness. Only by subsequently cultivating the idea of a possible reconciliation with God can he take a distance from the painful position of the Other's object of jouissance.

In Aimée's case a similar logic can be found (Lacan, 1966b, p. 215). The knowledge by which Aimée is driven is that Huguette Duflos and a number of other Parisian celebrities intrude upon her life and aim to cause harm to her and her son. The celebrities incarnate a grotesque jouissance of which Aimée and her son are the passive victims: the celebrities *see* into her life, in their works they *voice* allusions to her and, most disturbingly, they aim to *take* her child. Contrary to Schreber, Aimée doesn't cope with this position qua object of the Other by elaborating a delusional metaphor, but by actively putting a stop to the invasion of jouissance in the form of an attack.

Within this view the crux of paranoia does not reside in the elaboration of a delusion but, as de Clérambault (1942) indicated and Lacan (1966c) underscored in his tribute to de Clérambault, in a specific type of elementary phenomenon. Essential to the structure of paranoia is the position of the subject as an innocent victim of a jouissance-driven Other. This position is not based on belief, but on interpretation: palpable manifestations of the object *a* in the paranoid person's life repeatedly 'demonstrate' that the Symbolic universe is driven by a mad and maddening force, of which one is the tangible object.

Schizophrenia

In schizophrenia the situation is different. Contrary to paranoia, where the experience of the object *a* is interpreted as a sign that an Other has his eye on the subject, *no connection is made between object a and Other.* As a consequence the *jouissance emanating from the object* a *is experienced as a senseless ravaging force, and the impact of the Other qua carrier of the Symbolic order is nil.*

In schizophrenia *jouissance* is not a devouring force coming from without, but a destructive power that overwhelms the subject from within. Senseless manifestations of the objectal dimension invade reality and devastate the imaginary experience of subjective consistency. The feeling of being a person and having a coherent body that is demarcated from the outside world evaporates into thin air. What remains is a situation of complete chaos against which there is no defence. Brutal manifestations of the object *a* that have 'nothing to do anymore with any subject'[24] (Lacan, 1966b, p. 214) overwhelm the schizophrenic and only leave a feeling of fundamental despair. Lacan (1961–2, session 2, May 1962) argued that in schizophrenia 'desires are properly speaking mad'.[25] Desire is not organized by an anchor like the external object *a* in neurosis, and contrary to paranoia no Other is held responsible for the vital changes through which the person lives. What stands to the fore are senseless drive manifestations with which the subject of the signifier feels no familiarity.

Schreber's 'bellowing miracle' demonstrates very well the despairing impact of the brutally manifesting object *a* (Lacan, 1966b). In his *Memoirs* he makes clear that the senseless screams emanating from his mouth perplex him. Far from being intentionally produced, these screams are 'miraculous' manifestations of which his body is the carrier, but with which he feels no connection. Indeed, the moment screams emanate from his mouth Schreber is no longer a signified subject, but a mere scene upon which the voice is manifested. The bellowing miracle shows that the voice qua object *a* is not a vague semblance for Schreber, but an overwhelming inner force that confronts him with a jouissance over which he has no control.

Amongst the other miraculous phenomena to which Schreber bears witness, the references to bodily disintegration in relation to specific organs are particularly interesting. In my interpretation these disintegrations reflect how an oral object *a* ravages all experience of consistency. For example, Schreber (1903, pp. 144–5) indicates that at the start of his illness a lungworm absorbed the lobes of his lungs, that his abdomen was rotting and that at several moments in time his stomach simply disappeared. These phenomena indicate that, to his utter dismay, holes are created in his body. Organs that in a previous stage were part of Schreber's body are suddenly eaten away and vanish into nothingness. Contrary to what takes place in paranoia, no attributions to the jouissance-laden activities of an overwhelming Other are made. An unmotivated force simply destroys his body.

A central point in Lacan's discussion of the Other in schizophrenia is that its impact qua carrier of the Symbolic order is nil. For some reason, language has no grip on reality and on the body, and fails to have the organizing impact it usually has (Lacan, 1972b). In other subject structures, like paranoia or neurosis, signifiers have an organizing value and provide an orderly scheme from which the experience of the body can take shape: 'language is the first thing to which the body finds itself completely subordinated'[26] (Lacan, 1972b, p. 22). Language enables a person to experience the body as composed of different parts that make up a systemic whole. In schizophrenia this organizing effect remains lacking, because for the schizophrenic the system of language itself is 'mad'[27] and disorganized (Lacan, 1972b, p. 22).

The absence of a support in language affects the way in which the social bond takes shape or, better, fails to take shape: language does not provide a means to tame the drive, nor does it provide a consistent interface for establishing continuity in social relations. As a result, social isolation and solitude prevail. Lacan (1973, p. 474) emphasized this by saying that 'the so-called schizophrenic is specified by gaining no support by any established discourse':[28] in schizophrenia cultural representations provide no adequate basis for articulating one's identity in relation to others, and do not provide consistency. He states that the schizophrenic subject's fundamentally ironic attitude is 'directed to the root of each social relationship' (Lacan, 1966d, p. 209), and this is because of the impossibility of believing that a support for articulating the subject can be found in the Symbolic. Contrary to the neurotic, who prefers to ignore the inconsistency of the Other by focusing on the dimension of the law, the schizophrenic only sees inconsistency, and finds no support in common discourse (Miller, 1993, 2004b).

The Ravishing of Lol Valerie Stein

During his discussion of psychosis in the 1960s, Lacan refers to the fictional character Lola Valerie Stein, also called Lol, the protagonist of Marguerite Duras's novel *The Ravishing of Lol Stein* (Duras, 1964). Lacan discussed this novel in Seminar XII (Lacan, 1964–5, session 24 June), and wrote a text about it in which he pays tribute to the genius of Duras: 'Marguerite Duras proves to know, without me, what I teach'[29] (Lacan, 1965, p. 193; Hoens, 2005). Duras convincingly described how the object *a* might function in social interactions. She showed how a person for whom the object *a* is not extracted, like Lola Valerie Stein, can cope with the desire of others, and how, in the end, she might also go mad by specific desire-related events. What is interesting about this discussion is that it sheds a new light on the possibility of stabilization in psychosis. In his earlier work Lacan indicated that conventional identification and the elaboration of a delusional metaphor might create stability. What his discussion of Lola Valerie Stein adds is that stability can be obtained by cultivating an *a-subjective position* in social relations.

Sketched briefly, *The Ravishing of Lol Stein* brings the story of Lola Valerie Stein, told from the perspective of Jacques Hold. Jacques Hold is in love with Lol, and near the end of the book they have an affair, which unhappily provokes an episode of mental confusion in Lol, with paranoid thoughts and experiences of depersonalization. The book is a journalist-like account, in which Jacques Hold reconstructs the events that eventually lead to Lol's breakdown and reflects upon her psychological and relational functioning before the crisis. In this context, Lol's alliance with her friend Tatiana Karl is discussed; an abruptly ended romantic relationship is reviewed; details about the relationship with her mother and her marriage are described; and Lol's attitude towards Jacques Hold's affair with Tatiana Karl is considered.

As he examines the novel Lacan takes the final phase of the book where 'Lol starts being mad'[30] (Lacan, 1965, p. 195) as his central reference, and wonders what it is that first protected her against this madness. The answer he comes up with is that in earlier phases of the book Lola Valerie Stein found protection in situations that enabled her to 'be with three'[31] (Lacan, 1965, p. 195). Situations in which two other persons are involved, and in which she, as a third, is not expected to play an active role in relation to desire, help her tie together reality. Dual situations, by contrast, in which she is personally faced with a desirous Other brutally confront her with what Lacan (1965, p. 195) calls 'her emptiness',[32] and destabilize her completely. In his homage to Duras, Lacan (1965) did not elaborate the topic of emptiness, but in his Seminar (Lacan, 1964–5) he did. There he argues that *Lol's being is not adequately named.* Her being does not transcend signified existence, where she could fully participate in Symbolic relationships. For that reason, Lol is an a-subjective character, who remains an outsider to the circuit of desire in which the other characters are engaged. This lack of anchoring in the Symbolic is expressed in both Lol's use of discourse, where it seems that she often finds no words to articulate her own identity, and in her absent-minded contact with others. Lacan (1965, p. 191) calls her 'a wounded figure, exiled from things'.[33] While others connect, Lol is ravished from the scene. She drifts along the surface of human interaction.

For instance, this a-subjective position comes to the fore early in the novel, which starts with details of Lola Valerie Stein's teenage years. At a party the seemingly smooth engagement with her fiancé Michael Richardson abruptly comes to an end: a beautiful woman, Anne-Marie

Stretter, enters the scene ostentatiously, and Michael Richardson falls in love with this woman. He starts dancing with Anne-Marie Stretter, and all of a sudden loses interest in Lol. Lol's reaction to this event is *a-subjective* in that she doesn't take a position as a desiring individual: she is fascinated by the situation – not scandalized, jealous or happy to finally be rid of him, which are all reactions we would expect in a case of neurosis. From a distance Lol merely stares at the couple. A subjective reaction, by contrast, is displayed by Lol's mother, who arrives when the party comes to an end. When she sees what has happened to her daughter she is furious. At a certain moment she lays her hand on Lol. Lol can't stand this physical touch and passes to the act, knocking her mother down. The spell of fascination is broken and Lol collapses.

In his discussion of the incident at the party, Lacan doesn't empha-size Lol's failure to signify her existence, but indicates that by occupying the a-subjective position, and becoming totally absorbed in her fascina-tion with the dancing couple, Lol copes with the desiring relation that unfolds between her fiancé and Anne-Marie Stretter. By being the mere *observer*, Lol positions herself as an a-subjective observer in relation to the desiring couple, and gains a feeling of being: 'this [Lol's] being is never really specified, personified, presentified in her novel, in so far as she only exists in the form of this core object, this object *a* of something that exists as a gaze, but which is a gaze, a scattered gaze, a gaze-object, a gaze that we repeatedly see'[34] (Lacan, 1964–5, session 24 June). Indeed, Lol's a-subjective position as observer is functional: it helps her deal with social situations and avoid the position of the object *a* in relation to a ferocious Other. By observing others and by explicitly positioning her-self as the 'excluded third' (Lacan, 1965, p. 196) she avoids being the passive object of the gaze. With her outrageous reaction, by contrast, Lol's mother destroys this a-subjective position vis-à-vis the desiring couple and creates a dual situation. Out of great concern, she actively addresses Lol, expresses her wish that the scene at the party hadn't taken place and physically touches her. Lol can't cope with this direct appeal by her mother, which urges Lol to manifest herself as a subject, and attacks her mother.

Another triangular situation, which Lol actively organized, consists of her relationship with Jacques Hold, the narrator of the story, and Tatiana Karl, 'her best friend during her school years' (Duras, 1964, p. 1). Jacques Hold is fond of Lola Valerie Stein, but has an affair with Tatiana. Lol sup-ports this affair and puts herself in the position of observer, where she watches love scenes between them. Lacan views this situation as subjec-tively interesting for Lol, and claims that 'a knot is made again there'[35] (Lacan, 1965, p. 192). Indeed, by occupying the a-subjective position of observer Lol revives from her lifeless marriage. However, this triangular situation does not last, and ends up in a dual relationship when Jacques Hold falls in love with Lol. He seduces her, they plan to make love, yet at the moment Hold undresses Lol she literally goes mad. She suddenly thinks the police are in the building and that people are being beaten on the stairway, and starts to refer to herself as Tatiana Karl and Lol Stein at the same time. The direct confrontation with Hold's desire is a situation she cannot cope with.

What is most notable about these triangular situations is that *each time three jouissance-related positions are differentiated*, attributed to different people. The three positions involved are: a desiring subject, the image of a desired object and an excluded third who merely observes the situation. In the triangular scenes described, Michael Richardson and Jacques Hold are desiring subjects, while Anne-Marie Stretter and Tatiana Karl are desired objects. These women are not described in psychological terms, but in terms of images and appearances: the shape of their bodies being most significant. In each of the triangular situations Lol occupies the position of observer, looking at how a man is affected and excited by the body of a woman. In this context, Lacan (1965, p. 195) states that Lol 'is not the one who sees', or the 'voyeur',[36] meaning that the image that is created by looking at the couple doesn't affect her as a subject; the *perceptum* of her friends making love has no effect on Lol as a *percipiens*. On the contrary, 'That which happens realizes her', argues Lacan (1965, p. 195). In my interpretation this means that Lol gains consistency in the act of observing itself.

Characteristically, within these triangular situations sexuality obtains bearable proportions. An example of how this works for Lol is the situation in which Jacques Hold seduces Tatiana Karl and takes her to a hotel, while Lol waits outside and watches how Jacques Hold undresses her. This scene doesn't provoke subjective reactions in Lol. She simply stares at how a man goes into raptures over the body of another woman. It seems that by excluding her own physical being from sexually charged situations, Lol finds a place where she feels safe. The observed sexual seduction had nothing to do with the image of her own body. It appears that by evading physical interaction with a man who is attracted to the female body, Lol feels at ease and maintains a feeling of identity. Obviously abstinence guarantees that she is not overwhelmed by *jouissance*: the a-subjective position as observer protects her from being the object of *jouissance* of the Other. At the same time her position qua gaze seems to provide her with a surplus *jouissance*, and a bearable level of sexual excitation. Through her a-subjective position Lol delimits her own being and creates an experience of consistency.

The scene at the end of the book, where Lol goes insane, is different from these triangular situations in that there she occupies the position of observer as well as the position of the desired object. Whereas in the triangular situations both positions are distinguished, they converge at the moment Jacques Hold undresses Lol. Although Lol didn't object to what was happening at first, Hold's physical touch proved to be overwhelming. The sexual excitation emanating from Hold's desirous position devastated her consistency and she lost grip of reality. What then comes to the fore is a paranoid position, in which Lol is the object of an overwhelming jouissance that no longer has anything to do with Jacques Hold as a person.

While in neurosis holding on to the position of observer can also be identified, neurotic reactions clearly differ from Lol's position as an excluded third in that they always reflect a subjective position in relation to desire. For example throughout the case study of Dora, a young woman diagnosed as hysteric, Freud (1905) describes her as an active observer of the woman her father was having an affair with. She monitors her father's mistress, not only concerned with the issue of what it is that makes a woman feminine and desirable in relation to a man, but also with the aim of discovering how she herself should behave as a woman (Verhaeghe, 1999). This is quite different from Lol's a-subjective position.

What is innovative about Lacan's discussion of this fictional case is that it bears witness of a positive view of the object *a* in psychosis. Although the story does not have a happy ending, it shows that Lola Valerie Stein's position as observer doesn't necessarily exclude her from social bonds. As long as desiring others do not come too close and she can maintain her abstinent position, she is not a victim of the non-instalment of a belief in the Other as a reference for making sense of desire. Lol's abstinent sexual attitude is a sublime coping mechanism by means of which she keeps the pressure emanating from desiring others at bay and prevents herself from being the object of jouissance of a cruel Other. The only problem is that she did not remain faithful to this non-physical sexual attitude, which suited her so well.

Conclusion

To conclude, the shift Lacan makes in his work from the 1960s can be described as double. On the one hand the Name-of-the-Father is redefined, such that the idea of foreclosure no longer concerns the material lack of a signifier, but a non-instalment of a belief in the Other as guarantee. On the other hand the object *a* and jouissance are introduced as concepts that address the dimension of being that fails to be named via the signifier. Lacan stresses that in psychosis the jouissance represented by the object *a* is an overwhelming force, clear manifestations of which are observed in daily life. He argues that instead of suffering from a personal lack of enjoyment, which is the case in neurosis, the subject in psychosis suffers from being overwhelmed by a strange jouissance. While in neurosis the object *a* is externalized and attributed to the Other, it is not extracted from the subject in psychosis. Together with the differential status of the unconscious, which is experienced as internal in neurosis and external in psychosis, the object *a* is henceforth the main criterion for differentiating between both structures.

Interestingly, Lacan's reflections on the non-extracted object *a* bring him to make differentiations between different clinical structures within the broader domain of psychosis. Paranoia and schizophrenia are thereby described as two different modes of relating to a non-extracted object *a*. Yet, as many Lacanian scholars have indicated, further differentiations between clinical structures can be added to these.[37] However, as the case of Lola Valerie Stein makes clear, the non-separation of the objectal dimension does not necessarily imply that psychosis is pathological. Within the structure of psychosis, normality or mental stability is just as achievable as it is in neurosis.

What I find most interesting about Lacan's focus on the object *a*, and his redefinition of the Name-of-the-Father in terms of an act of faith, is that it enables us to break with a deficit model of psychosis. Lacan's first theory of foreclosure implied that, at the level of the Name-of-the-Father, psychosis fails whereas neurosis succeeds. The idea of the extraction versus non-extraction of the object *a*, and of the instalment or non-instalment of a belief in the Other as guarantee, by contrast, does not focus on failure, but on diversity: extraction/belief and non-extraction/non-instalment of belief are two positions for the object and the subject, and nothing more. Importantly, Lacan's discussion of Duras's story of Lola Valerie Stein even takes a positive view on the a-subjective dimension in psychosis: it shows that, conditional upon the cultivation of bodily restrictions, such as sexual abstinence in Lol's case, the individual is not duped by the non-extraction of the object *a*. Without cultivating a romanticized image of psychosis, it could even be argued that the non-separation of the objectal dimension also has its advantages, in the sense that as long as Lol holds on to triangular situations she remains free from the desire-related problems from which her associates seem to suffer. In terms of Lévi-Strauss's (1962) book *La Pensée*

Sauvage, and Miller's (2004b) work *L'Invention Psychotique,* on invention in psychosis, it could be argued that the triangular situations Lol
creates bear witness of an individual solution in the field of the social.
By removing herself from desire-laden situations, she invents a singular
way of dealing with others. Lol's solution is singular in that it is not
based on ideas she has acquired. Fixed ideas of how she should position
herself in social situations simply don't work, and even prove to have
a counterproductive effect. It is only by cultivating her own triangular
logic in the private situations of life that Lola Valerie Stein finds a *modus
vivendi* that suits her.

Part IV
Fourth Era: The Age of the Knot

7
Psychosis within the Logic of Knotting and Linking

The logic of connection

From Seminars XIX (1971–2) and XX (1972–3) a remarkable change can be discerned in how Lacan conceptualizes the relationship between the registers of the Real, the Symbolic and the Imaginary. Whereas in his earlier work a *dialectical logic* on the relation between these registers was predominant, in the 1970s Lacan begins to discuss this relationship within a *triangular or three-dimensional logic*. He henceforth aims to conceptualize how the Real, the Symbolic and the Imaginary mutually connect.

In his earlier dialectical approach, two registers were each time opposed to one another, the Symbolic being the main point of reflection on human functioning. During the 1950s, Lacan was mainly interested in the relationship between the Imaginary and the Symbolic, where he assumed that the actual meaning and content of mental representations should not be the main focus of attention. What is important is the interplay between signifiers and the way reality is constructed according to the law. Guided by the idea of a foreclosure of the Name-of-the-Father, psychosis was understood in terms of the absence of the crucial signifier that embodied the law. As a result of foreclosure, phallic meaning is not generated in the dialectical tension between the Imaginary and the Symbolic, and thus questions concerning identity and personal existence that operate at the level of the unconscious do not give rise to an articulation of the subject in terms of desire. Instead, such questions overwhelm the subject from without via hallucinations and elementary phenomena.

In the 1960s the dialectical tension between the Real and the Symbolic came to hold a prominent place for Lacan. Still starting from a primacy of the Symbolic, his interest concerns the way in which speech transforms corporeal jouissance, and the question of how the object *a* takes shape in the dialectics between the Real and the Symbolic. The object *a* represents both the impact and the powerlessness of language in relation to the drive. At this time psychosis was still studied in terms of the foreclosure of a signifier, but instead of being thought of as an inherently unique signifier, the Name-of-the-Father was conceptualized as a uniquely used signifier. In psychosis the object *a* is not separated from the subject, nor is it integrated in the ego or in the subject: as a mere element of strangeness, the object *a* is manifested in reality.

In the 1970s, this dialectical view on the relation between the Real, the Symbolic and the Imaginary is replaced by an approach that focuses on the *intermingling* and *connection* between the three registers. At the basis of this change, Lacan's view on the functioning of language shifts somewhat. Before the 1970s Lacan was guided by the Hegelian belief that 'the word is the murder of the thing' (Lacan, 1956c; Miller, 2002a) and that the signifier brings structure to jouissance by introducing it to the Symbolic. At this point he makes a conjunction between both, which brings him to define 'a jouissance of the signifier' (Miller, 2007c, p. 72). Crucial concepts Lacan uses to illustrate jouissance in speech are '*lalangue*' and '*parlêtre*'. These French neologisms are often left untranslated, but could be translated as 'llanguage' (Lacan, 1972–3) or 'thetongue' and 'speakingbeing', respectively. Through these concepts Lacan stresses the libidinous aspect of language. In his work prior to the 1970s, Lacan saw the signifier as a differential element through which the subject and the world are represented. What he subsequently adds is that, apart from the meaning they entail, signifiers are also laden with the drive. To speak, even when there is nothing to say, or to remain silent, even when something should be said, implies a jouissance that cannot be elucidated via structuralist theories. Hence Lacan turned to a new set of constructs that allow him to trace a mode of drive gratification that has nothing to do with the message speech conveys, but with the *act* of enunciation itself. Taking both aspects of speech together, in Seminar XX Lacan (1972–3) suggests that each signifier carries both structure and drive: On the one hand a signifier is nothing but 'a difference from another signifier', on the other hand it is a sign of jouissance (Lacan, 1972–3, p. 142); a sign that refers to the speaker's being.

By introducing the concept 'llanguage' or 'thetongue' Lacan indicates that, apart from its inherent structure, language has a radical non-signified or private quality. This is expressed in the phonetic and echolalic aspects of speech (Lacan, 1971–2, session 9 February 1972, 1972–3, pp. 101, 138–9). These characteristics bear witness of a *jouissance that is internal to language use*, and have nothing to do with lexicalization, signification or grammar. The moment a person speaks, signifiers function as carriers of jouissance that had previously operated only at a corporeal level for the subject. In other words, while jouissance cannot be adequately represented via language, it finds expression in the process of *enunciation itself*. Through enunciation, jouissance is connected to signifiers. There might be other ways for interpreting this idea, but in my understanding this principally implies that words should not be thought of a neutral logical signs, but as bodily invested elements. The words we use are not just communicative carriers of messages. They also embody a jouissance or an affective value we, as speakers, don't fully grasp. Signifying articulation drains jouissance from the body and connects jouissance to the signifier, which is why words play a vital role in regulating corporeal arousal. Lacan (1972–3, p. 139) therefore suggests that llanguage is the basis of our affective experience, and provides a basic feeling of being (Lacan, 1971–2, session 8 March 1972). To emphasize the role of signifying articulation he even argued that llanguage is as vital as an organ, without which human life would not be possible (Lacan, 1972b). Note that at this level, Lacanian theory on the jouissance that is internal to language use has some parallels with contemporary works on embodied language (Vivona, 2009), which implies that a critical comparison between both perspectives would be worthwhile.

In terms of Lacan's (1969–70, p. 56) distinction between the oral, anal, scopic and invocative object *a*, I suggest qualifying the form of jouissance that is at stake in llanguage as *vocal*. What comes to the fore in llanguage is a *vocalization* that demonstrates how the drive manifests in the individual. This drive expression has no explicit communicative value at the level of the message; however, this does not mean that llanguage has no communicative effect. Llanguage bears witness of how the subject meets the limits of communication via signifying chains. It refers to the jouissance attached to the signifier that cannot be transposed into a signified.

Lacan (1976d) argued that in each person, jouissance is not distributed evenly across the signifying chain. Certain signifiers are charged with jouissance and make up a kind of private idiom that manifests in productions of the unconscious: 'The unconscious is the fact that being, by speaking, enjoys' (Lacan, 1972–3, pp. 104–5). Dreams, lapses, jokes, symptoms and elementary phenomena convey signifiers that repetitively turn up in speech, and that obviously have a special significance for a person. These signifiers make up a set of senseless repetitive elements through which jouissance incessantly takes shape. In this respect Lacan (1976d) characterized the human being as a 'speakingbeing' to the extent that he/she articulates his/her private llanguage.

Compared with his previous work, these ideas on language qua llanguage and the human being qua speakingbeing reflect an important shift. Whereas previously Lacan considered language as a tool in the construction of identity, aiding the subject to grow to full stature, his later view is less romantic and stresses that, apart from any communicatory value, signifiers possess the speaker. Signifiers cannot simply be grasped in terms of the constitution of the subject, but bear witness to a senseless repetition, the precise nature of which can only be studied at the level of the singular. In this respect the psychoanalytic study of llanguage differs from the classic linguistic study of language. Linguistics looks at universalities and particularities in speech. Psychoanalysis, by contrast, takes into consideration the unconscious and therefore studies singularities. In this respect, each individual's speech reflects a highly personal relation to language, which is expressed in productions of the unconscious.

What is interesting about the concepts of llanguage and speaking-being is that they express the fundamental intermingling between the Symbolic and the Real. The Symbolic and the Real are no longer seen as antagonists, but as registers that are inextricably bound up with each other. Moreover, this binding between registers is seen as non-hierarchical. Contrary to previous phases of Lacan's work, in the 1970s special organizing qualities are no longer attributed to the Symbolic register. What organizes subjectivity is the actual link or interplay between the three registers, and not any one register in particular. This implies that Lacan actually dethroned the Symbolic in the later phase of his theory (Voruz and Wolf, 2007).

Towards mathematical formalization with knots and links

To conceptualize the triangular connection between the Real, the Symbolic and the Imaginary, from Seminar XX [1] onwards Lacan (1972–3) makes use of knot theory, a branch of topology that studies the spatial composition of knots (Adams, 2002). Lacan was familiarized with knot theory in the early 1970s through his association with a number of young French mathematicians, such as Thierry Soury and

Michel Thomé (Roudinesco, 1994). In Seminar XXIII on The Sinthome (1975–6), he gave a detailed explication of mathematical knot theory and its relevance for psychoanalytic theory. With knot theory he found a means of conceptualizing non-hierarchical links between these three elements. This constituted a new framework including axioms and rules whereby the relation between the Real, the Symbolic and the Imaginary, which he abbreviates as R, S and I, respectively, could be elucidated.

The choice of knot theory was as surprising for his students as it was for his contemporaries (Roudinesco, 1994): nobody before had used this branch of topology to facilitate reflection on the structure of human subjectivity. However, when one examines the trajectory of Lacan's work this progression makes sense. General mathematical theory, such as algebra and projective geometry, was a frame of reference that he had been using long before his interest in topological knot theory. Starting from his notion of the matheme, Lacan believed that the rigour of mathematics guaranteed a scientific exactitude that escapes common languages, and thus made frequent use of arithmetical terminology in an attempt to define more precisely basic psychoanalytical concepts. His subsequent interest in knot theory emerged largely because algebra had reached the limit of its usefulness for him at this point in his work (Lacan, 1975–6, p. 42). In his view, knot theory allows us to depict and 'write' the logic of relationships that cannot be comprehended without the support of a formal notation. It provided him with 'a model of mathematical formalization' (Lacan, 1972–3, p. 130) that enables us to reflect on subjectivity in three-dimensional terms (Lacan, 1975–6, pp. 28, 62). Moreover, knot theory offers a geometrical approach to concepts that enables one to bypass the Imaginary. For Lacan, mankind, with its inclination to two-dimensional reflection, is alienated to the Imaginary; one 'reflects' by building mental images. A problem with this kind of imaginary reflection is that it tends to frame complex problems in terms of univocal conclusions, which is always reductionist. Using knot theory, by contrast, acts like a barrier against the Imaginary, and helps us take into account the complexity of the relations between R, S and I. It provides us with 'a geometry of which one can say that the imaginary has no access to it'[2] (Lacan, 1975–6, p. 31). Moreover, Lacan explicitly thought of *knot theory* as a *formal language*, which in my interpretation led him to insist that knotting is not simply a metaphor. With this so-called formal language, Lacan aimed to illustrate how the three registers R, S and I could be linked in spatial terms. In this respect, he never had any ambition to derive numerical interpretations from knots, but solely used them in formal logical terms as a way for making his thinking about the three registers more rigorous.

Lacan stuck to the basics of the discipline and limited his reflections to simple knots and links. Next to the trivial knot or unknot, which can be represented as a closed loop without an entanglement contained within (Adams, 2002), he principally made use of the trefoil knot and of the Borromean rings. The trefoil knot (Figure 7.1) is one of the simplest of the non-trivial knots, and can be obtained by joining the loose ends of an overhand knot.

Figure 7.1   Trefoil knot

Contrary to Lacan's first discussion of knot theory (1972–3), the Borromean rings (Figure 7.2) cannot be qualified as a knot, but as a link, a point that he later affirmed (e.g. Lacan, 1975–6, p. 64). A link is obtained by entangling two or more knots. The simplest type of link is the so-called Hopf link, which consists of two rings that are linked precisely once (Adams, 2002). The Borromean rings, in their turn, consist of three mutually interlocked trivial knots, in which rings are linked because of their specific composition: ring B lies on top of ring A; ring C lies on top of ring B; but ring C lies under ring A. Removing any one ring will result in the disconnection of the other two rings (Adams, 2002; Soury, 1982). Conventionally, the Borromean rings are represented in three colours: red, green and blue, whereby each colour represents

Figure 7.2   Borromean rings

a dimension in three-dimensional space. The colouring of knots is most useful when knots are drawn or projected in two-dimensional space. Lacan made use of such colouring with the aim of differentiating between the three registers: the Real is represented by a blue ring, the Imaginary by a green ring and the Symbolic by a red ring (Lacan, 1975–6, pp. 52, 111, 116).

The central question Lacan was working with as he used knot theory is how the three rings are bound inextricably together, such that the triad becomes *a systemic whole that is more than just the sum of the parts*. The two main problems he aimed to address are how jouissance is organized by bringing R, S and I together: 'That which is written – what would that be in the end? The conditions of jouissance' (Lacan, 1972–3, p. 131); and how a basis is created for the articulation of the subject. In the 1970s Lacan clearly held on to his idea that 'the subject is that which a signifier represents in relation to another signifier' [3] (Lacan, 1975–6, p. 23). He then adds that what supports the subject is not an anchor point in the Symbolic, but the connection between the three rings. The link between the Real, the Symbolic and the Imaginary provides the conditions for a subject to appear (Lacan, 1975–6, pp. 50–3; Skriabine, 2004).

RSI

As he studied the triangular interconnection between R, S and I, Lacan partly redefined these registers. He stopped thinking of them as separate entities, and no longer considered their relation in dialectical terms: R versus S; S versus I; I versus R. He henceforth focused on their systemic connection whereby each register has a profound impact on the two others, making a so-called 'real gap' in their relationship (Lacan, 1975–6, pp. 24–5, 82–3, 117–18). [4] Consequently, the impact each register has in its link with the other registers is prioritized. Lacan argues that in the Borromean link between R, S and I, I constitutes consistency, while S constitutes a gap, and R constitutes ex-sistence: 'The fundamental character of this use of the knot is illustrating the three-fold nature resulting from a consistency that is only affected by the Imaginary, a fundamental gap that is related to the Symbolic, and an ex-sistence that belongs to the Real, and that is even its fundamental character' [5] (Lacan, 1975–6, p. 36; see also pp. 50, 56).

In Lacan's view, the main characteristic the Symbolic contributes to the link with R and I is that it constitutes a gap. For Lacan the Symbolic primarily creates gaps in the Real; language, so to speak, empties out the Real; 'language eats the Real' [6] (Lacan, 1975–6, p. 31). Language allows us to discern sense in the world, making the unforeseeable predictable. This is why language is efficacious (Lacan, 1975–6, p. 32). Yet, in the logic of the Borromean rings the effect of S on R cannot be separated from the effect of I. It is only because the green circle (I) defines an area in the blue circle (R), that the red circle (S) can create a void in the blue circle of the Real. This means that language effectuates a gap only due to the Imaginary tendency to build consistent images on the nature of the Real. However, as Lacan's concept of llanguage makes clear, the effect of the Symbolic on the Real is bidirectional: Language not only structures the Real, the Real also affects the Symbolic. Indeed, language is not only a communicative tool by means of which we structure the world; language is also affected by a Real jouissance it cannot grasp and can only be experienced as senseless in the light of the Imaginary search for meaning.

The characteristic that Lacan attributes to the register of the Real is 'ex-sistence'. In his earlier work Lacan used the concept ex-sistence to refer to a body of eccentricity within the subject, i.e. the unconscious (Lacan, 1957a) and the drive (Lacan, 1961). In the 1970s the Real is qualified as ex-sistent, thereby emphasizing an aspect of human experience that falls apart from the signifier and is not accessible by means of mental images. Indeed, a characteristic of the Real is that it delineates a gap or limit at the level of meaning or sense, which is defined by the intersection between S and I. The Real sets a limit to how meaning can be conceptualized; sense must always be approached with the notion of senselessness in mind. Similar to the Imaginary, the register of the Real can only be conceptualized in terms of its relation with S and I: 'The Real only exists through the limitation it meets in the Symbolic and the Imaginary' [7] (Lacan, 1975–6, p. 50). It is therefore qualified as what we cannot get hold of, or that which cannot be written: 'There is no other possible definition of the Real than this: it's the impossible' [8] (Lacan, 1976e, pp. 55–6).

Consistency is the characteristic that the Imaginary contributes in the linking of the Borromean rings: 'It's in the Imaginary that I locate the support of what is consistency' [9] (Lacan, 1975–6, p. 50). In Lacan's view, the Imaginary allows the individual to have a stable representation of the world (Lacan, 1976e). If, for example, our knowledge was exclusively built on S, it would consist of only an abstract series of symbols that function to grasp how R is organized, but carry no meaning. Obviously this is not how people function. On the contrary, we approach our environment in pursuit of recurrent patterns of meaning. In line with the first era of his work, in which he accentuated the imaginary basis of the self-image, Lacan believes that this natural inclination towards images, appearances and unity is rooted in our experience of the body image. Man experiences the world 'just like this unity of pure form that the body represents for him' [10] (Lacan, 1976e, p. 54). Lacan (1975–6, 1976e) states that, in our self-experience, we approach the body as a kind of sphere; we perceive it as a closed unity that fascinates us. Its beauty provokes our admiration, and conversely we are filled with unease the moment we are confronted with disability or mutilation. Similarly, the notion of harmony in the world fills us with pleasure, while the experience of unexpected or unusual events provokes unease.

The knotting of RSI

In his discussion of the Borromean link between R, S and I, Lacan suggested that in the process of connecting the three rings, something is knotted. Indeed, because the registers R, S and I are connected an additional dimension is created, which Lacan calls *psychical reality* or the *symptom* and represents as a knot in the Borromean link (Lacan, 1974–5, session 11 February 1975, 1975–6, p. 19, 1976e, p. 56). By knotting R, S and I mental life is organized, such that in the experience of reality constancy can be perceived. Knotting creates orderly relationships between the registers, resulting in the subject's belief that the images (I) built around events and incidents (R) follow a certain logic (S).

Lacan did not use the Borromean rings simply as a metaphor, but as a formal language that could function to support theoretical reflection. Moreover, he suggested that the knot created in the Borromean rings can be deduced topologically. I believe this is why he referred to the Borromean rings with the neologism 'linkknot' [11] (Lacan, 1975–6, pp. 86, 111), stating that the Borromean rings 'naturally engender the trefoil knot' [12] (Lacan, 1975–6, p. 86). While Lacan did not really explain this idea during his seminar, from a topological perspective a trefoil knot can be deduced from the Borromean link. This is illustrated in Figure 7.3.

When a trefoil knot is projected onto a Borromean link, such that the four planes of the trefoil knot overlap with the intersections of the Borromean rings, we can see what Lacan probably intended: the central part of the Borromean link, which is composed by the crossing of two circles in the field of a third, follows the exact pattern of a trefoil knot. All of the understrands and overstrands that can be observed in the trefoil knot can also be seen in the Borromean link intersections between R and S in I, S and I in R and I and R in S. In the Borromean linking of the three rings, the intersections between R, S and I are stretched and

Figure 7.3   Trefoil knot deduced from the Borromean rings

fixed. Along this way a trefoil knot is created in the structure of the link itself.

What is important about this idea of the implicit trefoil knot is that the Borromean link can now be seen to have a fourfold structure (Lacan, 1975–6, p. 19): 'I argue that one has to consider that which makes up the Borromean link as fourfold . . . advancing the enigmatic link between the Imaginary, the Symbolic and the Real implies or supposes the ex-sistence of the symptom'. [13] In other words, the trefoil knot is the binding element through which stability is created in the link. The trefoil knot is the quality that is inherent to the systemic connection between R, S and I in the Borromean link.

Conceptually, Lacan qualifies the implicit trefoil knot as both *symptom* and *psychical reality*. Symptoms are not pathological elements from which the subject should be freed in order to be happy. No matter how irrational, symptoms function to tie R, S and I together; they prop up the subject's experience of reality, supporting his belief in his existence in the world. In my interpretation of Lacan's later works, this implies that symptoms have a systemic function. In this respect psychoanalytic treatment does not merely seek to remove symptoms, but to investigate how people can create an alternative way of knotting R, S and I that causes less suffering.

Parallel to this notion of the systemic function of symptoms, Lacan questioned conventional modes of how the experience of reality is conceptualized. He argues that our common experience of reality includes an aspect of madness we typically tend to neglect. People ordinarily experience life, human relationships and the world as meaningful, or at least expect them to be so. We commonly take the truthfulness of our mental representations for granted, and even the most sceptical amongst us tend to believe in the value of thought. Such beliefs are 'functional' in that they help people live their lives, but in Lacan's view they are also inherently 'mad' (1976d, p. 49); the only fundament of our belief in the world is an act of faith, which carries no truth value what-soever. In clinical contexts this viewpoint on the common madness of man implies that we should be careful not to allow our preconceived ideas about normality and deviance function as a standard for judg-ing patients. Both in diagnosis and treatment, the peculiarities of an individual's functioning should be explored and the systemic value of symptoms should be attended to.

From the Name-of-the-Father to knotting

In Seminar XXIII, Lacan (1975–6) also used his idea of the symptom and the implicit knot in the Borromean rings as a point of reflection on the Name-of-the-Father, which he began to consider as a typical neurotic symptom. The Name-of-the-Father is no longer seen as the privileged symbolic element that sets the paternal metaphor in motion, but as one possible mode of connecting R, S and I (Svolos, 2009). In this view the Name-of-the-Father is not the sine qua non for obtaining coherent psychical reality, but just one option for linking R, S and I. Prior to the 1970s this was not the case, and the Name-of-the-Father was seen as a crucial element in the Symbolic register. This line of reasoning gave rise to a *differential diagnostic classification*: either the Name-of-the-Father is installed, or not installed, which leads to neurosis or psychosis, respec-tively. With his focus on the knot in the relation between R, S and I, this viewpoint changes. Henceforth the Name-of-the-Father is no longer seen as a unique signifier but as a mode of knotting, and belief in the father function is just one manner of knotting the three registers.

In neurotic discourse the individual typically interprets his position in the world in terms of past events and tensions in the family: 'We see, like Freud said to us, that people irresistibly talk to us about their mama and their papa . . . they are always referring to something that they essen-tially associate to the way in which they have been raised by their family' [14] (Lacan, 1976a, p. 12). What is pivotal to neurotic discourse is a historical narrative about the family, in which the structure of the Oedipal myth can be recognized. In Lacan's (1975–6, 1976b, 1976c, 1976d) view an analyst's task consists of alleviating the hold of this nar-rative. Hence his idea that psychoanalysis, 'when it succeeds, proves that one can do without the Name-of-the-Father under the condition that one uses it' (Lacan, 1975–6, p. 136; Rabaté, 2001, p. 178). This means that the analyst should not validate the master position the analysant typically attributes to the analyst, in part by playing with the ambigu-ity and homophony of the signifier such that the analysant's tendency to define him/herself in terms of rigid Oedipal signifieds diminishes (Miller, 2007d).

In terms of the link between R, S and I, the neurotic belief in the father function can be equated with the trefoil knot that is inherent in the Borromean rings. At least this is what I conclude from the following statement, in which the term 'bo knot' refers to the knot implied in the Borromean rings: 'The father-version is the inevitable consequence of the fact that Freud gives all due to the father function; and that is the bo knot' [15] (Lacan, 1975–6, p. 150). In this line of reasoning, belief in the father figure is equated with the trefoil knot that is implicit in the three rings when they are connected along the standard of the Borromean link: in the Borromean link stable relations between the registers R, S and I are obtained by following the standard topological pattern; in neurosis psychical reality takes shape by adopting the Oedipal norm.

However, in Lacan's line of reasoning the Borromean linking of R, S and I should *not* be the theoretical standard for psychoanalysts in their clinical approach, but considered as an exception. His position in this context is quite extreme, arguing that in clinical practice the rings relate in a non-Borromean way in the majority of cases: 'In most cases the Symbolic, the Imaginary, and the Real are tangled, such that they melt into one another, and this due to the absence of the operation that distinguishes them like in the link of the Borromean knot' [16] (Lacan, 1975–6, p. 87). This implies that in his view from the 1970s, clinical practice cannot be framed in terms of a neurotic logic alone. Neurosis is not the standard, but an exception in relation to what he considers as more common, that is, a mode of subjectivity in which the Name-of-the-Father does not play a centrally organizing role, meaning psychosis (Lacan, 1975–6, 1976a). In making this claim Lacan evidently starts from a broad definition of psychosis (Gueguen, 2004; Miller, 1993; Soler, 2008), considering it as a circumstance in which the Oedipal narrative is not functioning in the articulation of the subject. In terms of Anglo-Saxon psychoanalytic theories, so-called self-pathology, i.e. problems ranging from schizoid pathology to subjective emptiness, that don't reflect Oedipally structured neurotic concerns (Kirshner, 2004) also seem to be covered by Lacan's renewed interpretation. [17]

However, what is particularly important about Lacan's late view on psychosis is that it points to a position in discourse that is character- ized by occupying a solitary position in relation to jouissance. What stands to the fore in psychosis is social detachment and profound diffi- culty regulating jouissance via common discourses or discourse derived from interaction with Others. In other words, the Name-of-the-Father is lacking and jouissance is not regulated through the standard knotting of R, S and I. This implies that inventing alternative modes of knotting R, S and I is a prerequisite for subjective consistency. Psychosis confronts a person with the challenge of actively searching for and clinging to conditions that make life liveable. In this context elementary phenomena bear witness of unregulated jouissance and the need to find new solutions for connecting R, S and I (Gueguen, 2004).

This expansion of the psychosis concept created quite some controversy among Lacan's students and colleagues, and functioned as a divisive element in the Lacanian movement (Roudinesco, 1994). The fact that Lacan described himself as psychotic, or at least as someone who tried to be so, added to this storm. In a lecture at Yale University he said the following: 'Psychosis is an attempt at rigor. In that sense, I would say that I am psychotic. I am psychotic for the sole reason that I always tried to be rigorous' [18] (Lacan, 1976a, p. 9). The audience was shocked by this statement (see: Lacan, 1976a, p. 29). Later on, a student returned to this and asked Lacan whether he was actually psychotic. His answer then was that he was not psychotic enough: 'If I were more psychotic, I would probably be a better analyst' [19] (Lacan, 1977, p. 13). For some, such remarks indicate that in his later work Lacan was either losing his footing or simply trying to fool his audience. I see it as a paradoxical or surrealist intervention aimed to negate the master position attributed to him in order to provoke critical reflection on what it is that makes up psychosis.

In my view, Lacan's expansion of the psychosis concept and his reference to himself as psychotic should be read as an appeal to stop thinking about psychosis and neurosis in terms of *two categorically distinct conditions*. What is pivotal in Lacan's later use of the terms neurosis and psychosis [20] is that they merely refer to different modes of connecting R, S and I, and not to strict nosological categories in which cases should be classified (Miller, 2002b). Neurosis and psychosis are not mutually exclusive classes, but possible modes of subjective functioning. In this view cases should be seen as complexities that cannot be classified univocally; the complexity we can discern in a human being's functioning always surpasses the explanatory power of theoretical classes. A theory of neurotic and psychotic functioning, by contrast, should be used as a means to reflect and intervene on what goes on at the level of the singular. It is a tool for considering the logic inherent to each person's functioning in terms of R, S and I.

In this respect I agree with Jacques-Alain Miller (2003, p. 12), who compares Lacan's earlier work with his later teaching, and states:

'Referring clinical practice to the knot undoubtedly gives us arrangements that are different but in continuity with one another. We have lost the security of the discontinuous and the clearly distinct, and the result is that the symptom, rather than what we called the clinical structure, which was a class, has become the elementary unit of clinical theory'. What is important in Lacan's later work is how R, S and I are knotted via a symptom. The logic of this knot can be considered in terms of neurosis and psychosis, and as work with a single person progresses, the particular logic presented must be ascertained. In this respect, Miller (1998) refers to the work of Lotfi A. Zadeh on fuzzy sets and systems, which provides an alternative to Aristotelian thinking in terms of dichotomous truth values (Zadeh and Kacprzyk, 1992). Whereas Lacan's earlier work on psychosis holds to the Aristotelian presumption that one is either a member of a class or not, his later reflections demonstrate that the boundary between neurosis and psychosis should be thought of as fluid and not categorical. This implies that, at a theoretical level, neurotic knotting cannot be strictly differentiated from psychotic knotting: nothing defines the neurotic use of the Name-of-the-Father as strictly distinct from a psychotic means of dealing with R, S and I. This viewpoint not only implies that the transition between both forms of knotting is fluid, but above all that no single criterion can be used for differentiating psychosis from neurosis. In the first two eras of Lacan's work, a search for an ultimate differential diagnostic criterion is implicitly present; first Lacan tried to define such a criterion in terms of a peculiar type of Imaginary identification, and subsequently he sought to describe it in terms of a peculiar type of language. In the 1970s, by contrast, this search for strict differential diagnostic criteria falls away and is replaced by reflection in terms of complexity. What then comes to the fore is that only by considering the *interplay* between diverse aspects of an individual's functioning in terms of R, S and I can a diagnosis be made. In this later approach, diagnostics is far removed from categorizing problems in terms of fixed criteria. What counts is the logic that is expressed in the complexity of a person's functioning. Such logic can only be discerned by attending to an individual's speech and behaviour, hence the importance attributed to the singular and to the ethics of Lacanian psychoanalysis.

This viewpoint has important clinical implications in that greater attention must be paid to the individual. As long as one starts from dichotomous diagnostic categories, clinical practice will focus on disorders, which leads to judgment on the particularities of these disorders. Psychosis and neurosis, or subcategories of these classes, are then considered in terms of fixed characteristics that require a special approach. The assumption of fuzzy boundaries, by contrast, implies a certain reserve vis-à-vis the application of disorder-specific knowledge. What is henceforth emphasized is case-specific reflection on how R, S and I are organized. Within this logic diagnosis and intervention cannot be thought of in categorical terms; they are attuned to the specific way in which the treatment of a patient takes shape.

Psychotic knotting and unknotting

Given the broad assumption that psychosis is defined by not using the Name-of-the-Father to connect R, S and I, two possibilities logically open up: either the rings that make up psychical reality are disconnected, or they are linked via a fourth ring.

The disconnection or unknotting of the rings is characterized by disintegration of mental life. In Seminar XX, Lacan (1972–3) describes this with reference to the interrupted sentences hallucinated by Schreber. These so-called code messages 'leave some sort of substance in abeyance' (Lacan, 1972–3, p. 128), meaning that the materiality of the signifier is lost. The concatenation of signifiers comes to a sudden halt, which in terms of the knot implies that the Symbolic loses its connection with the Imaginary: meaning is lost and the Real abruptly occupies the place opened up in the Symbolic. In the midst of the Symbolic, Schreber is confronted with a meaningless gap that is perplexing and can be closed only by completing the interrupted sentences. Completing the sentences is his way of obtaining consistency. In Seminar XXIII, Lacan (1975–6) further explored the idea of a disconnection between the rings and described psychosis as a situation for the subject in which R, S and I are not spontaneously linked. Commenting on his own doctoral thesis, he indicates that in paranoia the registers R, S and I are not clearly differentiated, but make up a continuity: 'Paranoid psychosis consists of this: the Imaginary, the Symbolic and the Real are one and have the same consistency' [21] (Lacan, 1975–6, p. 53). If R, S and I are not linked in a Borromean way an implicit fourth ring is not created. The rings spontaneously melt into one another and, as they are not clearly differentiated, it could be argued that they have the same consistency.

However, this starting point does not necessarily imply that the rings remain disconnected. Next to the neurotic knotting of R, S and I with the Name-of-the-Father, the rings can also be linked via an explicit fourth ring. Topologically speaking, to create an alternative connection between the rings, it suffices to put the three rings that represent R, S and I on top of each other, thus imitating the shape of a Borromean link, and to add a fourth ring at the crossing or crossings. Here the difference from the classic Borromean rings can be observed: the fourth ring is substantial and explicit, while in the Borromean link the fourth knot is implicit. Clinically speaking, this idea about the fourth ring in psychosis implies that Lacan believed it was possible to create a stable psychical reality even in the absence of the Name-of-the-Father. Nevertheless in order to create a stable platform for the articulation of the subject, a means of connecting the rings must be invented. To the extent that a person actually succeeds in being the artificer of such a fourth ring that connects the three others, psychical reality will be relatively stable and ordinary, and not dramatically deviant from neurotic reality. What is common to the implicit and explicit fourth knots is that they embody the principle of connection between the three other rings but only obtain this status because of their relation with the three other rings: 'It's always from three supports, which we will now call subjective, meaning personal, that a fourth one will receive footing' (Lacan, 1975–6, p. 52).[22]

In Seminar XXIII, Lacan (1975–6) qualifies the fourth ring not only as the symptom, but also as the 'sinthome', which he described as 'something that permits the Symbolic, the Imaginary and the Real to remain connected' [23] (Lacan, 1975–6, p. 94). 'Sinthome' is the more ancient spelling of 'symptom' (Lacan, 1975–6, 1982), and although Lacan switches between both terms the concept sinthome specifically refers to ways of dealing with jouissance that create stability in mental life. Whereas a symptom always has a signified that can be grasped in terms of metaphor and metonymy, this is not the case for the sinthome. The sinthome refers to a *savoir faire* that makes life endurable and provides a platform for the articulation of the subject. One reason why Lacan switches to the word sinthome is because it has interesting equivocal connotations. 'Sinthome' plays on the English word 'sin' and on the *French 'saint homme'*, which means 'saintly man', and refers to the person who does the right thing. In Lacan's (1975–6, p. 13, 1982) interpretation a sinthome unites both dimensions: on the one hand it refers to a person's 'sins' or frailties, and on the other hand it bears witness of a person's *savoir faire* in tying R, S and I together.

Joyce the sinthome

The pre-eminent case in which Lacan elaborated his ideas on the sinthome as an explicit fourth ring is James Joyce. In his reading, Joyce's psychical reality is not based on a belief in the Father or in convention, but rooted especially in the cultivation of his identity as a writer. Based on his literary activity, Joyce fostered his own *ego*, which indeed presented grandiose traits. According to Lacan, Joyce's ego did not play the role it plays in 'common mortals', but fulfilled an important *function in structuring reality* (Lacan, 1975–6, p. 147). In other words, stability was created to the extent that he identified with the idea of being 'Joyce, the great writer', hence Lacan's suggestion that Joyce *is* the sinthome (Lacan, 1975–6, 1979, 1982). By fostering a categorical belief in his identity as a writer a link between the registers R, S and I was created. What is remarkable about this view is that, contrary to his work in the 1950s, Lacan no longer dismisses the ego, stating that its potential as an organizing force in mental life should not be underestimated.

At the basis of this notion of the sinthome is the idea that the Name-of-the-Father did not provide Joyce with stability. While references to the father figure are not absent from Joyce's work, Lacan believes that in his novels and personal life, father figures or conventional beliefs are remarkably absent. From *A Portrait of the Artist as a Young Man* to *Finnegan's Wake*, the father is represented as a broken and worthless figure in whom one cannot have faith (Billiet, 2007). Furthermore, in *Ulysses* whenever a paternal figure comes to the fore the structuring role of the father function is negated. He presents his protagonist as an 'artificer' who makes his way alone, starting from detached pieces of discourse taken from others (Lacan, 1975–6, pp. 96–7). In Joyce's universe, the Symbolic contains no solid father function starting from which ideas and interactions take shape. Discourse is shattered and does not reflect internal consistency. Lacan (1975–6, p. 89) says that Joyce is marked by a 'paternal copping out', [24] and concludes that there is a 'paternal shortcoming' [25] (Lacan, 1975–6, p. 97) or a '*Verwerfung* de facto' [26] (Lacan, 1975–6, p. 89; Lysy, 2006). In terms of Lacan's broadening concept of psychosis it could be concluded that Joyce was indeed psychotic, which Lacan (1982) endorsed by saying that Joyce had no contact with his unconscious; however, making such a diagnosis was not the purpose of Lacan's analysis. What was more intriguing to him was the question of how Joyce actually succeeded in bypassing the father without ending up in complete confusion and isolation. In this respect, writing and assuming the artist ego played a crucial role.

What is remarkable about Joyce's writing, and particularly apparent in *Finnegan's Wake*, is that it 'cuts through the effects of meaning and truth' (Lysy, 2006, p. 70). Joyce explores the limits of sense and readability and, by playing with homophony and intertextuality, he undermines the Imaginary search for meaning and coherence. It could be argued that in his writing Joyce evacuates the dimension of the Imaginary, and that the Real encroaches upon the Symbolic (Thurston, 2004). Whereas in Lacan's view the Symbolic creates holes in the Real because it discerns order in chaos, Joyce's work functions in the reverse way, demonstrating how the Symbolic itself is marked by impossibility and chaos (Lacan, 1975–6, p. 151). Lacan further underscored his idea that the Imaginary was strangely evacuated from Joyce's life when he controversially described *A Portrait of the Artist as a Young Man* and *Ulysses* as a 'straight autobiography' (Rabaté, 2001, p. 163). More particularly, Lacan (1975–6, pp. 148–9, 1982) was struck by the fact that the body is an external instance to which Joyce is not intimately attached. His body is like a mere envelope that is not interwoven with the subject. Lacan deduced this idea from anecdotes from *A Portrait of the Artist as a Young Man* (1965), in which Joyce states that when Stephen was beaten by a group of friends, or by the prefect at school, he was actually not distressed. In a remarkable way the physical impact of the beatings has no subjective counterpart. In Lacan's interpretation Stephen disconnects from his body and bows to the pain inflicted by the other's violence. Anger also has a peculiar status for Stephen. Intense feelings of anger and rage he is at one time completely consumed by can disappear 'as easily as a fruit is divested of its soft ripe peel' (Joyce, 1965, p. 87).

Nevertheless, this eccentric status of the Imaginary does not imply that in psychical reality consistency cannot be experienced. Lacan (1975–6, p. 87) indicates that, although R, S and I were not linked via a belief in the father, in the case of Joyce the topological rings were not untied or intermingled. On the contrary, Lacan (1975–6, p. 88) believes that by cultivating his position as an artist Joyce adequately compensated for such poor embedding in conventional modes of making sense of the world. Joyce aimed to make a name for himself as a writer, and wanted to be the kind of artist everyone is fascinated by. In Lacan's interpretation this self-made man attitude provided him with a way of living that counterbalanced his poor insertion in established discourse. Joyce fully cultivated his enigmatic way of writing, which bears witness to a mixture between R and S, and assumed the ego of being a great writer, which Lacan (1975–6, p. 152, 1982) qualified as a sinthome, or an explicit fourth ring via which R, S and I are linked. Joyce's cultivation of his artist ego zeroed in on the uncharacteristic way in which R, S and I functioned, and was successful because it compensated for his lack of connection with the Imaginary. However, in his discussion of Joyce,

Lacan refers to a number of other facets in Joyce's functioning that also provided stability, meaning that his writing should not be seen as the only factor that helped him manage his poor embedding in convention. What is remarkable in this context is his peculiar relationship with his wife and his regulated drinking habits (Jonckheere, 2007).

What is particularly interesting about this discussion of Joyce is that it underscores a mode of linking R, S and I that doesn't build on a universal operator like the Name-of-the-Father, nor does it imply exclusion from the social bond. Using the model of the Borromean rings Lacan emphasized that, by inventing a singular mode of living, stability can be obtained in the relation between R, S and I, such that a stable platform for the subject is created. Furthermore, Joyce's case shows that a sinthome has a social function. No matter how little support established discourse might have given him, his art and his way of living connected Joyce to shared discourse.

Conclusion

The last era of Lacan's work is intriguing, and certainly the most innovative era of his oeuvre. His reflections are more complex than ever before and he challenges viewpoints previously articulated without always offering a clear-cut alternative. One of the most significant changes I discern in his later work is the shift from what I called a dialectical logic to a triangular logic. Prior to the 1970s, Lacan's work is dialectical to the extent that his focus on the three registers of R, S and I is based on the tension between the Symbolic and the two other registers. In line with Freud's idea on the *talking* cure, language and speech are the angle via which clinical practice is studied. With Lacan's introduction of knot theory this changes, bringing a triangular logic to the fore. Henceforth R, S and I are equivalent elements that are not inherently linked, but can be connected in a systemic way. Such a systemic connection always implies the creation of a fourth knot or ring, which functions to tie the others in a stable way. At the level of the Imaginary the creation of a systemic link between R, S and I creates an experience of consistency; in the Symbolic it enables the articulation of the subject; and at the level of the Real, jouissance is regulated. The concepts Lacan connects to this fourth ring are the symptom, the sinthome and psychical reality.

Within this new conceptual framework, the Name-of-the-Father is considered to be the symptom of neurosis, and defined as the implicit fourth knot that makes up the Borromean link. This means that the father function no longer refers to a unique, organizing signifier, but more broadly to making use of convention for the articulation of the subject and the regulation of jouissance. What is typical of psychosis is that such use of conventional discourse is lacking, which implies that to obtain a systemic connection between R, S and I a different solution must be found. In this context Lacan introduces the idea of the sinthome, which refers to a non-conventional way of dealing with reality that allows a systemic connection between R, S and I. This does not imply the kind of suffering a symptom typically entails. Lacan principally refers to the work of James Joyce to illustrate his concept of the sinthome that compensates for foreclosure. Lacan proposed that Joyce's use of language and his ego as a writer compensate for a deficient connection between the Imaginary, the Real and the Symbolic, which in his case prove to be intermingled.

This idea on the sinthome is particularly interesting in that it opens up discussion on how psychoanalytic therapy can facilitate the creation of a sinthome, so that stability at the level of psychical reality can be obtained. Several authors have addressed this question (e.g. Maleval, 2000; Miller, 2009; Naveau, 2004), but the principles that guide such intervention should be clarified and further documented with comprehensive case studies. This is a challenge for the Lacanian psychoanalytic movement.

The last phase of Lacan's work is also important because his concept of psychosis diverges quite markedly from commonly accepted psychiatric viewpoints. Above all, it refers to a discursive position that is marked by having no hold in established discourse. Underlying this idea I discern an epistemological change in Lacan's thinking about both psychosis and neurosis. In his later work neurosis and psychosis are not approached as logical classes, but as parameters of reflection on how singular cases should be approached. In other words, a theory of psychosis and neurosis should function as a point of reflection on the complexity of how each single case could take shape. Assuming that for some individuals a different clinical approach is required, clinicians must ascertain whether the individual's functioning bears witness of a psychotic or a neurotic logic. However, such an assessment should not be made in black-and-white terms. Theory must be used as a means to account for the complexity of each case and not as a vacuous method of diagnostic classification. In this respect, Lacan's discussion of Joyce is most interesting. James Joyce is not discussed primarily as an illustration of psychosis, but rather as an illustration of how psychoanalysts should refrain from dogmatic thinking. Theory should be used as a compass that orients the clinician in exploring the 'dark continent' of each case, never as a map that already shows us the way.

Notes

1 Psychosis as a Disorder at the Level of the Imaginary

1. This does not imply that Lacan disregards cases in which disintegration and chaos are more pronounced. Indeed, several cases taken from his clinical case presentations, which can be found in Seminar III, belong to this category.
2. 'réactions du sujet à des situations vitales'.
3. 'qui touche son affectivité de façon profonde'.
4. 'l'expérience originale qui détermine la psychose, est celle qui révèle au sujet sa propre insuffisance, l'humilie sur le plan éthique'.
5. 'Ces réactions sont caractérisées par leur insertion dans un développement psychologique *compréhensible*, par leur dépendance de la *conception* qu'a le sujet *de soi-même*, de la *tension* propre à ses relations avec le milieu *social*'.
6. 'cause efficiente'.
7. 'déterminante de la structure et de la permanence des symptômes'.
8. 'tout son pouvoir de sympathie'.
9. 'du déclenchement des symptômes'.
10. 'un épisode toxique endogène ou exogène, un processus anxieux, une atteinte infectieuse, un trauma émotionnel'.
11. 'tare biologique de la libido'.
12. In this respect Lacan disagreed with his contemporary Henri Ey. In the text Remarks on Psychic Causality, Lacan (1947, pp. 123–32) strongly criticized Ey's idea that cerebral processes and lesions can completely account for the cause of psychosis and explain its symptoms.
13. 'la clinique ne nous montre pas ces mécanismes'.
14. 'Certes, dans l'étude des psychoses, chaque jour semble apporter quelque corrélation *organique* nouvelle; qu'on y regarde de près: ces corrélations, que nous ne songeons pas à discuter, n'ont qu'une portée partielle, et ne prennent leur intérêt que du point de vue doctrinal qu'elles prétendent renforcer'.
15. 'phase aiguë'.
16. 'phase de méditation affective'.
17. 'phase d'organisation du délire'.
18. 'cause spécifique'.
19. 'le sens du délire'.
20. This was the mother of the psychoanalyst Didier Anzieu, who was later in analysis with Lacan. At the beginning of this analysis neither of them knew of their common relation with Marguerite Anzieu (see: Allouch, 1994; Roudinesco, 1994).
21. 'J'ai fait cela parce qu'on voulait tuer mon enfant'.
22. 'Nous étions deux amies'.
23. 'Un jour, dit-elle, comme je travaillais au bureau, tout en cherchant comme toujours en moi-même d'où pouvaient venir ces menaces contre mon fils,

j'ai entendu mes collègues parler de Mme Z. Je compris alors que c'était elle qui nous en voulait'.

24. This claim had already been made in his article on the structure of paranoid psychoses (1931).
25. 's'opposent à celles de notre sujet "comme à l'objet de son image inversée dans le miroir"'.
26. 'Des deux amies, l'une est l'ombre de l'autre'.
27. 'la femme qui à un degré quelconque, jouit de la liberté et du pouvoir sociaux'.
28. 'Aimée frappe l'être brillant qu'elle hait justement parce qu'elle représente l'idéal qu'elle a de soi'.
29. 'les doublets, triplets et successifs "tirages" d'un *prototype*'.
30. '*attribuée à l'objet*'.
31. 'Aimée frappe donc en sa victime son idéal extériorisé, comme la *passionnelle* frappe l'objet unique de sa haine et de son amour'.
32. 'un énorme besoin de compensation affective'.
33. In 1932 Lacan translated Freud's article Some Neurotic Mechanisms in Jealousy, Paranoia and Homosexuality (1922).
34. 'elles expliquent de façon lumineuse la structure de délire'.
35. 'le problème thérapeutique des psychoses nous semble rendre plus néces-saire une *psychanalyse du moi* qu'une psychanalyse de l'inconscient; c'est à dire que c'est dans une meilleure étude des *résistances* du sujet et dans une expérience nouvelle de leur *manœuvre* qu'il devra trouver ses solutions techniques'.
36. 'Lacan a éclairé d'une lumière scientifique un phénomène obscur pour la plupart de nos contemporains – l'expression paranoïa – et lui a conféré sa vraie signification'.
37. 'Une satisfaction psychique privilégiée'.
38. When using the concept identity, I start from Lacan's logical discussion of the concept. In his seminar on *Identification* (Lacan, 1961–2), Lacan indi-cates that identity can be defined as an entity that is equal to itself (i.e. $A = A$). Punning on this logical formula, he asks how it comes about that someone can start experiencing one as 'one-self': how does it hap-pen that I consider the idea of a 'me' as part of my own self? And why in fact do we say 'my-self'? Is it not self-evident that this 'my' is a part of the 'self'? And isn't it curious that the word 'self', which we use to make auto-references, is in many languages also used to refer to sameness? Along this way Lacan indicates that the experience of iden-tity is a result of the mechanism of 'identification', which functions as an answer to a question that lies at the basis of subjectivity: 'Who am I?'. In saying and believing that 'I am me' and that 'I' mirrors 'myself', people produce answers to this question (see Vanheule and Verhaeghe, 2009).
39. Lacan's (1945) text on 'logical time' makes clear that hesitation is the emi-nent characteristic of the way in which the neurotic deals with information that concerns his own being. The neurotic cannot see who he is and looks for clues about his own being in others. These clues never define the subject's being, but create the conditions based upon which a conclusion about one's own being can be made.

2 Towards a Structural Study of Psychosis

1. I was made aware of this example by Lieven Jonckheere (Jonckheere, 2003, pp. 11–12, 44–6).
2. In the English version of correspondence between Freud and Fliess, *que faire* is wrongly printed as *qué faire*. In the German version, *que faire* is spelled correctly.
3. In line with Lacan I write analysant with a 't' and not with a 'd'. The term 'analysand' denotes a passive position – it's the word used to refer to a person who undergoes analysis. 'Analysant' points to an active position; it is the active form of the French verb *analyser* (to analyse). Lacan prefers the expression analysant because of the active role it gives to the one who decides to engage in a psychoanalysis (Lacan, 1972a).
4. 'c'est du langage que nous tenons cette folie qu'il y a de l'être'.
5. This idea returns in Lacan's discourse theory (Lacan, 1969–70): the subject is not conceptualized as the agent or determining force of discourse, but as a pawn in the structure of discourse.
6. See also Parker (2003) for an excellent discussion of this signifying function.
7. 'Dans la paranoïa, le signifiant représente un sujet pour un autre signifiant'.

4 A Novel Approach to Hallucinations

1. 'Un homme qui a la conviction intime d'une sensation actuellement perçue, alors que nul objet extérieur propre à exciter cette sensation n'est à portée de ses sens, est dans un état d'hallucination'.
2. 'perception sans objet à percevoir'.

5 Delusions Scrutinized

1. In the I-schema (Lacan, 1959, p. 476), the zeroed-out father is symbolized by 'P0'. In this symbol 'P' refers to Father, *Père* in French, and '0' refers to the zeroing-out of the father function.
2. In the I-schema (Lacan, 1959, p. 476), the missing phallus is symbolized by 'Φ0'. In this symbol 'Φ' refers to the phallus while '0' refers to the zeroing-out of the phallus.
3. Lacan (1959, p. 468) says the autonyms qua Created are attributed to an ultimate Creator, God, and that via autonyms all kinds of Creatures come into existence.
4. Lacan (1959, p. 471) suggests that that 'unmanning' is a bad English translation of the German *entmannen*. He prefers translating it as 'emasculation'.
5. Schreber (1903, p. 61) indicates that twice before he experienced the 'miracle of unmanning' on his body: 'The rays of the lower God (Ariman) have the power of producing the miracle of unmanning; the rays of the upper God (Ormuzd) have the power of restoring manliness when necessary'.
6. These opposing positions are reminiscent of Freud's (1910) theory of object choice in men, albeit in Schreber's case the positions refer to his own identity, and not to the identity of objects.

7. In terms of the I-schema (Lacan, 1959, p. 476), the role of retaining integrity is visualized by making a graphical connection between 'loves his wife' and '*m*', which is the letter that symbolizes the ego (*moi*) and '*a*', which refers to the mirror image.

6 The Object *a* and Jouissance in Psychosis

1. Prior to the 1960s Lacan occasionally used the concepts 'jouissance' and 'object *a*'. Jouissance is extensively discussed in Seminar VII (Lacan, 1959–60; De Kesel, 2009; Miller, 1999), where it refers to lust beyond satisfaction. The object *a* in its turn is occasionally used to refer to the imaginary object upon which desire is oriented (Miller, 1999, 2004a).
2. 'sujet de la jouissance'.
3. 'le sujet hypothétique à l'origine de cette dialectique'.
4. 'le sujet encore non-existant, qui a à se situer comme déterminé par le signifiant'.
5. Further discussions on the topic of jouissance can be found in Fink (2002) and Verhaeghe (2002).
6. The pleasure principle denotes the tendency to avoid and reduce the displeasure evoked by an overwhelming rise in somatic tension, and the tendency to optimize the experience of pleasure.
7. This scheme can be found in the French edition of the seminar; however, instead of O and barred O Lacan (1962–3, p. 189) uses A and barred A. A is the abbreviation of the French word *Autre*. *Autre* means Other, which we abbreviate as O.
8. 'le sujet a à se constituer au lieu de l'Autre sous les espèces primaires du signifiant'.
9. 'c'est par la voie de l'Autre que le sujet a à se réaliser'.
10. 'l'Autre barré'.
11. 'Ce qui est maintenant de mon côté, c'est ce qui me constitue comme inconscient, à savoir Å, l'Autre en tant que je ne l'atteins pas'.
12. 'toute l'existence de l'Autre se suspend à une garantie qui manque, d'où l'Autre barré'.
13. In the 1950s Lacan had often claimed the opposite, suggesting that for the subject the Other of the Other exists (e.g. Lacan, 1957–8, p. 192).
14. 'Le *a* est ce qui reste d'irréductible dans l'opération totale d'avènement du sujet au lieu de l'Autre.. il est justement ce qui représente le S dans son réel irréductible'.
15. '*Petit a*, c'est l'être en tant qu'il est essentiellement manquant au texte du monde'.
16. In his first elaborations, Lacan (1962–3, 1963) also says that the phallus is an object *a*. Yet, from Seminar XI onwards this is no longer the case (Lacan, 1964).
17. Hence Lacan's suggestion that in anxiety, 'the object little *a* drops' ('Dans l'angoisse, l'objet petit *a* choit') (Lacan, 1963, p. 78).
18. In Seminar XX this line of reasoning changes completely, in that Lacan then suggests that the use of language as such bears witness of jouissance.

19. In the same vein he also indicates that the fundamental fantasy, which is the neurotic's unconscious scenario of how to relate to the Other, primarily bears witness of an attitude towards the object *a*, rather than a direct relation with O (Lacan, 1960); hence the following matheme to formally depict the fantasy: $\$ \diamond a$.

20. This pluralizing of the Name-of-the-Father also brings Lacan to reconceptualize the status of the identity-related questions with which the subject is confronted at the level of the unconscious. Whereas in the 1950s, with his formula of the paternal metaphor, Lacan suggested that questions concerning the existential position of the subject can be adequately answered with the aid of the paternal signifier, in the 1960s he states the opposite. What he then argues is that human identity is always marked by an 'existential gap' that cannot be signified (Lacan, 1963, p. 75). In reference to Kierkegaard, he says that crucial elements concerning subjectivity cannot be named and that, at the limits of Symbolic predictability, the subject meets the dimension of jouissance in his own body as well as in the Other (Lacan, 1961–2, 1962–3, 1963).

21. 'le névrosé, comme le pervers, comme le psychotique lui-même, ne sont que des faces de la structure normale'.

22. 'identifiant la jouissance dans ce lieu de l'Autre comme tel'.

23. 'Dieu ou l'Autre jouisse de son être passivé'.

24. 'n'a plus avec aucun sujet rien à faire'.

25. 'les désirs sont à proprement parler fous'.

26. 'le langage est le premier à quoi le corps se trouve absolument subordonné'.

27. 'affolé'.

28. 'le dit schizophrène se spécifie d'être pris sans le secours d'aucun discours établi'.

29. 'Marguerite Duras s'avère savoir sans moi ce que j'enseigne'.

30. 'Lol devient folle'.

31. 'être à trois'.

32. 'son vide'.

33. 'figure de blessée, exilée des choses'.

34. 'cet être n'est vraiment spécifié, incarné, présentifié dans son roman que dans la mesure où elle existe sous la forme de cet objet noyau, cet objet *a* de ce quelque chose qui existe comme un regard, mais qui est un regard, un regard écarté, un regard-objet, un regard que nous voyons à plusieurs reprises'.

35. 'un nœud qui se refait là'.

36. 'n'est pas le voyeur'.

37. Ideas on how the object *a* is manifested in other forms of psychosis can be found in the work of Miller (1993) and Soler (2008).

7 Psychosis within the Logic of Knotting and Linking

1. From Seminar XV (1967–8), Lacan began to argue in favour of the triangular conception of the relations between R, S and I. For example, in the session of 6 December 1967 he uses a triangle to depict the relation between the registers. It is only from Seminar XX (1972–3) that knot theory is used to conceptualize this triangular relationship.

2. 'une géométrie que l'on peut dire interdite à l'imaginaire'.
3. 'Le sujet est ce qu'un signifiant représente auprès d'un autre signifiant'.
4. The basis of this idea is the distinction between a false gap (*faux trou*) and a real gap (*vrai trou*) (Lacan, 1975–6; Soury, 1982). Lacan suggests that by taking one or two rings from the Borromean link, one could assume that in the inner space of a ring, or in the interspace between two rings a hole can be found. However, as long as a third ring that lays on top of one ring and under the other is not added, one cannot know whether the interspace is full or empty. Nothing differentiates the inner space of the rings and the interspace from the contour the circle makes, which means that it gives an illusion of emptiness; emptiness is suggested, but nothing proves it. This is why Lacan qualifies it as a false gap. In order to determine a real gap we need an additional circle that passes through the interspace and thus bears witness of the three-dimensional status of the void.
5. 'Le caractère fondamental de cette utilisation du nœud est d'illustrer la triplicité qui résulte d'une consistance qui n'est affectée que de l'imaginaire, d'un trou fondamental qui ressortit au symbolique, et d'une ex-sistence qui, elle, appartient au réel, qui en est même le caractère fondamental'.
6. 'le langage mange le réel'.
7. 'le réel n'a d'existence qu'à rencontrer, du symbolique et de l'imaginaire, l'arrêt'.
8. 'Il n'y a pas d'autre définition possible du réel que: c'est l'impossible'.
9. 'ce soit dans l'imaginaire que je mette le support de ce qui est la consistance'.
10. 'comme cette unité de pure forme que représente pour lui le corps'.
11. 'chaînoeud'.
12. 'engendre naturellement le nœud de trèfle'.
13. 'Je dis qu'il faut supposer tétradique ce qui fait le lien borroméen...Poser le lien énigmatique de l'imaginaire, du symbolique et du réel implique ou suppose l'ex-sistence du symptôme'.
14. 'Nous voyons, comme Freud nous le dit, les gens irrésistiblement nous parlent de leur maman et de leur papa...ils sont toujours ramenés à quelque chose qu'ils associent essentiellement à la manière dont ils ont été élevés par leur famille'.
15. 'La père-version est la sanction du fait que Freud fait tout tenir sur la fonction du père. Et le nœud bo, c'est ça'.
16. 'chez la plupart le symbolique, l'imaginaire et le réel son embrouillés au point de se continuer les uns dans les autres, à défaut d'opération qui les distinguent comme dans la chaîne du nœud borroméen'.
17. The more recent concept 'ordinary psychosis' picks up on this renewed definition of psychosis. An excellent discussion of the concept can be found in issue 19 of the journal *Psychoanalytical Notebooks*, which is entirely devoted to ordinary psychosis.
18. 'La psychose est un essai de rigueur. En ce sens je dirais que je suis psychotique. Je suis psychotique pour la seule raison que j'ai toujours essayé d'être rigoureux'.
19. 'Si j'étais plus psychotique, je serais probablement meilleur analyste'.
20. I restrict my line of reasoning to neurosis and psychosis, but it could of course be extended to perversion as well.

21. 'L'imaginaire, le symbolique et le réel sont une et même consistance, et c'est en cela que consiste la psychose paranoïaque'.
22. 'c'est toujours de trois supports, que nous appellerons, en l'occasion, subjectifs, c'est à dire personnels, qu'un quatrième prend appui"
23. 'c'est le quelque chose qui permet au symbolique, à l'imaginaire en au réel de continuer de tenir ensemble'.
24. 'démission paternelle'.
25. 'carence du père'.
26. '*Verwerfung* de fait'.

References

Adams, C.C. (2002) *The Knot Book* (Providence: American Mathematical Society).

Alajouanine, T., P. Delafontaine and J. Lacan (1926) 'Fixité du regard par hypertonie prédominant dans le sens vertical avec conservation des mouvements automatico-réflexes, aspect spécial de syndrome de Parinaud par hypertonie associée a un syndrome extrapyramidal avec troubles pseudobulbaires', *Revue Neurologique*, 2, 410–18.

Allen, P., F. Laroi, P.K. McGuire and A. Aleman (2008) 'The Hallucinating Brain: A Review of Structural and Functional Neuroimaging Studies of Hallucinations', *Neuroscience and Behavioral Reviews*, 32, 175–91.

Allouch, J. (1994) *Marguerite ou l'Aimée de Lacan* (Paris: E.P.E.L.).

American Psychiatric Association (2000) *Diagnostic and Statistical Manual of Mental Disorders. Fourth Edition. Text revision* (Washington, DC: American Psychiatric Association).

Apollon, W., D. Bergeron and L. Cantin (2000) 'The Treatment of Psychosis' in K.R. Malone and S.R. Friedlander (eds.) *The Subject of Lacan – A Lacanian Reader for Psychologists* (Albany: State University of New York Press), pp. 209–27.

Atkinson, J.R. (2006) 'The Perceptual Characteristics of Voice-Hallucinations in Deaf People', *Schizophrenia Bulletin*, 32, 701–8.

Badiou, A. (1982) *Theory of the Subject* (London and New York: Continuum).

Badiou, A. (2009) *Logics of the World – Being and Event II* (London and New York: Continuum).

Badiou, A. (2010) *Second Manifesto for Philosophy* (Cambridge and Oxford, UK: Polity Press).

Berrios, G.E. (1991) 'Delusions as "Wrong Beliefs": A Conceptual History', *British Journal of Psychiatry*, 195 (suppl. 14), 6–13.

Berrios, G.E. (1996) *The History of Mental Symptoms. Descriptive Psychopathology since the Nineteenth Century* (Cambridge: Cambridge University Press).

Billiet, L. (1996) *Het gebroken Oor* (Ghent: Idesça).

Billiet, L. (2007) 'Een eerste psychoanalytische Kennismaking met "Finnigans Wake"', *iNWiT*, 2/3, 173–88.

Bleuler, E. (1911) *Dementia Praecox or the Group of Schizophrenias* (New York: International Universities Press).

Brüne, M. (2005) '"Theory of Mind" in Schizophrenia: A Review of Literature', *Schizophrenia Bulletin*, 31, 21–42.

Butler, R.W. and Braff, D.L. (1991) Delusions: A review and integration. *Schizophrenia Bulletin*, 17, 633–47.

Cambridge Advanced Learner's Dictionary (2008) (Cambridge, UK and New York: Cambridge University Press).

Chiesa, L. (2007) *Subjectivity and Otherness – A Philosophical Reading of Lacan* (Cambridge, MA: MIT Press).

Cox-Cameron, O. (2000) 'Lacan's Doctoral Thesis: Turbulent Preface or Founding Legend?', *Psychoanalytische Perspectieven*, 41/42, 17–45.

Dali, S. (1933) 'Interprétation paranoïa-critique de l'image obsédante: L'Angélus de Millet', *Le Minotaure*, 1, 65–7.

Dali, S. (1973) *Comment on deviant Dali* (Paris: Robert Lafont).

David, A.S. (2004) 'The Cognitive Neuropsychiatry of Auditory Verbal Hallucinations: An Overview', *Cognitive Neuropsychiatry*, 9, 107–23.

de Clérambault, G.G. (1987 [1942]) *Oeuvres Psychiatriques* (Paris: Frénésie Editions).

De Kesel, M. (2009) *Eros and Ethics* (Albany: State University of New York Press).

Deleuze, G. and F. Guattari (1983 [1972]) *Anti-Oedipus – Capitalism and Schizophrenia* (Minneapolis: University of Minnesota Press).

de Saussure, F. (1916) *Course in General Linguistics* (New York: Philosophical Library).

Deutsch, H. (1942) 'Some Forms of Emotional Disturbance and their Relationship to Schizophrenia', *The Psychoanalytic Quarterly*, 11, 301–21.

Dolar, M. (2006) *A Voice and Nothing More* (Cambridge, MA: MIT Press).

Duras, M. (1964) *The Ravishing of Lol Stein* (New York: Pantheon Books).

Eco, U. (1976) *A Theory of Semiotics* (London: Macmillan).

Esquirol, E. (1838) *Des Maladies Mentales Considérées sous le Rapport Médical, Hygiénique et Médico-Légal. Volume 2* (Paris: J.B. Baillère).

Ey, H. (1932) 'Compte rendu', *L'Encephale*, 2, 851–6.

Ey, H. (1934) *Hallucinations et Délire* (Paris: Félix Lacan).

Ey, H. (1973a) *Traité des Hallucinations. Tome 1* (Paris: Masson).

Ey, H. (1973b) *Traité des Hallucinations. Tome 2* (Paris: Masson).

Fink, B. (1995) *The Lacanian Subject: Between Language and Jouissance* (Princeton: Princeton University Press).

Fink, B. (2002) 'Knowledge and jouissance' in S. Barnard and B. Fink (eds.) *Reading Seminar XX* (Albany: State University of New York Press), pp. 21–45.

Fink, B. (2007) *Fundamentals of Psychoanalytic Technique: A Lacanian Approach for Practitioners* (New York: W.W. Norton and Company).

Freud, S. (1900) 'The Interpretation of Dreams' in J. Strachey (ed. & trans.) *The Standard Edition of the Complete Psychological Works of Sigmund Freud*, Vols 4–5 (London: Hogarth Press).

Freud, S. (1905) 'Fragments of an Analysis of a Case of Hysteria' in J. Strachey (ed. & trans.) *The Standard Edition of the Complete Psychological Works of Sigmund Freud*, Vol. 7 (London: Hogarth Press), pp. 1–122.

Freud, S. (1910) 'A Special Type of Choice of Object Made by Men' in J. Strachey (ed. & trans.) *The Standard Edition of the Complete Psychological Works of Sigmund Freud*, Vol. 2 (London: Hogarth Press), pp. 163–75.

Freud, S. (1911) 'Psycho-Analytic Notes on an Autobiographical Account of a Case of Paranoia' in J. Strachey (ed. & trans.) *The Standard Edition of the Complete Psychological Works of Sigmund Freud*, Vol. 12 (London: Hogarth Press), pp. 9–82.

Freud, S. (1913) 'Totem and Taboo' in J. Strachey (ed. & trans.) *The Standard Edition of the Complete Psychological Works of Sigmund Freud*, Vol. 13 (London: Hogarth Press), pp. 1–161.

Freud, S. (1915) 'Instincts and their Vicissitudes' in J. Strachey (ed. & trans.) *The Standard Edition of the Complete Psychological Works of Sigmund Freud*, Vol. 14 (London: Hogarth Press), pp. 109–40.

Freud, S. (1918) 'From the History of an Infantile Neurosis' in J. Strachey (ed. & trans.) *The Standard Edition of the Complete Psychological Works of Sigmund Freud*, Vol. 17 (London: Hogarth Press), pp. 3–122.

Freud, S. (1920) 'Beyond the Pleasure Principle' in J. Strachey (ed. & trans.) *The Standard Edition of the Complete Psychological Works of Sigmund Freud*, Vol. 18 (London: Hogarth Press), pp. 1–64.

Freud, S. (1922) 'Some Neurotic Mechanisms in Jealousy, Paranoia and Homosexuality' in J. Strachey (ed. & trans.) *The Standard Edition of the Complete Psychological Works of Sigmund Freud*, Vol. 18 (London: Hogarth Press), pp. 223–32.

Freud, S. (1925) 'Negation' in J. Strachey (ed. & trans.) *The Standard Edition of the Complete Psychological Works of Sigmund Freud*, Vol. 19 (London: Hogarth Press), pp. 233–9.

Freud, S. (1955) 'Extracts from the Fliess Papers' in J. Strachey (ed. & trans.) *The Standard Edition of the Complete Psychological Works of Sigmund Freud*, Vol. 1 (London: Hogarth Press), pp. 173–281.

Garrabé, J. (1979) 'Prolégomènes à un Manifeste de la Surpsychiatrie', *L'Évolution Psychiatrique*, 44, 5–28.

Garrabé, J. (2005) 'Clérambault, Dali, Lacan et l'Interprétation paranoïaque', *L'Évolution Psychiatrique*, 163, 360–3.

Gueguen, P.G. (2004) 'Symptomatic Homeostasis in Psychosis', *Psychoanalytical Notebooks*, 12, 65–76.

Grigg, R. (2008) *Lacan, Language and Philosophy* (Albany: State University of New York Press).

Guiraud, P. (1933) 'Compte Rendu', *Annales Médico-Psychologiques*, 1, 230–1.

Hegel, G.W.F. (1977 [1807]) *The Phenomenology of Spirit* (Oxford: Oxford University Press).

Hoens, D. (2005) 'When Love is the Law: On the Ravishing of Lol V. Stein', *Umbr(a)*, 1, 105–19.

Hoornaert, G. (2008) 'Little Hans and the Construction of the Out-of-Body Object', *Bulletin of the NLS*, 4, 28–31.

Hyppolite, J. (1953) 'A Spoken Commentary on Freud's *Verneinung*' in J. Lacan (1988 [1953–54]) *The Seminar of Jacques Lacan, book I: Freud's Papers on Technique* (New York and London: W.W. Norton), pp. 289–97.

Jakobson, R. (1971 [1953]) 'Results of the Conference of Anthropologists and Linguists' in *Selected Writings II: Word and Language* (Paris and The Hague: Mouton), pp. 554–67.

Jaspers, K. (1997 [1959]) *General Psychopathology – Volume I* (Baltimore: John Hopkins University Press).

Jonckheere, L. (2003) *Het Seksuele Fantasma Voorbij* (Leuven: Acco).

Jonckheere, L. (2007) 'Nora als Sinthoom van Joyce?', *iNWiT*, 2/3, 189–238.

Joyce, J. (1965) *A Portrait of the Artist as a Young Man* (New York: Penguin).

Katan, M. (1950) 'Structural Aspects of a Case of Schizophrenia', *The Psychoanalytic Study of the Child*, 5, 175–211.

Kojève, A. (1947) *Introduction à la Lecture de Hegel* (Paris: Gallimard).

Kraepelin, E. (1913) *Psychiatrie, ein Lehrbuch für Studierende und Ärtzte, Band III* (Leipzig: Engelman).

Kraepelin, E. (1920) *Psychiatrie, ein Lehrbuch für Studierende und Ärtzte, Band I* (Leipzig: Engelman).

Kusnierek, M. (2008) 'Jacques Lacan's Theory of Perception', *Bulletin of the NLS*, 3, 22–35.

Kirshner, L.A. (2004) *Having A Life: Self Pathology after Lacan* (New York: Routledge).

Kirshner, L.A. (2005) 'Rethinking Desire: the *Objet Petit a* in Lacanian Theory', *Journal of the American Psychoanalytic Association*, 53, 83–102.

Lacan, J. (1931) 'Structure des Psychoses Paranoïaques', *Semaine des Hôpiteaux de Paris*, 7 July, 437–45.

Lacan, J., J. Lévy-Valensi and P. Migault (1931) 'Écrits "Inspirés": Schizographie', *Annales Médico-Psychologiques*, 2, 508–22.

Lacan, J. (1932) *De la Psychose Paranoïaque dans ses Rapports avec la Personnalité* (Paris: Seuil).

Lacan, J. (1933) 'Motifs du Crime Paranoïaque – Le Crime des Sœurs Papin', *Minotaure*, 3/4, pp. 25–8.

Lacan, J. (2001 [1938]) 'Les Complexes Familiaux dans la Formation de l'Individu' in J. Lacan and J.A. Miller (eds.) *Autres Écrits* (Paris: Seuil), pp. 23–84.

Lacan, J. (2006 [1945]) 'Logical Time and the Assertion of Anticipated Certainty – A New Sophism' in J. Lacan and J.A. Miller (eds.) *Écrits* (New York and London: W. W. Norton), pp. 161–175.

Lacan, J. (2006 [1947] 'Presentation on Psychical Causality' in J. Lacan and J.A. Miller (eds.) *Écrits* (New York and London: W.W. Norton), pp. 123–58.

Lacan, J. (2006 [1949]) 'The Mirror Stage as Formative of the Function of the I' in J. Lacan and J.A. Miller (eds.) *Écrits* (New York and London: W.W. Norton), pp. 75–81.

Lacan, J. (1953) 'Le Symbolique, l'Imaginaire et le Réel' in J. Lacan and J.A. Miller (eds.) *Des Noms-Du-Père* (Paris: Seuil), pp. 9–63.

Lacan, J. (1988 [1953–54] *The Seminar of Jacques Lacan, Book I: Freud's Papers on Technique* (New York and London: W.W. Norton).

Lacan, J. (1988 [1954–55]) *The Seminar of Jacques Lacan, Book II, The Ego in Freud's Theory and in the Technique of Psychoanalysis* (Cambridge: Cambridge University Press).

Lacan, J. (1993 [1955–56]) *The Seminar 1955–1956, Book III, The psychoses* (New York and London: W.W. Norton).

Lacan, J. (1994 [1956–57]) *Le Séminaire 1956–1957, Livre IV: La Relation d'Objet* (Paris: Seuil).

Lacan, J. (2006 [1956a]) 'The Situation of Psychoanalysis and the Training of Psychoanalysts in 1956' in J. Lacan and J.A. Miller (eds.) *Écrits* (New York and London: W. W. Norton), pp. 384–411.

Lacan, J. (1956b) 'Intervention sur l'Exposé de Claude Lévi-Strauss: "Sur les Rapports entre la Mythologie et le Rituel" à la Société Française de Philosophie le 26 mai 1956', *Bulletin de la Société française de Philosophie*, 48, 113–19.

Lacan, J. (2006 [1956c]) 'The Function and Field of Speech and Language in Psychoanalysis' in J. Lacan and J.A. Miller (eds.) *Écrits* (New York and London: W. W. Norton), pp. 197–268.

Lacan, J. (1994 [1956–57]) *Le Séminaire 1956–1957, Livre IV: La Relation d'Objet* (Paris: Seuil).

Lacan, J. (2006 [1957a]) 'Seminar on "the Purloined Letter"' in J. Lacan and J.A. Miller (eds.) *Écrits* (New York and London: W. W. Norton), pp. 11–48.

Lacan, J. (2006 [1957b]) 'The Instance of the Letter in the Unconscious or Reason since Freud' in J. Lacan and J.A. Miller (eds.) *Écrits* (New York and London: W. W. Norton), pp. 412–42.

Lacan, J. (1998 [1957–58]) *Le Séminaire 1957–1958, Livre V: Les Formations de l'Inconscient* (Paris: Seuil).

Lacan, J. (2006 [1958]) 'The Signification of the Phallus' in J. Lacan and J.A. Miller (eds.) *Écrits* (New York and London: W. W. Norton), pp. 575–84.

Lacan, J. (1958–59) *Le Séminaire 1958–1959, Livre VI: Le Désir et son Interprétation* (Unpublished seminar).

Lacan, J. (2006 [1959]) 'On a Question Prior to any Possible Treatment of Psychosis' in J. Lacan and J.A. Miller (eds.) *Écrits* (New York and London: W.W. Norton), pp. 445–88.

Lacan, J. (1992 [1959–60]) *The Seminar 1959–1969, Book VII, The Ethics of Psychoanalysis* (New York and London: W.W. Norton).

Lacan, J. (2006 [1960]) 'The Subversion of the Subject and the Dialectic of Desire in the Freudian Unconscious' Psychosis' in J. Lacan and J.A. Miller (eds.) *Écrits* (New York and London: W.W. Norton), pp. 671–702.

Lacan, J. (2006 [1961]) 'Remarks on Daniel Lagache's Presentation: "Psychoanalysis and Personality Structure"' in J. Lacan and J.A. Miller (eds.) *Écrits* (New York and London: W.W. Norton), pp. 543–74.

Lacan, J. (1961–62) *Le Séminaire 1961–1962, Livre IX, L'Identification* (Unpublished seminar).

Lacan, J. (2004 [1962–63]) *Le Séminaire 1962–1963, Livre X: L'Angoisse* (Paris: Seuil).

Lacan, J. (2005 [1963]) 'Introduction au Noms-du-Père' in J. Lacan and J.A. Miller (eds.) *Des Noms-du-Père* (Paris: Seuil), pp. 67–104.

Lacan, J. (1973 [1964]) *The Seminar 1964, Book XI, The Four Fundamental Concepts of Psycho-Analysis* (New York: Karnac).

Lacan, J. (1964–65) *Le Séminaire 1964–1965, Livre XII: Problèmes Cruciaux pour la Psychanalyse* (Unpublished seminar).

Lacan, J. (2001 [1965]) 'Hommage fait à Marguerite Duras, du Ravissement de Lol V. Stein' in J. Lacan and J.A. Miller (eds.) *Autres Écrits* (Paris: Seuil), pp. 191–7.

Lacan, J. (2006 [1966a]) 'Science and Truth' in J. Lacan and J.A. Miller (eds.) *Écrits* (New York and London: W.W. Norton), pp. 726–45.

Lacan, J. (2001 [1966b]) 'Présentation des Mémoires d'un Névropathe' in J. Lacan and J.A. Miller (eds.) *Autres Écrits* (Paris: Seuil), pp. 213–18.

Lacan, J. (2006 [1966c]) 'On my Antecedents' in J. Lacan and J.A. Miller (eds.) *Écrits* (New York and London: W.W. Norton), pp. 65–72.

Lacan, J. (2001 [1966d]) 'Réponses à des Étudiants en Philosophie' in J. Lacan and J.A. Miller (eds.) *Autres Ecrits* (Paris: Seuil), pp. 203–11.

Lacan, J. (1966 67) *Le Séminaire 1966–1967, Livre XIV, La Logique du Fantasme* (Unpublished seminar).

Lacan, J. (1967) *Petit Discours aux Psychiatres de Sainte-Anne* (Unpublished paper).

Lacan, J. (1967–68) *Le Séminaire 1967–1968, Livre XV, L'Acte Psychanalytique* (Unpublished seminar).

Lacan, J. (2001 [1968]) 'Allocution sur les Psychoses de l'Enfant' in J. Lacan and J.A. Miller (eds.) *Autres Écrits* (Paris: Seuil), pp. 361–72.

Lacan, J. (2001 [1969]) 'Note sur l'Enfant' in J. Lacan and J.A. Miller (eds.) *Autres Écrits* (Paris: Seuil), pp. 373–4.

Lacan, J. (1991 [1969–70]) *Le Séminaire 1969–1970, Livre XVII, L'envers de la Psychanalyse* (Paris: Seuil).

Lacan, J. (1970) 'Of Structure as an Immixing of an Otherness Prerequisite to Any Subject Whatever' in R. Macksey and E. Donato (eds.) *The Languages of Criticism and the Sciences of Man: The Structuralist Controversy* (Baltimore and London: John Hopkins Press).

Lacan, J. (1971–72) *Le Séminaire 1971–1972, Livre XIX,... Ou Pire* (Unpublished seminar).

Lacan, J. (1972a) 'Du Discours Psychanalytique' in Anonymous (ed.) *Lacan in Italia 1953–1978. En Italie Lacan* (Milan: La Salamandra), pp. 32–55.

Lacan, J. (1981 [1972b]) 'Séance extraordinaire de l'École Belge de Psychanalyse', *Quarto*, 5, 4–22.

Lacan, J. (1998 [1972–73]) *The Seminar of Jacques Lacan, Book XX, Encore* (New York and London: W.W. Norton).

Lacan, J. (1973) 'L'Étourdit' in J. Lacan and J.A. Miller (eds.) *Autres Écrits* (Paris: Seuil), pp. 449–95.

Lacan, J. (1974–75) *Le séminaire 1974–1975, Livre XXII, R.S.I* (Unpublished seminar).

Lacan, J. (1975) *Entretiens avec Jacques Lacan at Institut Français London* (Unpublished paper).

Lacan, J. (1975–76) *Le séminaire 1975–1976, Livre XXIII, Le Sinthome* (Paris: Seuil).

Lacan, J. (1976a) 'Conférences et Entretiens dans des Universités Nord-Américaines: Yale University, Kanzer Seminar, 24 novembre 1975', *Scilicet*, 6/7, 7–31.

Lacan, J. (1976b) 'Conférences et Entretiens dans des Universités Nord-Américaines: Yale University, 24 novembre 1975, Entretien avec des Étudiants, Réponses à leurs Questions', *Scilicet*, 6/7, 32–7.

Lacan, J. (1976c) 'Conférences et Entretiens dans des Universités Nord-Américaines: Yale University, Law School Auditorium, 25 novembre 1975', *Scilicet*, 6/7, 38–41.

Lacan, J. (1976d) 'Conférences et Entretiens dans des Universités Nord-Américaines: Columbia University, Auditorium School of International Affairs, 25 novembre 1975', *Scilicet*, 6/7, 42–52.

Lacan, J. (1976e) 'Conférences et Entretiens dans des Universités Nord-Américaines Massachusetts Institute of Technology, 2 décembre 1975', *Scilicet*, 6/7, 53–61.

Lacan, J. (1979) 'Joyce le Symptome II' in J. Lacan and J.A. Miller (eds.) *Autres Écrits* (Paris: Seuil), pp. 565–70.

Lacan, J. (2005 [1975–76]) *Le Séminaire 1975–1976, Livre XXIII: Le Sinthome* (Paris: Seuil).

Lacan, J. (1977) 'Ouverture de la Section Clinique', *Ornicar?*, 9, 7–14.

Lacan, J. (1982) 'Joyce le sinthome I', *L'Âne*, 6, 3–5.

Lévi-Strauss, C. (1949) *The Elementary Structures of Kinship* (Boston: Beacon Press).

Lévi-Strauss, C. (1958) *Structural Anthropology* (New York: Basic Books).

Lévi-Strauss, C. (1962) *The Savage Mind* (London: Weidenfeld and Nicolson).

Lysy, A. (2006) 'Joyce and the Name-of-the-Father' in Anonymous (ed.) *Scilicet of the Name-of-the-Father* (Paris: World Association of Psychoanalysis), pp. 68–70.

Lysy, A. (2008) 'The Body – in the Flesh', *Bulletin of the NLS*, 3, 17–21.

Masson, J.M. (1985) *The Complete Letters of Sigmund Freud to Wilhelm Fliess 1887–1904* (Cambridge and London: The Belknap Press).

Merleau-Ponty, M. (1945) *The Phenomenology of Perception* (London: Routledge and Kegan Paul).

Maleval, J.C. (1991) *Folies hystériques et Psychoses dissociatives* (Paris: Payot).

Maleval, J.C. (2000) *La Forclusion du Nom-du-Père* (Paris: Seuil).

Malone, K.R. and J.L. Roberts (2010) 'In the World of Language but not of It Lacanian Inquiry into the Subject of Discourse Psychology', *Theory and Psychology*, 20, 835–54.

Miller, J.A. (1979) 'Supplément topologique à la "Question Préliminaire"', *Lettres de l'EFP*, 2, 127–38.

Miller, J.A. (1993) 'Clinique ironique', *La Cause Freudienne*, 23, 7–13.

Miller, J-A. (1998) 'Psychose ordinaire et Clinique floue', Ornicar? Digital, 2. Available at: http://membres.multimania.fr/jlacan/ornicar/ornicardigital/Articles_d_Ornicar_digital/psychose_ordinaire_et_clinique_floue_Jacques_Alain_Miller_28998.htm [Accessed 1 October 2010].

Miller, J.A. (1999) 'Paradigms of Jouissance', *Lacanian Ink*, 17, 8–47.

Miller, J.A. (2001) 'The Logic of the Perceived', *Psychoanalytical Notebooks*, 6, 9–30.

Miller, J.A. (2002a) 'A Contribution of the Schizophrenic to the Psychoanalytic Clinic', *The Symptom*, 2. Available at: http://www.lacan.adamscom/contributionf.htm [Accessed 1 October 2010].

Miller, J.A. (2002b) 'Intuitions milanaises I', *Mental*, 11, 9–21.

Miller, J.A. (2003) 'Intuitions milanaises II', *Mental*, 12, 9–26.

Miller, J.A. (2004a) 'Introduction to Reading Jacques Lacan's Seminar on Anxiety', *Lacanian Ink*, 26, 6–67.

Miller, J.A. (2004b) 'L'invention psychotique', *Quarto*, 80/81, 6–13.

Miller, J.A. (2005) 'Notice de Fil en Aiguille' in J. Lacan (ed.) *Le séminaire 1975–1976, Livre XXIII, Le sinthome* (Paris: Seuil), pp. 199–247.

Miller, J.A. (2007a) 'Jacques Lacan and the Voice' in V. Voruz and B. Wolf (eds.) *The Later Lacan – An Introduction* (Albany: State University of New York Press), pp. 137–46.

Miller, J.A. (2007b) 'L'esp d'une Hallucination', *Quarto*, 90, 19–26.

Miller, J.A. (2007c) 'The Sinthome, a Mixture of Symptom and Fantasy' in V. Voruz and B. Wolf (eds.) *The Later Lacan – An Introduction* (Albany: State University of New York Press), pp. 55–72.

Miller, J.A. (2007d) 'Interpretation in Reverse' in V. Voruz and B. Wolf (eds.) *The Later Lacan – An Introduction* (Albany: State University of New York Press), pp. 3–9.

Miller, J.A. (2009) 'Ordinary Psychosis Revisited', *Psychoanalytical Notebooks*, 19, 139–67.

Miller, J.A. (2010) 'The Responses of the Real', *(Re)-turn – A Journal of Lacanian Studies*, 5, 9–31.

Mills, J. (2003) 'Lacan on paranoiac Knowledge', *Psychoanalytic Psychology*, 20, 30–51.

Milner, J.C. (2002) *Le Périple structural, Figures et paradigmes* (Paris: Seuil).

Muller, J.P. and W.J. Richardson (1982) *Lacan and Language* (Boston: International Universities Press).

Munro, A. (1999) *Delusional Disorder, Paranoia and Related Illnesses* (Cambridge: Cambridge University Press).

Naveau, P. (2004) *Les Psychoses et le Lien social – Le Noeud défait* (Paris: Anthropos).

Nobus, D. (2000) *Jacques Lacan and the Freudian Practice of Psychoanalysis* (New York: Routledge).

Parker, I. (2003) 'Jacques Lacan, Barred Psychologist', *Theory and Psychology*, 13, 95–115.

Parker, I. (2010) *Lacanian Psychoanalysis – Revolutions on Subjectivity* (London and New York: Routledge).

Pluth, E. (2007) *Signifiers and Acts – Freedom in Lacan's Theory of the Subject* (Albany: State University of New York Press).

Quintilian (1856) *Institutes of oratory*. Available at: http://honeyl.public.iastate.edu/quintilian/ [Accessed 15 May 2010].

Rabaté, J.M. (2001) *Jacques Lacan* (New York: Palgrave).

Ragland-Sullivan, E. (1986) *Jacques Lacan and the Philosophy of Psychoanalysis* (Urbana and Chicago: University of Illinois Press).

Roudinesco (1994) *Jacques Lacan* (New York: Columbia University Press).

Rümke, H.C. (1960) *Psychiatrie II: de Psychosen* (Amsterdam: Scheltema and Holkema).

Santiago, A.L. (2009) 'The Semblant and the Postiche Object', *Papers - Electronic Journal of the Action Committee of the School-One 2009–2010*, 1, 13–17.

Sauvagnat, F. (2000) 'On the Specificity of Elementary Phenomena', *Psychoanalytical Notebooks* [Online], 4, Available at: http://www.londonsociety-nls.org.uk/sauvagnat_phenomena.htm [Accessed 16 September 2010].

Schreber, D.P. (1903) *Memoirs of My Nervous Illness* (New York: New York Review of Books).

Shepherdson, C. (2008) *Lacan and the Limits of Language* (New York: Fordham University Press).

Skriabine, P. (2004) 'The Clinic of the Borromean Knot' in E. Ragland and D. Milovanovic (eds.) *Lacan: Topologically Speaking* (New York: Other Press), pp. 249–67.

Soler, C. (2008) *L'Inconscient à Ciel ouvert de la Psychose* (Toulouse: Presses Universitaires du Mirail).

Soury, T. (1982) 'Introduction aux dessins et schémas topologiques de Monsieur Lacan', *Quarto*, 5, 24–45.

Stasse, P. (2008) 'From the Drive to Object a', *Bulletin of the NLS*, 3, 36–41.

Stump, E. (2003) *Aquinas* (New York: Routledge).

Svolos, T. (2001) 'The Great Divide: Psychoanalytic Contributions to the Diagnosis and Management of Psychosis', *Lacanian Ink*, 18, 42–59.

Svolos, T. (2009) 'Ordinary Psychosis', *Psychoanalytical Notebooks*, 19, 79–82.

Thurston, L. (2004) 'Specious Aristmystic: Joycean Topology' in E. Ragland and D. Milovanovic (eds.) *Lacan: Topologically speaking* (New York: Other Press), pp. 314–27.

Tracy, D.K. and S.S. Shergill (2006) 'Imaging auditory Hallucinations in Schizophrenia', *Acta Neuropsychiatrica*, 18, 71–8.

Trichet, Y. (2011) *L'entrée dans la Psychose* (Rennes: Presses Universitaires de Rennes).

Van Haute, P. (2002) *Against Adaptation: Lacan's Subversion of the Subject* (New York: Other Press).

Vanier, A. (2011) 'The Object between Mother and Child' in L. Kirshner (ed.) *From Winnicott to Lacan* (New York: Routledge).

Vanheule, S., A. Lievrouw and P. Verhaeghe (2003) 'Burnout and Intersubjectivity: A Psychoanalytical Study from a Lacanian Perspective', *Human Relations*, 56, 321–39.

Vanheule, S. and P. Verhaeghe (2009) 'Identity through a Psychoanalytic Looking Glass', *Theory and Psychology*, 19, 319–411.

Vanheule, S. (2011) 'A Lacanian Perspective on Psychotic Hallucinations', *Theory & Psychology*, 21, 86–106.

Ver Eecke, W. (2006) *Denial, Negation, and the Forces of the Negative: Freud, Hegel, Lacan, Spitz, and Sophocles* (Albany: State University of New York Press).

Verhaeghe, P. (1999) *Does the Woman Exist? From Freud's Hysteric to Lacan's Feminine* (New York: Other Press).

Verhaeghe, P. (2001) *Beyond Gender: From Subject to Drive* (New York: Other Press).

Verhaeghe, P. (2002) 'Lacan's Answer to the Classical Mind/Body Deadlock: Retracing Freud's *Beyond*' in S. Barnard and B. Fink (eds.) *Reading Seminar XX* (Albany: State University of New York Press), pp. 109–40.

Verhaeghe, P. (2004) *On being Normal and other Disorders* (New York: Other Press).

Verhaeghe, P. (2009) *New Studies of old Villains. A Radical Reconsideration of the Oedipus Complex* (New York: Other Press)

Villagran, J.M. and G.E. Berrios (1996) 'A Descriptive Model of Delusion', *Neurology Psychiatry and Brain Research*, 4, 159–70.

Vinciguerra, R.P. (2010) 'The object Voice', *Psychoanalytical Notebooks*, 20, 41–9.

Vivona, J.M. (2009) 'Embodied Language in Neuroscience and Psychoanalysis', *Journal of the American Psychoanalytic Association*, 57, 1327–60.

Voruz, V. and B. Wolf (2007) *The Later Lacan – And Introduction* (Albany: State University of New York Press).

Zadeh, L.A. and J. Kacprzyk (1992) *Fuzzy Logic for the Management of Uncertainty* (New York: John Wiley and Sons).

Žižek, S. (1993) *Tarrying with the Negative* (Durham: Duke University Press).

Index

Act of faith, 12, 26, 109, 136, 147, 161
Adams, C.C., 154, 156
Adoration, 28–30
A-father, 77–8
Affect, 86, 145
Aggression, 20
Aggressiveness, 20
Aimée, 2, 10, 13–21, 27–8, 30, 138, 140, 173
Alajouanine, T., 12
Algebra, 155
Algorithm, 37
Alienation, 26, 41, 75
Allen, P., 81, 84
Allouch, J., 14–15, 172
Allusion, 28, 33, 54, 59
Alter-ego, 28
Anal, 132–3, 139, 153
Anal drive, 133
Analysis, 3, 9, 35, 89, 98, 167, 172, 174
Analyst, 40, 45–6, 72–3, 161, 163
Anthropology, 51
Anxiety, 12, 14, 38, 51, 59, 101, 105, 109, 127, 134, 175
Anzieu, D., 14, 172
Apollon, W., 72
Aquinas, T., 83
Aristotle, 164
As-if mechanism, 73, 75
a-subjective position, 143–6
Atkinson, J.R., 84
Aufhebung, 117–18, 127
Aulagnier, P., 127–8
Autonym, 108–10, 112–13
Autonymous speech element, 109

Badiou, A., 37, 126
Bedeutung, 46

Being, 1, 4, 15, 17, 19, 23–4, 26–9, 42, 46, 54, 56–7, 59–61, 64, 68–9, 72, 77, 79, 85–6, 91–3, 96, 100, 107, 110–113, 115–18, 121, 125–3, 137–41, 143–7, 151–4, 166–8, 173
Bejahung, 66–8, 71, 105, 136
Belief, 12, 33, 37, 59–60, 82, 96–7, 109, 112, 134, 136–7, 140, 146–7, 152, 159–62, 167–8
Berrios, G.E., 81, 96, 112
Billiet, L., 75, 167
Biological models of psychosis, 10–14
Bleuler, E., 10, 100
Body, 23, 27, 29, 42, 44, 102, 104, 106–7, 109, 116–19, 128–31, 135, 137, 139, 141–2, 145, 153, 158–9, 168, 174, 176
Borromean link, 157, 159–60, 162, 166, 170, 177
Borromean rings, 156, 158–62, 166, 169
Braff, D.L., 97
Brüne, M., 69
Butler, R.W., 97
Button tie, 37, 44, 48, 53–5, 104, 106

Case-oriented approach, 47
Case presentation, 77, 86, 90, 92, 172
Castration, 67
Categorical diagnostics, 165
Causality, 2, 21, 25, 172
Cause, 11, 14, 21–7, 34, 50, 65, 87, 102, 134, 137, 140, 172
Chiesa, L., 59
Code phenomena, 91–5
Communication, 48, 71, 93, 109–10, 121, 153
Complex, 4, 14–15, 18, 22, 29, 50, 57–8, 61, 73, 79, 127, 131, 155, 169
Comprehension, 11, 82
Conceptually-based practice, 34

Condensation, 28, 51–2
Conflict, 10–11, 14, 16, 18, 70, 74–6, 117
Consistency, 33, 96, 106–7, 114, 119–20, 126, 131, 135, 141–2, 145–6, 157–8, 163, 165, 167–9
Content-based approach to delusions, 97
Contingence, 27, 64, 113
Convention, 28–9, 36, 40, 69, 93, 167, 169, 170
Coping, 107, 119, 146
Cox-Cameron, O., 14–15, 19
Creativity, 56
Criminal, 75

Dali, S., 21, 25
David, A.S., 82
Deaf, 84
Death, 28, 56, 64, 70, 106–7, 128
Déclenchement, 11, 76, 172
De Clérambault, G.G., 2, 9, 11, 84, 100–3, 108, 140
Decompensation, 76–9
Defense, 18–20, 23, 67, 94, 99, 107, 141
De Kesel, M., 175
Deleuze, G., 50
Delusion, 14, 16–19, 26, 71, 86, 96–103, 110–116, 121, 140
Delusional metaphor, 4, 73, 96, 100, 106, 113, 115–19, 121–2, 140, 142
Delusional signifier, 116–18
Dementia praecox, 89
Depersonalization, 14, 143
Depression, 14
De Saussure, F., 3, 33, 35–7, 39–40, 46
Desire, 29, 58–63, 65–6, 68–71, 75–6, 79, 107, 114–15, 131, 133–4, 136–7, 141–3, 145–8, 151, 175
Despair, 104, 141
Detachment, 162
Deutsch, H., 73
Diachronic, 39–40, 43, 52, 87
Diachrony, 39, 41–2
Diagnosis, 96, 161, 164–5, 167
Diagnostic and Statistical Manual of Mental Disorders, 97
Dialectic, 61, 102, 128

Differential diagnostic classification, 161
Disbelief, 12, 30, 112
Discourse, 25, 37, 40, 44–9, 60, 69–70, 74, 76, 97, 102–4, 108, 110–111, 115, 121, 130, 135, 142–3, 161–2, 167–70, 174
Discourse theory, 174
Disorder, 9–30, 79, 114, 165, 172
Displacement, 51–2
Disregulated Other, 114
Divided Other, 130
Divided subject, 129–30
Division, 44, 85, 129–31, 133, 135, 138
Division of the Other, 129, 133, 135, 138
Division of subject, 133
Dolar, M., 132
Dora, 146
Dreams, 39–40, 51, 70, 138, 153
Dr. Flechsig, 103, 106
Drive, 2, 4, 29, 66, 88, 94, 125–6, 129, 131–3, 141–2, 152–3, 158
Drive gratification, 4, 126, 152
Duras, M., 142–4, 176

Ego, 2, 16, 18, 20–4, 26–30, 33, 40, 44, 63, 66, 76, 78, 85, 112, 120, 130, 152, 167–8, 170, 175
Elementary phenomenon, 101, 140
Embodied language, 153
Enjoyment, 24, 28–9, 88, 125, 147
Enunciated subject, 48–9, 54, 56, 68–9, 71, 75–6, 88–91, 95, 113, 121
Enunciating subject, 48–9, 54, 56, 69, 75–6, 89, 106, 113
Enunciation, 135–6, 152–3
Epistemology, 25, 170
Erogenous zone, 13
Erotomania, 14, 17, 18–19, 30, 140
Erroneous idea, 96
Esquirol, E., 81–2
Estrangement, 14, 77, 101, 103, 106, 110
Ethics, 164
Ethnography, 33
Ethology, 22

Event, 10, 25, 34, 47, 58, 77, 82, 90, 96, 98, 101, 107, 144
Excluded third, 144–6
Excrement, 133
Existence, 42, 54, 59–60, 64–71, 73–4, 76–7, 79, 81, 88, 90, 96, 100, 105, 113
Exogamy, 60
Ex-sistence, 157–8, 160, 177
Exterior intimacy, 110–111, 121
Extraction object a, 105
Ey, H., 9, 20, 81, 84, 172

Family, 21–2
Fantasy, 71–2, 176
Father, 3–4, 14, 22, 24, 50–1, 57–71, 73, 75–9, 81, 90–1, 93, 98, 100, 112–17, 121, 126, 135–9, 146–7, 151–2, 161–70, 174, 176
Father-version, 162
Feminization, 20, 99, 118
Fertile moment, 26
Fink, B., 46, 72, 175
Flechsig, 103, 106, 116, 140
Fliess, 38, 174
Formal language, 155, 159
Formation of the unconscious, 138, 153
Fourth knot, 166, 169–70
Fragmentation, 29
Freud, S., 2, 9, 14, 18–20, 30, 33–4, 38, 42, 50–2, 57, 61, 66–7, 78, 89, 91, 94, 98–9, 112, 120–1, 129, 131, 146, 161–2, 169, 173–4, 177

Garrabé, J., 21, 25
Gaze, 133, 139, 144–5
Geometry, 155
Gestalt, 22–3, 26, 74, 84
Giving nothing, 133
God, 23, 71–2, 91, 93, 99, 103–4, 106, 109, 111, 114–18, 139–40, 174
Grandeur, 14, 19
Grandiosity, 18
Grigg, R., 66
Guarantee, 42, 58, 98, 126, 130, 133–4, 136–7, 139, 145, 147, 155
Guattari, F., 50

Gueguen, P.G., 162–3
Guiraud, P., 20

Hainamoration, 27–30, 60, 63, 107
Hallucination, 67, 81–7, 89–91, 95
Hallucinatory, 66–7, 81–2, 86, 89, 91, 95
Hate, 19, 28–30, 58
Hegel, G.W.F., 28, 61
Hoens, D., 142
Holophrasis, 108
Homosexual, 18–20, 30, 173
Hoornaert, G., 134
Hyppolite, J., 66
Hysteric, 146

Ideal ego, 23–4, 26–7, 33, 76
Ideas of reference, 14
Identification, 1–3, 9–30, 34, 62–3, 65–6, 68, 73–6, 78, 140, 142, 164, 173
Identity, 23, 26, 36, 46–8, 54, 56, 61–2, 64, 66, 68–71, 73–7, 79, 88–9, 90–2, 95, 102, 106, 113–15, 120–1, 127, 133, 139, 142–3, 145, 151, 154, 167, 173–4, 176
Image, 1–2, 16–18, 22–4, 26–30, 35, 38–9, 41, 44, 51, 83, 88, 118, 132–3, 145, 147, 159, 173, 175
Imaginary, 2–5, 9–30, 33–5, 37, 44, 58, 60–1, 63, 68, 72–9, 84, 107, 110, 114–16, 119–20, 127, 129, 141, 151–2, 154–5, 157–8, 160, 164–6, 168–70, 172–3
Imago, 23
Incest, 60
Ineffability, 104
Inhibition, 14, 101
Inmixing of subjects, 102
Insane, 27, 72, 146
Interpretation, 3, 14, 23, 27, 29, 40, 42, 51–2, 54, 57, 60, 64, 69, 75, 78–9, 80, 82, 93, 97–9, 114, 119, 122, 126–7, 133, 140–1, 145, 155, 160, 162, 166, 168
Intervention, 51, 80, 87, 122, 163, 165, 170
Intimate exteriority, 110, 121
Intrusion, 16, 22, 29–30, 112, 139

Intrusion complex, 22, 29
Invention, 4, 148
Invocative drive, 132–3, 153
Ironic, 142
Ironical, 23, 84, 110
Irony, 51
Irrefutable, 111–12, 116
I-schema, 174–5

Jakobson, R., 3, 33, 39–41, 51–2, 55
Janet, 16
Jaspers, K., 10, 98
Jealouissance, 27–30, 60, 63
Jealousy, 14, 18–19, 28–30, 173
Jonckheere, L., 169, 174
Jouissance, 4, 28, 88, 125–48, 152–4,
    157–8, 162–3, 166, 169–70,
    175–6, 180
Joyce, J., 4, 10, 126, 166–70
Jung, 23, 40, 98

Kacprzyk, J., 164
Katan, M., 99, 102
Kirshner, L.A., 131, 162
Klein, M., 80, 131
Knot, 4, 144, 151–2, 154–78
Knot-theory, 4, 154–7, 169, 176
Knowledge, 13, 24–7, 40, 45, 67, 119,
    138, 140, 158, 165
Kojève, A., 28, 61
Kraepelin, E., 25, 100
Kretschmer, 10, 16
Kusnierek, M., 82

Lacan, J., 1–5, 9–30, 33–49, 50–80,
    81–95, 96–122, 125–47, 151–70,
    172–7
Lalangue, 152
Language, 1, 3–4, 25, 33, 35–42, 44–6,
    48–50, 52, 54, 56, 79, 93–4,
    100–2, 104, 108–9, 114, 125–6,
    130–2, 134–5, 141–2, 152–5,
    157–9, 164, 169–70, 173, 175
Law, 17, 27, 34, 50, 60–2, 71, 75, 78,
    117–18, 121, 128, 136, 151
Lévi-Strauss, C., 3, 33, 51, 57, 147
Libidinous activity, 132
Linguistics, 33, 35–6, 44, 46, 50, 54,
    56, 65, 100, 102, 105, 108, 154

Link, 4, 36, 67, 97, 104, 107, 112, 118,
    154, 156–7, 159–60, 162, 166,
    167, 169–70, 177
Linkknot, 159
Llanguage, 152–4, 158
Logical time, 173
Lol V. Stein, 4, 10, 126
Love, 17–20, 28–30, 58–9, 64, 70, 86,
    90, 120, 143–5, 175
Lust, 28–9, 175
Lysy, A., 132, 167

Macalpine, I., 99
Madness, 24–5, 27, 30, 42, 45, 114,
    117–18, 143, 160–1
Mad Other, 116, 118, 121–2
Maleval, J.C., 66, 72, 81, 122, 170
Malone, K.R., 46
Marienkäfer, 38–9, 41
Martyr of the unconscious, 72, 79
Masson, J.M., 38
Master-slave dialectic, 61
Materialism, 3, 37–8, 42, 44–5, 47, 49,
    65, 97
Maternal, 58–61, 63, 66, 68
Maternal desire, 58–61, 63, 68
Matheme, 37, 129–30, 133, 138, 155,
    176
Meaning, 11, 14, 16, 21, 28, 33,
    36–40, 43–4, 48, 53–5, 59, 67–8,
    72, 86–9, 91–4, 105–6, 110–111,
    130, 136, 138, 145, 151–2, 158,
    160, 162, 165–9
Mental automatism, 9, 13, 42, 100–3,
    112–13
Merleau-Ponty, M., 2, 82–5, 95
Message, 43–4, 48, 53, 55, 62, 71–2,
    75, 87–95, 105, 119, 152–3
Message phenomena, 91–5
Meta-perspective, 27, 112
Metaphor, 4, 24, 50–1, 54–62, 65–70,
    73–5, 96, 100, 106, 110, 113–22,
    140, 142, 155, 159, 161, 166, 176
Metaphorization, 3, 4, 34, 50, 57–9,
    117–18, 121
Metonymy, 3, 10, 50–6, 100–8, 120,
    166
Mihilism, 27

Miller, J.A., 22, 37, 39, 47, 76, 81–2,
    105, 127, 132–3, 135, 137, 142,
    148, 152, 162–4, 170, 175–6
Mills, J., 26
Milner, J.C., 36, 46
Mirror, 16, 21–30, 41, 60, 74, 107, 173
Mirror stage, 21–6, 28–30, 41, 74, 107
Misrecognition, 26–7, 30
Morbid belief, 96
(m)other, 61–3, 68–9, 79, 115
Muller, J.P., 61
Munro, A., 96
Murder, 93, 106–7, 110, 116, 139, 152

Names-of-the-Father, 135–7
Narcissism, 60
Narcissistic, 21, 28
Naveau, P., 42, 170
Negation, 18
Neologism, 28, 93, 108, 152, 159
Neurosis, 4–5, 34, 44, 47–8, 64, 66,
    70–2, 75, 78, 81, 94, 128, 131,
    133–42, 144, 146–7, 161–4,
    169–70
Nipple, 132–3
Nobus, D., 66
Non-Bejahung, 67–8
Non-extraction object a, 105, 138, 147
Non-separated object, 137
Normality, 128, 134, 147, 161

Object, 125–48, 175–6
Object a, 4, 105, 125–48, 152–3
Objectal, 132, 134, 139–40, 147
Oedipal, 28, 50, 58, 61, 161–2
Oedipus complex, 22, 50, 57–8, 61,
    73, 79, 127
One-father, 78
Oral drive, 132–3
Ordinary psychosis, 76
Organ, 65, 81, 153
Organo-Dynamism, 9
Organogenesis of psychosis, 13
Other, 2, 24, 28, 34, 39–44, 49, 60,
    62–6, 71, 75, 79–80, 92–3, 103,
    107, 114–22, 126–47, 162, 175–6
Other of the Other, 126, 131, 134–5
Overdetermination, 42
Overstrand, 159

Papin sisters, 19
Paranoia, 138–40
Paranoiac, 20, 138
Paranoid knowledge, 27, 138
Parenthood, 64
Parker, I., 46–7, 174
Parlêtre, 152
Partial object, 4, 126–8, 131–3
Passivity syndrome, 9, 100–1
Paternal, 58–63, 66–70, 74–5, 91, 96,
    100, 107, 115, 117, 135–6, 161,
    167
Paternity, 77, 90–1, 113–14
Perception, 3, 19, 35, 66, 81–5, 94, 97,
    99, 174
Perceptual, 81–2
Perceptum, 83–7, 145
Percipiens, 83–6, 145
Perplexity, 13, 69, 85, 89, 96, 101,
    103, 110
Persecution, 14, 18–19, 30, 131
Personality, 10–11, 13, 15–16, 45
Perversion, 128
Phallic, 63–5, 67–71, 75–6, 90, 114,
    118, 151
Phallus, 20, 58, 60, 62–5, 174–5
Phenomenology, 45, 82
Pleasure, 4, 125–6, 128–9, 139, 159,
    175
Pleasure principle, 128–9, 175
Plus-de-jouir, 134
Pluth, E., 46
Poetry, 110
Post-Freudian, 14
Praecox experience, 110
Pre-delusional state, 102, 104
Primordial father, 78
Procreation, 64
Projection, 19–20, 34, 67–8, 99, 121,
    133–4
Psychasthenia, 15
Psychiatry, 9, 11, 20, 79, 94, 96, 108,
    110
Psychical causality of psychosis, 25
Psychoanalysis, 1–2, 9–10, 13–14, 20,
    24, 33–4, 40, 49, 72, 80, 94, 127,
    154, 161, 164, 174
Psychoanalyst, 2, 25, 50–1, 80, 98–9,
    122, 125, 127, 162, 171

Psychodynamic, 9, 47
Psychosis, 1–5, 9–30, 33–49, 50–1, 58–9, 64, 66–73, 75–7, 79–80, 81, 83–4, 90, 93–4, 96, 98, 100, 102–3, 106–8, 112–15, 120, 125–48, 151–7, 172–4, 176–8
Psychotic outbreak, 10, 13, 26, 99
Punctuation, 36, 43–4, 47, 51, 88–9, 91–2

Questions of existence, 65, 67–71, 77, 81, 121–2, 136
Quintilian, 51–2, 54

Rabaté, J.M., 161, 168
Ragland-Sullivan, E., 33, 51
Ravishing, 4, 126, 142–6
Real, 2, 4–5, 67, 70–2, 77–9, 87–8, 90, 113, 117, 126–32, 151–2, 154–5, 157–8, 162, 165–6, 168–70
Reality, 4, 21, 25, 27, 35, 47, 49, 66, 75–6, 81–2, 84, 89, 94, 96–8, 109, 120, 132, 134–5, 137, 139–41, 143, 146, 151–2, 159–62, 165–70
Recognition, 24, 61–2, 119
Referent, 46
Regression, 21, 107
Rejection, 34, 67
Remainder of jouissance, 134
Repression, 5, 18, 52, 70–1
Resilience, 119–20, 122
Resistance, 19–20
Retroaction, 46
Revelation, 72, 93, 109, 112, 138
Richardson, W.J., 61, 143–5
Rival, 28–9, 60, 63
Rivalry, 29, 63
Roberts, J.L., 46
Roudinesco, E., 9–10, 14–15, 155, 163
Rümke, H.C., 110
Rupture in metonymy, 102–3, 107

Santiago, A.L., 132
Satisfaction, 4, 22, 29, 126, 128
Sauvagnat, F., 101
Schizophrenia, 4, 21, 73, 110, 126, 138, 140–2, 147
Scholastic, 83

Schreber, D.P., 91–4, 97, 99, 103–4, 106–7, 109–20, 122, 140–1, 165
Science, 37, 49, 119
Scopic drive, 132–3, 139, 153
Scybalum, 132–3
Self-made man, 168
Self-pathology, 162
Self-punishing paranoia, 17, 30
Semblable, 22, 28–9, 129
Sense of life, 107, 114, 139
Sensoria, 10, 83–4
Sex, 64, 66
Sexual, 10, 64–5, 69, 71–2, 79, 113, 118, 145–7
Sexuality, 11, 70, 145
Shepherdson, C., 126
Shergill, S.S., 84
Signification, 35–6, 39, 42–5, 49, 51, 54–5, 60, 63, 71, 75, 82, 85, 87–93, 95, 100, 102, 104–5, 109, 111, 131, 133, 136, 153
Signified, 35–8, 40–2, 45, 47–8, 52–6, 58–64, 68, 70, 74, 76, 78, 91, 93, 100, 104–7, 110, 114–15, 118–19, 121, 137, 141, 143, 152–3, 162, 166, 176
Signifier, 2–4, 33–49, 50–80, 81–95, 96–122, 125–37, 141–2, 146–7, 151–4, 157–8, 161, 165, 170, 176
Signifying chain, 39–40, 42, 44–55, 70, 77, 81, 85–90, 93, 95, 100, 109, 111, 113, 120, 125–6, 130, 156
Singular, 4, 13, 80, 85, 148, 154, 163–4, 169–70
Singularity, 154
Sinthome, 155, 166–70
Skriabine, P., 157
Social bond, 50, 57, 62, 110, 119, 121, 142, 146, 169
Social life narrative, 74–6, 78–9, 90
Soler, C., 162, 176
Sound, 27, 35–7, 39, 41, 97, 104, 132–3
Sow, 86–7, 89
Speakingbeing, 152, 154
Speech, 1, 34–49, 51–6, 69, 75, 82, 86–9, 92–105, 108–14, 120, 122, 130–1, 133, 135–6, 152–4
Stabilization, 126, 142

Stasse, P., 132–3
Structural, 3, 9, 33–51, 54, 56, 58, 91, 97–102, 108, 114, 137, 174
Structuralism, 25
Stump, E., 83
Subject
  of jouissance, 127–33, 138
  of the signifier, 106, 127–8, 134, 141
Subjectivity, 1, 4, 34, 43–4, 46–54, 56, 64–5, 69, 71–3, 76, 78, 80, 87, 90, 92, 96, 100, 106–7, 111, 113, 122, 130, 137, 154–5, 162, 173
Subjet-Other relationship, 34
Super-ego, 18
Surplus of jouissance, 134
Surrealist, 21, 25, 163
Svolos, T., 72, 161
Symbolic, 3–5, 27, 29, 33–5, 44, 50–1, 60–3, 65, 67–9, 71–2, 74, 76–8, 89, 91, 95–6, 107, 113–16, 121, 125–8, 130–2, 134–6, 138, 140–3, 151–2, 154–5, 157–8, 160–2, 165–70, 176
Symptom, 1, 4, 11, 15, 20, 37, 39, 64–5, 70–3, 76, 79–80, 89, 94, 96, 138, 153, 159–61, 164, 166, 169–70
Synchronic, 40–1
Synchrony, 41–3, 55
Syntagm, 39–40
Syntax, 36, 39
Systemic, 2, 4, 143, 157, 160–1, 169–70

Taboo, 57, 60, 78–9
Taking in nothing, 133
Testimony, 72, 110
Theorists of mind, 69
Thetongue, 152
Three-dimensional, 151, 155, 157, 177
Thurston, L., 168
Topographical regression, 107
Topology, 127, 154–5
Totem, 57, 78
Tracy, D.K., 84
Transference, 37, 51, 54

Treatment, 1, 3, 11–13, 20, 34, 64, 70, 72, 77, 80, 83–4, 106, 108, 115, 118, 126, 134, 160–1, 165
Trefoil knot, 156, 159–60, 162
Triangular, 61, 144–8, 151, 154, 157, 169, 176
Trichet, Y., 102
Triggering of a psychotic episode, 76

Unchained signifier, 86–7, 90, 95
Unconscious, 3, 17–18, 20, 37–40, 42, 46, 49, 51–2, 63–73, 76, 79, 87, 94, 99, 122, 130, 138, 147, 151, 153–4, 158, 167
Understanding, 13, 40, 42, 44, 52, 61, 82–5, 93, 98, 122, 153
Understrand, 159
Unfinished sentence, 91–2
Unglauben, 112

Van Haute, P., 42
Vanheule, S., 16, 21, 61, 81, 173
Vanier, A., 131
Ver Eecke, W., 66
Verhaeghe, P., 16, 21, 66, 75, 98, 110, 126, 135, 146, 173, 175
Verneinung, 18
Verwerfung, 67, 167
Villagran, J.M., 112
Vinciguerra, R.P., 132
Vivona, J.M., 153
Vocal, 36, 105, 153
Vocalization, 105, 135
Voice, 91, 133, 135, 139–41
Voruz, V., 154

Weaning complex, 22
West Indian man, 77
Wolf, B., 67, 154
Wolf man, 67
Woman, 15, 17, 64, 66, 70–1, 73–5, 86–92, 116, 118, 143–6
Wordlessness, 105

Zadeh, L.A., 164
Žižek, S., 139

CPSIA information can be obtained at www.ICGtesting.com
Printed in the USA
BVOW031201080312

284589BV00003B/2/P